TWO

PATHS

TOWARD

PEACE

TWO
PATHS
TOWARD
PEACE

DONALD SCHERER

AND

JAMES W. CHILD

Temple University Press

Philadelphia

Temple University Press, Philadelphia 19122
Copyright © 1992 by Temple University. All rights reserved
Published 1992
Printed in the United States of America

Library of Congress Cataloging-in-Publication Data
Scherer, Donald.
  Two paths toward peace / Donald Scherer and James W.
Child.
    p. cm.
  Includes bibliographical references and index.
ISBN 0-87722-882-5 (alk. paper)
1. Violence—Moral and ethical aspects. 2. Pacifism.
3. Peace. I. Child, James W., 1941– . II. Title.
BJ1459.5.S34 1992
172'.42—dc20

                                        91-17434

The quotation on pages 57–58 is from *The Target Is
Destroyed*, by Seymour M. Hersh. Copyright © 1986 by
Seymour M. Hersh. Reprinted by permission of Random
House, Inc.

The poetry on page 286 is from *Summer Knowledge:
Selected Poems*, by Delmore Schwartz. Reprinted by
permission of Robert Phillips, Literary Executor for the
Estate of Delmore Schwartz.

To the memory of my father, James L. Child

J.W.C.

To William Lloyd Garrison, Sr., Leo Tolstoy,
Mohandas Gandhi, and Martin Luther
King, Jr., whose path I have endeavored to
trace and extend

D.S.

CONTENTS

Acknowledgment   ix

Introduction   3

The Pacifist's Vision / *Donald Scherer*   3

The Cost of Uncritical Pacifism / *James W. Child*   5

Two Paths to Peace / *James W. Child and Donald Scherer*   10

Part I: A Critical Examination of Justified Violence

1. A Defense of Justified Violence / *James W. Child*   15

2. A Critique of Justified Violence / *Donald Scherer*   36

Part II: A Critical Examination of Pacifism

Introduction   67

3. Problems with Traditional Forms of Pacifism / *James W. Child*   72

4. Creating a New Pacifism / *Donald Scherer*   91

Part III: The Moral and Metaphysical Foundations of Pacifism and the Justified Violence View

5. On Justifying Violence / *James W. Child*   129

6. A Viable Pacifism / *Donald Scherer*   169

Part IV: The Work of Peacemaking

Introduction   207

7. On Avoiding War / *James W. Child*   209

8. Toward an Enriched Peace / *Donald Scherer*   232

Afterword / *James W. Child*   267

Notes   271

Index   311

ACKNOWLEDGMENT

One of the great pleasures of this enterprise for the authors has been the degree to which each of us has interacted with and influenced the thought of the other. We believe that this is obvious from the text. Nonetheless, the chapters signed by each author are his own work for which he alone takes both full credit and full responsibility. Moreover, the substance of the total joint project is equally the work of both. Don Scherer's name appears first because he carried virtually the whole administrative burden of manuscript preparation and of dealing with the Temple University Press. In a work as complex as this that burden was substantial. Moreover, Jim Child notes that Scherer's belief in this work and his indefatigable persistence in urging its completion were indispensable to its being completed.

We authors would like to thank a number of people who read early versions of the manuscript and from whose comments we profited greatly. They include Tom Attig, David Braybrooke, J. R. Burholder, Christopher Morris, and Malham Wakin. Needless to say, we alone are responsible for any mistakes or confusions. Margy DeLuca provided highly competent and tireless work in the word processing of the numerous drafts of this work.

J.W.C.
D.S.

TWO
PATHS
TOWARD
PEACE

DONALD SCHERER
JAMES W. CHILD

Introduction

The Pacifist's Vision / *Donald Scherer*

I did not grow up in a traditional peace church, but as a youth, thinking about the justification of war and more broadly, of violence in general, I always found violence difficult to justify. I remember at age nine tutoring a classmate who was having problems learning the multiplication tables. I insisted on his walking to and from school with me so that I could drill him. Since he often accepted my help without protest, even cheerfully, I interpreted his occasional disinterest as reflecting embarrassment at his limitations or merely myopic interest in other childhood pleasures. But perhaps I misinterpreted and he was frustrated by my insistence, for one day, on the way home from school, after we had parted at his house, the class bully accosted me in an alley. Why he should want to trouble me I did not immediately guess, but, whatever his motives, I could see no greater good coming out of my fighting back than out of my allowing him his way. If someone chose to harm me, how could my harming him be a better alternative?

He wrestled me to the ground where he lay upon me—punching me, as I recall. I know I was crying, which probably contributed to his

3

thinking he had taught me a lesson, a sentiment he expressed: Maybe now I would leave his friend alone between home and school. But as I walked home, still crying, my tears reflected the different lesson I was stretching to comprehend. I was no small kid; I could have defended myself with some ability, had I tried. And it was easy for me to see that I could quit helping my friend if he didn't want the help. But I couldn't see why anyone had to fight about it. If he wanted help, why couldn't the bully let me give it to him? And if he didn't want the help, why didn't he just ask me to leave him alone?

And how harmful the fighting seemed! Why should an expression of enmity stand between me and the bully? Though I usually raced home, I walked slowly that day, trying to grasp the harm I saw in the fighting. It wasn't that I was injured: where I grew up, nine year olds weren't all that effective at harming each other. The harm seemed to be that, in fighting, we made ourselves needless enemies. I wondered whether anybody needed enemies. And while many adults agreed with me that my little fight was probably unnecessary, they assured me that fights among adults were different. (In the spring of 1950, this adult view was quite widespread.) Being an audacious child, I expressed my doubts, to which people replied that I must be a pacifist, but I didn't care about names.

I wondered what would make a conflict not only unavoidable, as things stood, but unchangeably so, no matter how things might be rearranged. And as I started paying attention to adult discussions, I learned that exactly which fights are unavoidable was (and remains) a matter of some dispute. Lots of people were ready to tell me that sometimes you just have to fight. Fighting, they held, is something you can be forced to do. Then one of them would give me an example, but another would say no, that wasn't really a very good example. Fighting is sometimes necessary, the other would allow, but in the cited case some other maneuvers were possible. I would look back to the first of them, his eyes gleaming, his teeth clinched, shaking his head at the views of the second. Where was the compulsion to fight? The second was shrugging his shoulders, not feeling any pugnacious compulsion. As I listened to adult discussions, it seemed to me almost any fight was avoidable in someone's eyes. And I began to wonder if we could all come to see with those eyes.

Among the people I knew then, many expressed admiration for "anyone with the principles to be a pacifist," though most felt reservations about how unqualified the pacifist position seemed: "What would you do if someone broke into your home? Would you stand idly by if your mother were being raped?" A young man inclined to pacifism hears this question put in terms of his mother or sister; with the passage of time, the question is rephrased in terms of one's wife or daughter. The question remains stark, however, and can easily back one away from a view that seems to ignore not only the rights of innocents but also one's feelings for loved ones.

Indeed, questions like these have moved many peace-loving persons into the defense of the use of "minimal necessary violence" and "just wars." But I have not so easily acquiesced. Instead, I have wondered how unqualified the position of the pacifist must be. Every schoolchild knows that one of the best ways to make a position look foolish is by making it look absolutist to the extreme of fanaticism. And so I have pondered whether some qualifications might be built into the definition of pacifism. Must one define pacifism as the position that in *every* circumstance within *every* social setting, *every* individual is wrong and blameworthy if that individual uses *any* force against *any* other human being? I think not.

Instead, I present a new conception of pacifism, but one that preserves the traditional pacifist emphases on the avoidance of violence and the cultivation of a reign of peace. The view I introduce is a teleological pacifism. Because it is teleological, it is concerned to effect a deliberate evolution of social practices. By teleological pacifism, then, I initially mean the view that it is desirable for persons to be committed to such improvement of social practices and institutions as will promote a true reign of peace. In the course of this book I clarify and refine this concept.

The Cost of Uncritical Pacifism / *James W. Child*

My first memories as a child are of wartime Washington, D.C. My father was a naval officer who worked in the Naval Bureau of Ordnance on designs for mines and depth charges. He wasn't happy, however, because he wanted a combat assignment. Though repeatedly rejected as too old, he kept trying. Finally, orders came through: an assignment in the Pacific to a destroyer as executive officer. We all knew that his ship would be involved in the invasion of Kyushu, the first of the Japanese home islands. The most recent invasion of a fortified Japanese island in the Pacific, Okinawa, had been horribly bloody. The navy had suffered worse casualties than the army or marines because of the dreaded kamikaze planes. Their favorite target was the bridge of destroyers. Kyushu, we were sure, would make Okinawa seem tame by comparison.

I remember vividly the day my father came home from his office thrilled that he could leave his hated desk. He could, as he said, "finally do something." What he meant, though, is that at last he could *fight*. And I remember the fear in my mother's eyes. We didn't know it then— it was July 1945—but the atomic bomb had been successfully tested, and in a few weeks the war would be over.

The housing project in which we lived during those years was occupied by families of all the armed services. It was always alive with news of the war, with rumors, and with intense feelings. I remember terrible racism toward the Japanese and a sad neighbor woman, whose fighter-pilot husband had been killed over Germany. Several disabled veterans lived nearby. One man, I remember, had lost a leg at Normandy. Down the rowhouse half a block lived a marine captain who had won the Congressional Medal of Honor and a battlefield commission at Guadalcanal, a noble figure held in awe by neighborhood kids. There was, among the people in the neighborhood, an exhilaration about being so close to war, and in retrospect that is frightening. But there was also a deep moral conviction that we were *right*.

A few years later, when I began to think and read seriously, World War II became a touchstone for my study of history and then later of international law and philosophy. Had it been the noble effort I remembered, brave soldiers serving at great risk in a just cause? Or had it been merely another miserable chapter in the human race's perennial fratricide, driven by dark and sinister instinctual atavisms? Could it possibly have been both?

Sometimes, I believe, we have to use lethal violence, and sometimes it is morally appropriate that we do so. Pacifism, while invariably well intentioned, risks tragic moral mistakes. At least this is what I have concluded after a lifetime of thought on the subject. How does my analysis of World War II fit into that conclusion? The story goes, I believe, something like this.

In the 1930s pacifism specifically, and a much more general and uncritical antimilitary mindset, gripped the great European democracies,

France and Great Britain. Heaven knows it was understandable. Only two decades earlier, a generation of the young men of both countries had been maimed or killed in the trenches and shell craters of Flanders, Champaigne, and Lorraine. Conditions in the trenches were bestial almost beyond imagining. Men ate, slept, and lived in the company of rats and corpses. Mud and disease were constant companions. The cost of the war dwarfed anything in the past and reduced all the belligerents to poverty. The democracies were economically and spiritually bled white. Yet at the end of the day one could ask, "What was all the death and horror *for?*" And no compelling answer was forthcoming.

It is impossible for us, children of a second world war and the nuclear era, to appreciate the mind-wrenching effect of World War I on decent society and civilized minds. The brutality and destructiveness of nationalist militarism had been labeled forever for what it was, morally and rationally beyond the pale. But as Aristotle long ago taught, the essence of moral rectitude is in following a mean between two extremes. In both countries where pacifism became fashionable, the vision of this mean was lost. It is understandable in that climate that one could come to believe that nothing is worth fighting for, that the world is so morally ambiguous and humankind so morally ambivalent that violence, always offensive to sensitive souls, is never justified. In the famous Declaration of the Oxford Union, young men concluded this and took a pledge never to fight for "King and Country." The military was socially despised and ridiculed, and politically starved for even reasonable funding. The voices of Winston Churchill and Charles de Gaulle, who insisted that military defense had a legitimate role in a free society, were ignored.

Remember, this was the 1930s! Not all the world was so passionately pacifist and antimilitary. All the world seldom is, and therein lies a deep lesson. The Soviet Union was building "socialism in one country" under one of the most brutal and bloody tyrants in history. In that process it engaged in a large military buildup. Toward the end of the decade it would conquer the Baltic states and invade Finland in an effort to extend its suzerainty. Italy was arming rapidly, only to embark on an attack against hapless Ethiopia. Japan, already in 1929 a major world power, undertook a military and naval buildup of massive proportions. The Japanese invaded Manchuria and then China in pursuit of empire. At that time, the leaders of the Soviet Union, Italy, and Japan were people not amenable to reconciling conflict through communication and peaceful means. They were extremely unpleasant types who believed that offensive military violence was a legitimate tool of national policy and that it was appropriate that strong nations bend the will of weak people to their own, using violence to do so.

But most of all, during the 1930s, there grew up, practically next door to France and Britain, in the most civilized heart of Europe, in the land of Goethe and Kant and Beethoven . . . Well, we know what grew up there. A world monster. In 1939, free people and decent civilized societies stood almost defenseless before him. Holland, Belgium, Norway, Denmark, and, finally, France fell. Britain very nearly did the same. For almost two years, from September 1939 to June 1941, the four great totalitarian empires were in a de facto alliance against the democracies. (Moscow was linked first to Berlin, and through it to Tokyo and Rome by the Russo-German Non-Aggression Pact, under which it had cooperated with Germany in the invasion and the dismemberment of Poland and under which it continued to supply Adolf Hitler's war machine.) Had Hitler not turned his fury on his erstwhile Soviet ally, and had Britain and the great British fleet fallen into his hands, who can say what our fate would have been. As completely unprepared as we were, the United States might well have been conquered. At the least, we would have morally compromised our most basic values in a world dominated by monstrous men and malevolent movements. It would have changed our society and our way of life utterly. And millions of the world's citizens would have been condemned to live in the totalitarian nightmare states. How close we came to losing it all, to the end of Western civilization and the onset of what Churchill called "a new dark age, made more sinister by the lights of perverted science." So great a penalty did we nearly pay for steering too close to the pacifist extreme. So costly can be a misunderstanding of the appropriate limited uses, as well as the potentially terrible abuses, of violence in the management of social and international life.

What I remember was the end of the great struggle, when Germany and Japan were in their death throes, though, of course, we didn't know that. The fact of the war, that it happened, was tragic beyond calculation. It produced untold death and human misery, some microscopic part of which I saw around me in Washington. Still, given the facts they had no hand in making, the soldiers and sailors and marines I looked up to were *right* to make war. The moral intuition I had then has sustained the onslaught of much doubt and argument, yet I feel more convinced than when I started.

But if some causes are morally worth fighting for, then pacifism is mistaken. I believe that it is. Moreover, if in following pacifism where it was not appropriate, we failed to stop the depredations of a military aggressor where we could and should have, it could have led us into *moral error*, even tragic moral error. Or so I argue. Indeed, the appeal of this project to me grew first and foremost out of my heartfelt conviction that Donald Scherer and pacifists generally are simply morally mistaken.

Nevertheless, even if I succeed in showing that pacifism risks moral error, more needs to be done. It cannot be that because violence, including war, can sometimes be justified, that there are no moral restrictions on its application. (Although certain thinkers, called "realists," have actually argued for a similar position.) Indeed, the very justifiability of violence including war implies that some set of norms must govern its application, norms that first limit it and then justify it within those limitations. In addition to an argument against pacifism, indeed as part of that argument, this study is an effort to discover and set out norms for the morally appropriate use of violence.

What has all this to do with our lives today? A very great deal, as it turns out. Of course, there is always, in any society, a question of violent crime and violent police and citizen response to it. This is all the more pressing in our society with crime as rampant as it is. But open questions on the issue of war and peace remain even as the cold war, we may hope, draws to a close. The Soviet Union is a boiling kettle, and it is not beyond the realm of possibility that a different leadership or a renegade armed service or some geographical schism might raise a new military threat. We must remember that the Soviet Union still possesses the world's largest military establishment and approximately thirty thousand nuclear weapons.

Moreover, issues of military force and war can arise independently of cold-war adversaries. Only a few short months ago, Panama was a case in point. As I write these lines, the world is holding its breath in anticipation of what might happen in the Persian Gulf. Unfortunately, the issue of pacifism versus the just use of force and violence will probably always be with us. At least, it shows no signs of departing soon.

Two Paths to Peace: A Dialectic Approach /
James W. Child and Donald Scherer

All sorts of people affirm that something is seriously wrong with a world as full of violence as our own. Those who condemn violence include advocates of greater police authority and defenders of civil liberties, believers in the use of military force and advocates of an exclusive reliance on nonviolence in international relations. Violence is condemned on all sides, yet our world is full of it. Why? Surely one reason is that hotheads and passionate souls are sometimes not constrained, even by their own better judgment. But there is another reason. Though all condemn violence as inherently bad, no one can deny that it is sometimes an expedient instrument. It seems inevitable, then, that violence will be used, by some people, at some times, regardless of its moral quality. In the light of such a strong, widespread tendency, all of us must ask how best to respond to the use of violence and to the threat of its use.

Here we find the root of an ancient argument: Is it ever possible to justify morally the use of violence? With perhaps more eloquence, pacifists say no. With perhaps more realism, the advocates of justified violence say yes. But is either view sustainable? Does either respond to the challenges the other poses? What does each say about the prospect of reducing violence and effecting a more peaceful world?

The two authors of this book begin with opposite inclinations about justifying violence. But, unlike many books written by authors of contrasting viewpoints, the focus of this book is on the dialogue and a resulting dialectic. The book is designed to show the reader how the interplay of moral claims incorporated into each of these positions leads to a refined view that meets higher moral standards than either traditional versions of pacifism or traditional Just War views.

Our constructive goal is to combine the moral strength pacifists and just-war theorists each claim into a view theoretically justified and practically fecund. We have therefore tried to write for the large audience of people in countries throughout the world who we believe can play a constructive role in promoting peace. The reduction of violence and the promotion of peace are difficult goals, but we have written this book in an attempt to provide a moral basis from which to discourage violence and promote peace.

James Child begins Part I by developing a unified view of both inter-personal and international violence. He holds that some uses of violence can be morally justified, both within the rule of law and in defensive wars. He rests this view partly on a view of why violence is bad, which in turn rests on premises about what violence is. But, although Donald Scherer largely agrees about what makes violence bad, he takes issue with defining violence in terms of intention and in terms of the speed with which it is inflicted. Contrarily, he argues that including intention and speed of infliction in the definition hides problems in Child's view. For the view Child develops affirms that violence is bad and that, accordingly, defensive violence, when justified, must be a last resort. Scherer thus aims to show that the motive of security behind Child's view compromises whether violence remains a last resort. Moreover, Scherer argues, violence tends to elicit more violence, in an unterminating, intensifying spiral.

Part II opens with a joint exposition of a traditional variety of paci-fist positions. Thereafter, Child develops several critical arguments directed against what he sees as the common core of traditional pacifism. A central theme of these arguments is the moral inadequacy of a view that fails to recognize obligations to protect innocent victims from threatened violence. In various ways, Scherer agrees that not attempting the restraint of violently aggressive persons is morally deficient. Therefore, he devotes his portion of the chapter to the recasting of a personal pacifism in which the capacity for nonviolent force is magnified, and special responsibilities for promoting peace are assigned to persons of a pacifist disposition.

Whatever departures Child and Scherer make from more traditional views in the first two parts, Child still maintains that his is the sole position that adequately responds to the immorality of aggressively inflicted violence. And, similarly, Scherer attempts to show his as the only position that does not end up justifying violence, having originally agreed that it is a bad thing. Accordingly, in Part III, while adjusting his own view to Scherer's criticisms, Child buttresses his attempt to justify violence by arguing that violence can help deescalate and even terminate cycles of violence. He also urges that Scherer's focus on policy makes his view inadequately responsive to the victim of violence. Yet, even in the face of these arguments, Scherer argues for the importance and feasibility of sustaining a policy perspective in the midst of violence. In so doing, he also explicates what special qualifications help make pacifists effective peacemakers outside an established rule of law.

Explicitly, then, this book is a dialogue designed to exhibit how difficult it is for both the pacifist and the defender of justified violence to meet the demands of morality on which the other insists. How is the advocate of Just War to respond to the ubiquity of violence, the tendency of violence to escalate, and the ease with which adversaries justify their use of violence against each other? But, similarly, how can the pacifist respond to the plight of the innocent victim of aggression, to the success of the rule of law in minimizing violence, and to the fact that all the normal intercourse of peaceful civil society has its foundation in a threat of violence?

Interestingly, the modifications of traditional theories that Child and Scherer force on each other seem practically fecund. Child and Scherer agree that there are rational courses of action that move toward a more peaceful, less violent world. In Part IV, the authors go to great lengths to explain and exemplify how to take many safe steps toward a less violent world. Their common theme is that within a moral framework, considerable room exists for the improvement of international relationships. Child uses his theory to suggest steps toward an acceptable reduction of potential violence between adversarial nations. Scherer shows how, within a security-conscious context, a social niche can develop for expanding Mohandas Gandhi's pacifist politics from the intrasocial conflict that Gandhi and Martin Luther King, Jr., confronted to the intersocial conflict between adversarial nations.

In the authors' eyes, then, the dialogue of this book moves two traditional views about the justifiability of the use of violence from contraries to complementary theses about both the reduction of violence and the promotion of peace. The point of the dialogue is to show the reader why the original views require modification, how the modification makes them complementary, and what practical policy directions these theoretical adjustments portend.

PART I

A CRITICAL

EXAMINATION OF

JUSTIFIED VIOLENCE

1 *JAMES W. CHILD*

A Defense of Justified Violence

Principled Views on Violence

How might we describe violence in moral terms? How can we evaluate acts of violence and the perpetrators of those acts? When, if ever, might violence be permitted? On what principles would it be permitted? How would those principles be justified?

These questions, particularly when about moral principles, cannot be answered by social science. For social science tells us how things *are*, not how they *ought* to be. The notion of "ought" is more often broached by legislators, courts, and lawyers because our society must ultimately answer "ought" questions and tries to answer them in the form of law. Philosophers must delve still deeper. Judges and courts decide what our behavior ought to be, given the rules (i.e., the laws). But philosophers must ask, not what the rules governing violence are, but what they ought to be. What is the moral foundation for any such rules?

More particularly, my focus in this work is on violence viewed from a perspective of a party to a conflict and from a contemporaneous perspective: "If violence is occurring or about to occur, what sort of response is justified?" I defend the limited use of violence in the face of opposing violence. Accordingly, I do not focus on violence from a retrospective perspective. Unlike courts, I do not concern myself with the issues of punishments and reparations that a retrospective perspective addresses.

It is very important that we distinguish violent resistance to violent attack and the rights thereto from *violent punishment*. Punishment for an act occurs after it is completed and its consequences are assessed. It cannot be justified as defense.[1] Thus, punishment of any kind is not what I seek to justify. I can say, however, that I believe there is no right to impose violent punishment. That is, violent punishment is simply wrong. This would include whipping, torture, and even capital punishment. For, as we later see, a key tenet of my view is that violence is justified only to stop violence. Someone subject to punishment is, by definition, restrained and unable to impose violence on others.

Violence as Morally Good

It may seem strange to us, but a deep tradition in Western thought sees violence as a fundamental good to be glorified and pursued, either for its own sake or because of its direct positive benefit. War, for example, has been viewed as a source of tribal, imperial, or national glory, a forum for the expression of courage, heroism, and manhood where whole populations or nations are tested and made better and more fit. In ancient times, the gods of the victorious nations were considered to be stronger and better than those of the vanquished. Some philosophers even saw war as a grand historical stage on which victorious people, nations, or classes represented the cutting edge of history and progress. Wars, then, became the physical manifestation of moral and metaphysical progress.

Often, violence is glorified not by philosophic argument but by vivid description. Homer's accounts of the battles of the heroes of the Trojan War quicken the blood and produce a positive reaction to violence and its perpetrators.[2] We *feel* that violence is good, but that feeling is not based on rational argument or moral principle. Similar feelings are elicited on reading violent and martial passages from the stories of Samson and Joshua in the Bible[3] or the Anglo-Saxon poem *Beowulf*.[4] These works exemplify a classic, yet effective, appeal to emotion. Indeed, while hardly high art, movies featuring "Rambo" and "Dirty Harry" are part of this deep and (at least until recently) honored tradition. Yet it is obvious that appeals to emotion carry absolutely no intellectual cogency.[5]

There are fewer instances of philosophic arguments generally in favor of violence. Still, a number of philosophers (e.g., Heraclitus, Plato, Hegel, Nietzsche, Marx, and, in our own time, Frantz Fanon and Jean Paul Sartre) at times talk as though violence may be good in itself or as an instrument to some transcendental goal. These thinkers have very different views of violence. Some see it as good in itself, some as promoting manhood, courage, and other martial (and therefore "good") virtues. Some believe it central to the drama of historical progress. Others see it as essential to the liberation of the human spirit. Yet, in the relevant works or passages, they seem to agree on one thing: Everything else being equal, their particular brand of violence is a good thing to be exercised by the appropriate people in the appropriate martial, historical, or political context.

Despite our society's fascination with "Rambo" and "Dirty Harry," most thoughtful people today reject the view that violence is in any way good. Violence, virtually all of us agree, is bad; it is sometimes necessary perhaps, but invariably bad. Why? This is a central question, to be sure, but our approach to it is through an even more basic question.

What Is Violence?

First, we must know what violence is. To aid us, we may turn to legal theory where the notion of violence, and the related concept of force, have a central place. Violence in our legal system is uniformly regarded as bad, not always wrong but always to be discouraged. Except in highly limited and carefully defined instances, it is criminal or tortious, or both.

To see this, we must limit our inquiry a bit. For we are interested here in violence against persons. There are related questions about violence against property and interesting interim cases of violence against animals. But our interests are limited to violence against and between persons. In the first instance, this means living, breathing human beings. In the second, we want to extend our concern to legal persons, organizations made up of human beings, each playing a role in some institutional context. This last category could conceivably include corporations, tribes, or military units, among many other sorts of things. Our interest, however, focuses on only one kind of organized, legal person: the nation-state. After all, in our time it is primarily nation-states that wage war on one another. For our purposes, war is the most important, though by no means the only or even most basic, form of violence. International law governs the activity of waging war, and it treats nation-states as legal persons.

One of the best definitions of violence that fits the framework of our law has been formulated in slightly different forms by Ronald Miller, Robert Audi, and most thoroughly by Robert Holmes, and I rely on their work here.[6] Let us begin by setting out a definition that is partially descriptive and partially stipulative. It does not include, for example, violence as used in "violent storm." Nonetheless, I claim that this definition does capture an important, and for us central, part of the proper range of the concept.

First, violence is a quality of intentional actions of persons directed against other persons. An act of violence against a person (1) is itself capable of causing pain, injuring or killing the person acted upon (*the consequential condition*); (2) is done with the *intent* of putting in pain, disabling, injuring, or killing the person acted upon (*the intentional condition*); and (3) involves great force and vigor (*the delivery condition*).

Each of these conditions is going to give us trouble, but this constitutes a good starting point. We should note several key characteristics of this definition. First, unlike some definitions of violence, ours does not presuppose that violence is necessarily wrong. One's purpose in intentionally killing another might be to bring about some acceptable situation, where bringing it about is morally justified. Second, an act of violence is an intentional action; it is not a mere happening (e.g., a storm). Moreover, it must intentionally bring about or aim at bringing about pain, injury, or death and not be an act directed at some other end that "by accident" is violent.[7] Third, our definition excludes acts that cause solely psychological harm and efforts to do the same.[8] Fourth, we purposely exclude notions of violence often used to characterize human institutions.[9] Descriptions of capitalism, colonialism, or even slavery that label them as violent use a different sense of "violence" (which may itself be coherent or incoherent) from what we employ here. This does *not* mean, however, that certain human institutions do not rely on practices that include the customary and regular commitment of acts of violence. Slavery, for example, is almost always accompanied by brutal forms of corporal punishment (e.g., flagellation), which certainly involve acts of violence.

As said earlier, this definition is not defended as complete, although

Holmes[10] does a splendid job of conceptual analysis to arrive at something very close to our definition as "primary cases" of violence. We
instead temporarily engage in linguistic legislation. Then we rely on
an emergent demonstration throughout this analysis to show that our
notion of violence is central to accounts of the wrongfulness of violence
and to the ways we typically justify it. Indeed, if correct, our notion of
violence should emerge as the central one (though perhaps not the only
one) in law and morals.

Why Violence Is Bad

What is wrong with violence? Plenty of things. First, violence hurts.
One need not hold the view that the absence of pain or the presence of
its contrary, pleasure, is the *only* good to believe that human pain and
suffering is very bad indeed. There may be other goods than pleasure
and, more important, other bads than pain, but human pain is clearly
bad. Pain is simply bad for its own sake, without further analysis. Unless we are profoundly disturbed, we all want, and *should* want, our
fellow humans not to be in pain. Philosophers as diverse as David Hume
and Jean Jacques Rousseau have made basic to their views a sympathy
between people, most obviously made manifest in an aversion to the
pain of others. In our time, Thomas Nagel has explicitly treated pain
as an elemental, negative feature of our moral world.[11] We follow Nagel
in this basic normative assumption. From this it seems to follow that,
at least prima facie, people should not be put in pain, and we should
avoid putting them in pain if at all possible.

If it is clear, as I believe it is, that pain is to be avoided and prevented
whenever possible, then it is surely even more clear that pain ought
not to be *inflicted*. That is, pain ought not be intentionally brought
into existence, at least not without an extremely good reason, such as
a medical procedure that causes pain to save a life. Indeed, we want to
go further and hold that every human person has a *right* not to be put
in pain against her or his will.[12]

Even though pain is bad, and violence almost always produces pain,
the badness of pain is not the only reason that violence is bad. Indeed,
surprisingly, the production of pain may not even be the primary reason
that violence is bad. To see this point, let us do a short thought experiment. Consider a demented experimenter who describes a project
that she and her team are about to undertake. She plans to choose an

uninformed, nonconsenting subject. She will give this subject massive doses of local anesthetic (something like novocaine), then proceed to injure his body seriously—strike him with a moving vehicle at a fairly high speed, perhaps. The key, she tells you with her eyes aglow, is that he will feel no pain. You object that he will be in terrible pain when the novocaine wears off, as he recovers in the hospital. But no. The experimenter has thought of everything. She will have the subject locally anesthetized during the entire recuperation period, which is expected to last several months. There will simply be no pain in the experiment. There will injury and damage to the subject's body, to be sure, but no pain.

"So what is wrong with my experiment?" she asks. Note that any answer we provide will reveal things that are wrong with violence beyond its capacity to produce pain. For surely the subject's rights do not stop with a right not to be in pain. We all have a right to the physical integrity of our bodies. Violence is a "violent" contact with the body, forceful, swift, and injurious. If the recipient does not consent to such contact, then it by itself is wrong. Newton Garver points out that "violence" comes from the same Latin root as "violation," and he believes that this goes to the heart of the concept.[13] Doubtless, he is correct. Violence *violates,* and it is part of the essence of violence that it does so. Indeed, it violates in a number of ways. Accordingly, the "mad experiment" violates the subject's physical integrity. Anglo-American law recognizes a zone around each of us that is ours, not to be crossed by others without our consent. If you are struck without authorization, a key right of yours is violated. Even the lightest tap, if unauthorized and done in an insulting or threatening way, is battery and is an actionable tort.[14] If the threat attending it is great enough, it is also a crime.[15]

There is a very deep and intimate association between our bodies and ourselves as persons. Some violations of physical integrity bring home this intuitive moral connection more graphically than a simple, trivial touch. Think of rape. (The male reader is reminded that men, too, can be raped.) The law defines rape, not as a completed sex act, but as *penetration.*[16] That is how it should be. Now consider the report of many rape victims of a feeling of personal violation. "Not just my rights, but *I* have been violated," the victim often reports. And surely we can empathize with that; both her body and *her person* have been violated.

Consider another crime—torture.[17] The person in the torture chamber having his fingers mangled with pliers, for example, is being violated *as a person*. That crucial relationship between physical integrity and personhood has broken down. The tortured person, like the rape victim, is treated like a *thing*. Rape and torture are also often attended by conscious efforts to *humiliate*. Physically based violence, that is, can be intensified by psychological manipulation. Such humiliation only reinforces the dehumanizing nature of the violence perpetrated in these crimes. Rape and torture dramatize in an especially terrible way what is characteristic of all involuntarily applied violence: violation of one's bodily integrity and one's rights thereto.[18] And we must remember the intimate relationship between bodily integrity and personhood.

But this violation of bodily integrity does not exhaust the ways in which violence violates integrity. For there is the integrity of our *lives*. Let us return to our demented experimenter and her hapless subject. The subject will be hospitalized for weeks, perhaps months, while his body mends. Thus, more than his body, or even his person, has been damaged. His *life*, all his plans and projects, have been at least temporarily interrupted, some perhaps never to be resumed. His relationships with the members of his family have, no doubt, been changed. Unless the disturbed experimenter plans to pay for more than the subject's novocaine, he will have a heavy financial burden to bear. In short, *his autonomy as a free person* has been radically transgressed. Most of us believe that we have a right to lead our lives without this sort of interference with our autonomy, free to pursue our life's plans and projects. Certainly the poor subject in the experiment had that right violently interfered with.

These notions, the integrity of one's body and person and the integrity of one's life, are central to our notion of a person and a person's life as *worthy of respect* and possessing a certain *dignity*. It is these notions and the rights we have to their protection that separate us from things or objects.[19]

There is yet another kind of violation implicit in violence. For violence is not always an end in itself, it is often a means. The mugger hits you on the head to get your wallet or purse. The bank robber pistol-whips the bank manager to get the combination to the vault. Violence or the threat of violence is often used in this way *to reduce the will* of the victim to the *dominance* of the attacker's will.

Of course, social situations often put us under the dominion of the will of another. The student is to some very limited extent under the dominion of the professor. He decides what the student shall read and when the student shall be tested. The salesman is even more under the dominion of the will of the sales manager. She decides on whom he shall call, how he will sell his product, and, in most companies, how much he shall be paid. The marine recruit is even more under the dominion of the drill sergeant. Nevertheless, in each of these cases, *rules limit the authority* of the superior and especially what sorts of penalties or threats of penalties can be used to enforce the will of the superior on the subordinate. Generally, the threats of penalty are not threats of violence. Furthermore, these social roles (e.g., student, salesperson, and marine recruit) are *voluntary* or *consensual*.[20] People are in these roles because they have freely chosen to be.

But lawless, unbridled violence is different. The victim of the mugger or the bank robber is wholly, and without reservation, at the whim of the criminal's will. No rules effectively limit the criminal's behavior, nor is the victim a volunteer. The victim is there through coercion and the threat of violence or the consequences of its actual application or both. To be wholly under the dominion of another, backed by unlimited threats of violence and without any recourse, is one of the most basic definitions of slavery in Western law and political philosophy.[21] Another objectionable thing about violence, then, is that it allows those capable of it, and willing to initiate its use, to tyrannize the rest of us. It imposes time slices of slavery.

The clearest instances of the wrongness of violence, however, come with *lethal* violence. Violence often kills, and killing is often violent. Violence that kills constitutes the most total of all violations of basic rights. It is wrong to kill without very strong, very specific justification. This is because each human person has a right to life. Anyone who believes human beings have *any* rights agrees that we have a right to life. We may not know exactly how to analyze this very difficult notion,[22] but that does not vitiate our having the right.

There is another moral characteristic of humans, one that at least most of us believe in. People are equal simply because they are people. Equality can mean many things, but one of the most generally recognized notions of equality is moral equality. Your pain is as bad as my pain, your identical injury is as bad as mine, and so is the violation of any other of your rights. The moral personhood of which I spoke earlier is intrinsically *equal* moral personhood. Each of us has it and has it in the same degree. Relying on the philosophy of Immanuel Kant, Charles Fried has used this basic notion of moral equality to produce yet another argument against violence.[23] If I use violence to extract from you something I want—your wallet or information you have, for example—I am *using you for my ends*. Similarly, if I enjoy beating people and do that to you for the fun of it, I am also using you for my ends. In each case, you are only a means to the attainment of my ends. I use you as a thing, exclusively. In so doing, I deny your moral equality with me. I am, by my action, tacitly saying that you are worth less than I am, something that can be bent to my needs, never mind your value as a person. That denial of moral equality is wrong.

Thus we are now in a position to make the obvious badness of violence explicit. Violence is bad for the following reasons:

1. It usually causes pain, and
    a. Pain is bad; its presence in the world should be minimized. One of the most obvious and effective ways of minimizing pain is not intentionally to bring it about.
    b. People generally and presumptively have a right not to be put in pain, especially against their will.
2. It violates the dignity and integrity of human beings because it violates
    a. The right to bodily and personal integrity.
    b. The right to the integrity of one's life, that is, to live one's life and pursue one's goals without unjustified interference through injury.
    c. The right to the integrity of one's life in another way, that is, not to have one's will subjected to the unconditional and nonconsensual domination of another by violence or threats of violence.
    d. The right to life.
3. It denies our basic moral equality with other humans not being treated violently, especially including the perpetrator of the violence.

The reader should note two features of my analysis of violence, for they are going to be strongly controverted by Scherer in Chapter 2.

First, I very explicitly make violence or, more properly, an act of violence *intentional* in character. This directly leads to the next feature of my analysis of violence. What is bad about violence is that it *violates* persons, and our moral logic captures that by talking about violence violating *individual human rights, basic* individual rights. Typically (many would say exclusively), a person can violate another's rights only through intentional action. Moreover, the sorts of violent rights violations we discuss here are not only intentional acts, they are self-consciously and intentionally rights violative.[24] So the possession of these rights and the intentional character of violence come together in the possibility for intentional violent interference or invasion of those basic individual rights. This, as we later see, gives rise to second-order rights of self-defense and defense of others.

A Theory of Value and a Theory of the Right

Enough has been said to demonstrate that violence is a very bad thing. And we usually believe that whatever is bad is also wrong to bring about or to tolerate. This belief, however, risks a fundamental confusion. Badness is an expression of *value*. It tells us that a certain thing, in this case, violence has negative value. Getting from a theory of value to a decision about what we should do is not as obvious as it seems. Most philosophers believe that to do so requires a theory of the right.[25]

A theory of the right lays down rules by which we can specifically guide our action. Although violence is bad and has bad effects, according to most theories, it is not the only bad thing. Indeed, we have already discovered that pain is bad also, even pain not caused by violence. Suppose that in some given situation one had a choice of preventing the occurrence of violence but only by producing a greater amount of pain from some source other than violence. The mere fact that violence is bad and has bad effects is not enough to give one a rule by which to act in that situation, for pain, in this case greater pain, is also bad. Which ought one to choose: (1) violence that will produce some pain plus some other bad things (some other rights violations) or (2) more pain without rights violations? When one must choose between different sorts of good things, or as in this case different sorts of bad things, one needs a theory of right, that is, a theory of right and wrong action.

There are two fairly obvious ways of moving from a theory of value to a theory of right as regards violence. One is to define an absolute duty never to commit any violent act. Pacifists traditionally follow this path. Another way to link the strong negative value of violence with action is to formulate a presumptive duty never to commit a violent act without a very good reason. Thus, a rebuttable presumption against violence (or a prima facie duty not to be violent) is created. Violence is bad, but other things, including the prevention of greater violence, might justify or excuse violence. This is the path I choose and to which we now turn.

Rights of Defense against Violent Attack

The most traditional argument in favor of self-defense and the defense of others under violent attack is also the most consonant with the moral position I take in this book, namely, a *natural rights position*. If, simply because we are persons, we have rights to life, liberty, and personal integrity, not to be coerced with violence or threats of violence, then it follows that we must have second-order rights to protect those basic, first-order rights. (They are "second order" because they are rights having rights as their objects.) Jan Narveson has argued that not having such rights implies not having first-order rights.[26] Thus, a right that is unprotectable is no right at all. Narveson is correct, and we can demonstrate this somewhat differently from the way he does.

If our basic rights are claim rights, in Hohfeld's sense, they make claims against all humans. Scherer's right not to be violently attacked (a shorthand for the list of basic rights set out earlier) binds me and all others not to attack him. Thus it imposes a correlative duty on me and all others not to attack him. Thus we have derived the presumptive or prima facie duty not to attack others violently from the existence of those basic rights. But, if Scherer's right not to be attacked violently is a genuine right, my duty not to attack him *must be enforceable* by him and others in his behalf. If it is not, then in what sense is it a duty to him? Does this justify *violent* defense of basic rights? Isn't such violent defense rights violative itself? What happens to the attacker's basic rights? How are those conflicting rights (i.e., the defender's second-order right of defense and the attacker's basic rights) made consistent? This is a very difficult question, one that, at the deepest level, we shall not try to answer. Scherer's attack on my position is not directed at this point, indeed is not framed in terms of rights; and so pursuing this topic would take us too far afield.[27] We can, however, provide an answer at one level.[28] The attacker forces the defender to make a choice of rights violation, that is, acquiesce in the violation of his own or an innocent third-party's rights at the hands of the attacker or launch a defensive counterattack and violate the attacker's basic rights. (We assume throughout that these are the only options, i.e., there are no nonviolent alternatives. See the next section.) The attacker forces this choice wrongfully by his intentional action. The attack is wrongful by definition, since it is rights violative and unjustified. In this case, the wrongful party's rights must give way. This seems intuitively obvious for anyone who (1) accepts a set of basic rights as fundamental and (2) requires that sets of rights be compossible or mutually consistent.[29]

There is a subsequent question, however. If the defender is justified in a violent and rights-violative counterattack, *how extensive* may the rights violation be? One view, for example, is that the attacker's rights are forfeit and that anyone can do anything they want to him.[30] He is the moral equivalent of an "outlaw" in the old Norse and Anglo-Saxon law; that is, he is beyond the protection of the law and has no rights under it. My view, which I elaborate in the next section, is the opposite: The rights violation committed by a justified defender must be the *most narrow practically possible.* What this means and along what dimensions this narrowness must lie I flesh out in my moral theory of violence.

A corollary argument for limited rights of defensive violence stems from Charles Fried's argument set out earlier. Recall that Fried believes that unjustified violent attack is the use of a person (the victim) as an object and a consequent denial of her moral equality with the attacker. But a limited, defensive counterattack is not the denial of the attacker's moral equality. If it is, it too is wrongful and is an overreaction. An appropriate defense is merely the *reassertion and reestablishment of moral equality.*[31]

Nation-States and the Right of Defense

Let us now extrapolate the basic rights we all possess to the level of nations.[32] We organize ourselves into political entities, some of which are called nation-states. We do this to attain a number of ends, but the most obvious ones (and most political philosophers would say the most important) are to protect our lives, our safety, our freedom (i.e., our basic rights) from arbitrary and unjustified invasion through violence or coercive threats of violence. In such political organizations, we give up a lot. We must abide by many rules (laws), and we must pay (via taxes) for the services we receive.

There is, then, a quid pro quo between what we obtain and what we give up. We enter a *contract* with each other, or the political organization, to give up something in order to get something.

An important part of what we aim to get is protection from violations of our basic rights. These rights can be invaded in two ways. First, they can be invaded or threatened with invasion from within our society by fellow citizens. The state provides police forces to protect us from that. Second, our basic rights can be threatened by people from outside our nation-state. Often (although certainly not always) such people are organized as other nation-states. Thus, we have armed forces to forestall or arrest such extranational invasions.

Now comes a crucial move. The right of a nation to defend itself and to launch any military operation to that end is justified *only because it is protecting its people and their basic rights in their homeland.* The state can defend its territory with violent force *only because* that territory is also the property of its citizens and is indispensable in defending their lives and basic rights. National territorial integrity is derivative; protection of citizens in their homes fundamental.[33] For the present, we merely assume that in recognizing a right to self-defense, international law recognizes, as logically contained therein, a right of a nation to defend its citizens within its boundaries.

The Minimal Justified Violence View

As we have seen in the two preceding sections, it is much easier to defend defensive violence and defensive rights violation if they are rigorously limited. The theory I now advance justifies violence in large measure by limitation. I call this view the *Minimal Justified Violence View* (or, for short, the Justified Violence View). Its roots lie deep in the Western legal and moral tradition. At the interpersonal level, it underpins most of the traditional legal "defenses" for the use of violence in criminal law and the law of torts. These include self-defense, the defense of others, public (police) authority, prevention of a crime, and the defense of property. At the international level, the Justified Violence View serves as the foundation of the international law of war and of an important related tradition in moral philosophy called *Just War Theory*.

The Justified Violence View is fastened in history by two separate roots. The theory that governs interpersonal violence, at least in our society, evolved out of the common law of medieval England.[34] In contrast, Just War Theory has deep roots in Western religious and philosophic tradition.[35] Beginning in Saint Augustine's work, it followed a path through Saint Thomas Aquinas and canon law to rise up in the secular, international arena in the work of Grotius, the father of the modern law of nations. Indeed, it is fascinating that two such different histories could evolve along essentially separate paths into two bodies of rules having so much in common. I am inclined to put this conceptual and systemic similarity down to the intuitive moral force and natural coherence of the shared structures, although a partially shared background of Roman law and then later Church canon law might explain some shared features.

The Prerequisites for Justified Violence

Prerequisite 1. The use of violence is presumed to be wrong.

This means that no one is allowed to use violence gratuitously. Violence requires a *justifying reason* and is wrong without it. What reasons, then, in the form of prerequisites, must pertain for violence to be used?

Prerequisite 2. For violence to be justified, it can be used only to stop violence being illicitly (and therefore unjustifiably) used in an attack.

This prerequisite for the use of violence is a very controversial one and cannot be said to be part of our law. The police officer may also use violence to prevent the commission of a felony, and this includes nonviolent felonies or at least felonies in which the police officer is in no danger of personal attack. A police officer can use violence, for example, to apprehend an escaping felon (although in most jurisdictions it is no longer justifiable to use deadly or lethal violence, as it once was). There are other possible uses of violence by police officers that we could consider. As I define the Justified Violence View, however, it does not permit such uses. Its logic is a logic of *violence only against violence;* in other words, it permits only *defensive violence.*

Prerequisite 3. For violence to be justified even in pursuit of prerequisite 2, it must be *necessary,* or appear to

>be necessary to a reasonable person, to stop the
>violent attack.

Violence can never be used when a nonviolent technique or measure
will suffice to stop the attack. This *is* the presumption against violence
and violent acts given in prerequisite 1.

But prerequisite 1 implies, along with prerequisite 3, that whatever
violence is used must be *the least* necessary. This yields the following:

>*Prerequisite 4.* For violence to be justified even in the pursuit of
>prerequisite 3, it must be the *minimal* amount
>necessary, or appear to be the minimal amount
>necessary to a reasonable person, to stop the
>violent attack.

Prerequisite 4 has important consequences for the *means* chosen to
stop an attack, for it must always be a means capable of stopping an
attack with the minimal violence necessary. You cannot stop a violent
attack with a machine gun when a body block would have done the job.

There is yet another restriction on defensive violence.

>*Prerequisite 5.* For violence to be justified, it must be
>*proportional* to the violence used in the attack.

This is a distinct condition quite distinguishable from justifiability (in
prerequisite 2), necessity (in 3) and minimality (in 4), although it is
related to the latter and sometimes confused with it. Proportionality
can succeed in banning certain measures of defensive violence, even
if they meet the first four requirements. Only incidental violence can
be used against incidental violence. If someone threatens to shove you
and proceeds to try to do it, you can shove back, but you cannot break
both his legs. This is true even if your only alternative to acquiescing
(to his shove) is the breaking of his legs. You must acquiesce in the
shove. A special case of prerequisite 5 is a much more well-known principle of law. *Lethal violence can be used only against lethal violence*
(or reasonably anticipated lethal violence). If someone approaches you
with a yardstick, threatening you with a spanking, you cannot shoot
him dead with a gun. Again, this prohibition holds even if the gun was
necessary to stop the attack and is the minimally violent response you
can muster in that situation. Better that you suffer a spanking with a
yardstick than that your attacker die of gunshot wounds.

Lest the reader conceive the requirement of proportionality as too great a concession to a pacifist standard, you should rest assured that it is not. For the law has historically granted considerable leeway on the part of the victim to interpret the events in her favor. That is why I put a yardstick in the hands of my would-be attacker, for a yardstick could not be used in a lethal attack. If we make the weapon a baseball bat, and if the attacker is strong enough to wield it with lethal force, and if he behaves in a manner that would cause a reasonable person to infer deadly intent, the use of the gun would be justified. That is, the attacked victim gets the "benefit of the doubt." As long as a particular violent means of defense would *appear* necessary, minimal, and pro-portional, to a *reasonable person*, it is justified. This is true even if, were all the facts actually known, that violent means would not have been necessary.

One more principle follows from prerequisites 1 through 5, especially from prerequisite 3, the necessity requirement:

> *Prerequisite 6.* Before undertaking defensive violence, one has an affirmative duty, as time and circumstance allow, to search for nonviolent options that may be available to frustrate a violent attack.

To all possible nonviolent options? The standard must be that of a reasonable search for reasonable options. By "reasonable options" we mean both practical options and those that are morally reasonable. Thus, to pick an absurd example to make the point, one is not obligated to jump off a bridge to avoid violent resistance to being mugged.[36]

Thus we see how the general presumption that violence, being bad, is also presumptively wrong, could nonetheless lead to a theory of justified violence. And see how nicely and logically the presumption against violence shapes and limits justified uses of violence. But we have not yet asked and answered the most basic question: What *moral conditions* actually *justify* the use of violence, even where its use is so scrupulously circumscribed as it is in these rules? I set out as my moral starting point that people had *rights* not to be put in pain, not to have their persons and lives violated, not to be enslaved or coerced with threats of violence. It is obvious, then, that the justifying conditions for minimal violence have to do with the *protection* of those basic rights. But to be morally justified to protect those basic, first-order rights you need rights to protect rights, that is, *second-order rights* of self-defense and the defense of others. It is to these crucial second-order rights that we now turn.

Conflict, Conflict Resolution, and the Right to Resist

In formulating and analyzing rules governing violence, a central issue comes to the fore: What characterizes a situation of violent conflict? How and why do such situations occur? The law seems to presuppose that one person "started it" and is at fault. Does this assumption hold up? To find out, let us examine some of the constituent concepts. Before we analyze *violent* conflict situations, let us look at the broader class of conflict situations. We might define a *conflict situation* as existing between or among people when several people want to bring about states of affairs that are inconsistent with each other (i.e., that cannot all be brought about at the same time).[37] How can conflict situations come about? Broadly, there are two ways. First, they may be caused by events or situations beyond the control of the parties to the conflict; that is, they can *happen*. Second, the conflict can be the *intentional creation* of one or both parties; that is, they can be the action of an agent.

Included in the first category would be conflict brought about by natural causes. Imagine an area, let us say a valley, that is traditionally home to two tribes, wherein the carrying capacity of the valley makes a comfortable life for both possible. Subsequently, a climatic change occurs, causing drought and famine. Now there is carrying capacity for only one tribe. The conflict situation is the desire each tribe has to remain living in the valley, the *fact* that only one can live there, and the consequence that their desires are in conflict.

At the other extreme is the conflict intentionally created by a party to it. In interpersonal relations, the violent criminal is usually a good example. The mugger, the rapist, the violent assailant is a party *choosing* to create the conflict situation in the morally relevant sense. Unlike the victim, he could at any moment desist from (his creation of) the conflict, and it would go away.[38] In the affairs of nations, Hitler's aggressive demands and later his aggressive attacks are the purest example in modern times of a choice to create a conflict situation.

One must readily admit that the line between conflict situations that happen and conflict situations that are the intentional creations of agents is, like most important lines in law, politics, and morals, fuzzy at the boundary. This is especially true in international conflicts. Which party caused or is causing the Arab–Israeli conflict? We gain another perspective on this fuzziness by trying to discover the moral status quo ante. That is, what was the situation *before* the conflict situation arose or was brought about?[39] We might call this the *moral baseline*. This would be a situation where no manifest injustice was imposed on relevant parties. At least, none has recently been imposed by morally responsible agents. All rights are honored, all duties discharged.

Where do we begin in finding rights violated and duties undischarged, credit and blame? In the Arab–Israeli conflict, do we start the moral analysis today with the outrageous terrorist attacks against Israeli citizens in their homelands? Do we begin in 1948 with the eviction of the Palestinians from their homeland? Should the British or the United Nations or some other third party come in for moral evaluation based on actions or omissions occurring long ago? Perhaps we should say that impersonal "history" is the relevant moral cause, rather than look for intentional agents as cause. The contrast between the earlier questions and the last question is a crucial clue to the origin of any conflict situation. When the moral baseline is changed by the intentional action of an agent, it is fairly easy to determine. We find the point at which the agent intervened. Thus it is also fairly easy to see how things should be put right. If possible, we put things back the way they were before the agent created the conflict. When a situation has evolved through the impersonal forces of history, however, there can be no obvious, morally appropriate point to which we should return.

Suffice it to say, there are clear instances both in interpersonal and international conflict where one party makes demands backed by threats or undertakes unilateral changes that create the conflict. That is, sometimes a party creates the situation in which the wants of both parties are inconsistent one with the other. The mugger says, "Give me your wallet," as he levels a gun at you. Germany (in the person of Bismarck) says to France, "Give us Alsace-Lorraine." In both instances, there was no conflict situation until the mugger and Germany wanted something that was not theirs, that is, decided to change the moral baseline. Now we have two inconsistent states of affairs, that desired by the agent creating the violent conflict and that which now exists.

The key characteristic of this kind of conflict is that it is gratuitous. It need not have happened. One party undertakes to create it, without just cause or necessity, exclusively for his own interest. We might contrast this to the conflict, between the two tribes in our first example.

Understanding the possibility of gratuitous conflict intentionally brought about by one party, we can now define a central concept, that of aggression. An *aggressor* is someone who (1) seeks to force an outcome to a conflict situation that is solely (or at least primarily) in the aggressor's interest and has been intentionally brought about solely *for that interest*, that imposes a net cost or harm on another, and that is to be imposed without the other's free (i.e., uncoerced) consent; and (2) seeks to bring about acquiescence to his demands using violence or coercive threats of violence to violate the basic rights of the subject of the aggression. Note that condition 2 requires that all aggressors be violent aggressors because it includes *threats* of violence as well as acts of violence. (There may be something we could call "nonviolent aggression," but if it exists, it is not of immediate interest here.)

Now we come to a central thesis in the Justified Violence View. While the use of violence must be carefully constrained by prerequisites 1 through 6, there are instances when its use is morally justified. The most obvious and important one is in the *resistance to aggression*. That a party who is the victim of aggression has a right to self-defense or that third parties have a right to defend the victim against such aggression, or both, is what we endeavored to show in the section "Rights of Defense Against Violent Attack."

Acquiescence to aggression is one nonviolent option that I explicitly deny is required of those faced with aggression. Rather than be morally forced to acquiesce, there arises a clear right of *violent defense*, if necessary, against such aggression. One may choose to acquiesce, but that is supererogation.[40] Everything else being equal, one is not obligated to acquiesce. One thing is certain: At a bare minimum, the Justified Violence View *must* claim that, when an aggressor, by threat or action, demands a solution that imposes nonconsensual pain on you, violates your physical or personal integrity, seeks to dominate your will unconditionally, or seeks to take your life, you are unequivocally justified in using (minimal, necessary, proportional) violent force to resist. (Note: This does not mean that other threatened costs or harms could not also justify violent resistance to violent imposition of those costs or harms. They often could. But here we look at only the simplest case for defensive violence.)

Let us review the position set out thus far. If some person is the victim of an aggressor, that person's right of self-defense is the right to remove the conflict situation created by that aggressor by threat of violence or, failing that, by violence, assuming that the only nonviolent option open to the person is acquiescence. Similarly, the right of defense of others is the right to remove a conflict situation by threat of violence or actual violence if the only alternative is acquiescence in the violation of basic rights of persons.

The Justified Violence View of International Relations

In the section "Nation-States and the Right of Defense" we saw that the right to resist aggression violently, based on the basic rights of human persons, can be extrapolated to the rights of nation-states. Thus the Justified Violence View applies to the behavior of nations also, if we are allowed the simplistic but here harmless assumption that nation-states are persons. What does this view mandate for states? War making, which is the primary international form of violence, is justified only for *defensive* purposes. Just War Theory, the international version of the Justified Violence View, rejects the Clauswitzian notion of war as an instrument of policy. War is not a justifiable means of policy implementation, nor is it a justifiable vehicle for the pursuit of "national interest."

The Justified Violence View permits a state to make war only in three cases: (1) when the state is under attack, or about to be attacked (i.e., self-defense); (2) when another, innocent third-party state is under attack, or about to be attacked (i.e., defense of others); (3) when people within a country are being attacked or are about to be attacked by the governing powers of that country and genocide is threatened (i.e., crimes against humanity). Note that for both human persons and nation-states, our right of defense is the right to defend innocent victims of unjustified violent attacks, whoever that victim might be. Thus it is not equivalent to a right of self-defense, though it includes that. With this understanding, we may conclude from (1), (2), and (3) that war making is justified only in *resistance to immanent or occurrent aggression*.

Summary

The foundation of the Minimal Justified Violence View is its theory of the right. This theory rests on the kind of argument I have given herein for the conclusion that the intentional compromise of certain basic values is unequivocally unjustified. Having thus set out basic rights as protection of those values, I have argued, on the one hand, that violence is always unjustified unless several conditions (minimality, necessity, proportionality, etc.) are met. But I also have argued that violence meeting those conditions is justified in defense of the basic human rights of either oneself or others.

A Critique of Justified Violence

Alternative Practices and Deep Justification

The horror of a Hitler tells us that practices for controlling violence are necessary. Indeed the history of warfare; the age-old issues of tyranny, crime, and police brutality; and the worldwide problem of domestic violence amply demonstrate that violence all too often goes uncontrolled. Admittedly, when we compare contemporary intrastate mechanisms for the control of violence to, say, the blood feuds of early medieval Germanic culture, we see real moral progress. But our vastly violent world also suggests that contemporary practices for responding to violence may be inferior to others we might envision, develop, and implement.

In contrast to this ameliorative hope, the Minimal Justified Violence View is a conservative philosophical theory about justified responses to violence. The theory is based in philosophical reflection on the Anglo-Saxon legal tradition and on international law, which also has deep roots in our own legal tradition.[1] Accordingly, it analyzes and defends the principles underlying our social practices.

Unlike James Child, I find analyzing and defending the principles underlying extant social practices philosophically inappropriate. Such a provincial style of philosophizing too easily justifies too much by ignoring the power of normal socialization to supply the models that guide our prereflective thought. For the people of a given society become socialized to the problems and practices of their society. The concepts they use, instead of merely describing their experience, define for them their problems, prescribe for them their solutions, and consign to them lamentable residual problems they will tend to consider unfortunately unavoidable.

Accordingly, a conservative model of violence does more to condemn and justify than to contain and reduce the violence of our world. For within it, people will tend to see themselves as lacking constructive alternatives. Consider, for example, how Child defines an aggressor: "someone who (1) seeks to force an outcome to a conflict situation that is solely (or at least primarily) in the aggressor's interest and has been intentionally brought about solely *for that interest*, that imposes a net cost or harm on another, and that is to be imposed without the other's free (i.e., uncoerced) consent; and (2) seeks to bring about acquiescence to his demands using violence or coercive threats of violence."[2]

The terms of this definition set us up to accept the need for firmly resisting aggressors. But since socialization is a molding power, we should not be surprised to notice possibilities that this definition hides. For instance, the search for forced outcomes may be retributive, or otherwise provoked; or an apparent aggressor may only inadvertently force an outcome. By hiding such possibilities, Child's plausible definition implausibly characterizes aggression as a problem of immoral action.

But why, if the definition ignores these possibilities, does the definition strike us as plausible? Various components of our socialization help: (1) We assume a moral status quo ante, a set of claims and rights, known and accepted beforehand; (2) we assume established, acceptable procedures for resolving disputed claims and rights; and (3) we highly value the ability to undertake personal projects in a social environment where the assumptions mentioned here operate.

However desirable our social environment may be, the violence of our world should make us suspect that these assumptions cause troubles as well as provide us a framework. To be sure, sometimes no status quo ante is established. In the home, in the schoolyard, and in the international arena, the mechanisms that make our assumptions plausible have not gained systemic currency.

But this may seem to be no more than a practical problem of incomplete implementation. Therefore, it is a much more troublesome concern that sometimes procedures for resolving disputed claims mold and reinforce antagonistic and violent dispositions. So if our assumptions are incompletely implemented, do we know whether we ought to extend, rather than modify, our responses to violence? And if our procedures harden adversarial stances, might an alternative order have virtues ours lacks?

To see how differently a society may respond to violence, let us undertake a simple thought experiment. We may imagine having been asked to adjudicate a dispute within the so-called stateless tribes of traditional West Africa[3] in a situation where some hostility has occurred and perhaps some violence has been done.

Having been called in, we would first want to know "what the problem was." Accordingly, we would ask who did what and with what provocation and with what justification. When we had established a set of rights, we would aim at assigning responsibility, fixing blame, and determining punishment or reparation.

For their part, the West Africans would tell us about former ties, disturbed community structures, and the necessity of restoring relationships. *We* would see a problem focused in a past action for which responsibility must be assigned. *They* would see a disrupted relationship requiring restoration. *We* would see parties proved untrustworthy because of having abused the rights of others. *They* would see parties needing to reestablish community and mutual trust. *We* would be prepared to allow for the possibility of a permanent rift between the guilty and the innocent in order to punish the guilty and protect the innocent. *They* would forgo condemnation of the wrongdoer in order to reestablish the sense and structure of social intercourse between the conflicting parties.

These contrasts rest on the contrast between our concern for rights violated or duties not properly discharged versus their concern for community and communal ties to be reestablished. In our view, the aggressive character of some act should be established as the basis for determining appropriate treatment for the victim and the criminal. In their view, the tensions in the community should be identified so that the functioning of the entire community can be restored. Our focus is on the protection of the rights of the victim or the social need for protection against the wrongdoing of the criminal. They focus on the twofold tear a crime creates in the social fabric, a rift between criminal and victim, and an estrangement between criminal and other members of the society. Unlike some societies around them that countenance revenge or employ banishment as a punishment, these tribes tradition-ally see dispositions toward revenge and banishment as parts of the problem, not as keys to its solution.

The members of two such different societies may agree abstractly that life, health, safety, education, personal integrity, freedom from pain, liberty, and community are fundamental goods of human life. But if they prioritize these values differently, they will find different problems or concerns in a given social interaction. Thus, out of such concerns as the West Africans had, several patterns of response may arise and have arisen: Violators may be expected to provide compen-sation or restitution for their victims; they may be asked to provide services for their victims, who are expected to express gratitude for the efforts. The violators may be asked to do penance, contemplating the unhappiness of their broken relations. Their victims may be asked to offer forgiveness. Mediators may be employed to ascertain the needs of both violators and victims, and to propose solutions that may in-volve third parties in (partial) redistribution of land or other property. Elaborate social rituals expressing and reinforcing the reestablishment of communal ties may be performed.

Such practices form a reinforcing package: They become safer, more feasible, and more efficacious as they are taken in concert or in known sequence. Similarly, they give substance to the restoration of commu-nity harmony and develop what that value can involve if social practices cultivate it.

I conclude, then, that the values of our culture do not imply the re-sponses we make to violence. Other practices, indeed less alienating, more reconciliative practices, have been developed. Accordingly, since different prioritizations of values undergird the development of differ-ent practices for responding to violence, the question must be faced: How should we compare and evaluate alternative practices?

The Teleological Character of the
Justification of Action

My discussion of West African practices has two purposes. One purpose is to call attention to the value of the communal. In the light of this value I use a later section in this chapter, "Deficiencies of Rights Language," to analyze the danger of using the alienating terms of individualistic traditions to define the commonly human problem of violent conflict.

The other purpose is to show how the justification of action is fundamentally teleological. Here my target is not specifically the Minimal Justified Violence View with its rights-based concepts. Instead, my target is the shallowness of justification within many philosophical theories, rights theories included.

My contrast between our ways and traditional West African ways of dealing with conflict has emphasized that (1) a social practice presupposes a particular definition of "the human problem." The discussion has also shown that (2) a social practice includes several interactive components[4] for responding to the problem. These two philosophical data allow us to draw a conclusion of the first importance about the character of moral justification:

> Conclusion: We cannot read a moral justification off the
> application of a set of normative concepts that has
> wide currency.

Those concepts reflect not merely the fundamental human values, on which Child and I agree, but a particular society's prioritization of those values as reflected in its practices for responding to "the problem."

Thus the shallower justification of an action presupposes an established way of defining "the" human problem. The deeper justification first considers redefining "the problem." The shallower provides a general framework for justifying extant practices. The deeper criticizes extant practices in the light of how a new constellation of practices might allow common human values to be realized more fully.

Indeed, the use of shallow justification gives rise to an important practical difficulty that is most apparent in intersocietal dispute. For a shallow justification is inextricably tied to an ascribed prioritization of common human values and a set of procedures for realizing those values, to the extent, of course, that priorities, dispositions, and circumstances allow. To see this clearly, imagine a conflict between a society that entrenches certain practices manifesting one shallow justification and a society that entrenches divergent practices. Imagine, in the face of conflict, that the first society uses its shallow justification. The second society will perceive in that justification at least the strong appearance of question begging against its divergent practices. But the mere existence of such an appearance will often suffice to solidify an alienation between the societies and to broaden and intensify the bases for hostility.

Any culture intermixes definitions of "the problem" with practices for responding to it. Much of the evaluation of any particular definition of a problem, however, should rest on a teleological focus: The better definition of the problem will carry with it the more fruitful suggestions about conflict resolution. But notice: We cannot define the fruitfulness of suggestions for conflict resolution in the light of a given society's prioritization of common human values, for such a definition will be question begging. If, in contrast, we are to avoid such a definition, our recourse must be to define "fruitfulness" in terms of the realization of the common human values on which Child and I agree. Thus my procedure is to assume various particular definitions of a conflict. I then ask, "If the problem is so defined, what practices might be constructed for responding to the problem?" In this way, the success in realizing values becomes the criterion for evaluating both problem definitions and practices for responding to the problems.

In summary, then, we should not read the justification of responses to problems from socially entrenched problem definitions and socially entrenched practices for responding to them. Instead, we should lump a problem definition with the solution pattern it best justifies and then evaluate that lumping against its alternatives. Only then can we develop a philosophical justification deep enough to form a non-question-begging criterion for the resolution of conflict.

How, then, do I respond to Child? Child aims to state the rationale underlying liberal practices for controlling violence. I scrutinize and challenge such practices in the light of shortcomings I attempt to reveal in them and in the liberal philosophical tradition. Child aims to bring out what I also see as advantages of liberal practices for controlling violence. But I propose improved practices.

Alternative Priorities and the Problem of Violence

As we begin thinking about different sets of practices for resolving the "problem of violence," we should note some virtues of the West African focus on the relationships between persons in conflict: It moves away from the dichotomies that separate aggressor and victim. It incorporates the insight that human beings share the vulnerability of mortality, which is the basis of all human frailties. It affirms both the moral primacy of the commonalities binding the conflicting parties and the importance of maintaining amicable social relations. To the extent that a practice for responding to human-caused harm can incorporate these virtues, the practice will be the better. And in all these regards, the pacifism I develop follows the West African model and departs from our traditional Western deontological one.

In particular, the pacifism I develop emphasizes that human mortality, that fundamental frailty, is neither mine to the exclusion of you, nor yours to the exclusion of me. And inasmuch as human beings are all ultimately subject to it, so are they all appropriately worthy of protection from the frailties from which they suffer and worthy of respect for the strivings those frailties engender. Moreover, as self-aware creatures, human beings project what they may become, what they may make of themselves, and what may befall them. They accordingly come to value not only present, transitory experiences but what they see their more enduring identities to be and what they hope their lives to amount to. And the frustration of failure and the anxiety of possible failure gain poignancy from the quest for identity these mortals undertake.

These emphases coalesce to put a different gloss on Child's demonic experimenter, who sought to separate violence from pain. In accordance with this thinking, we may explain the experimenter's perversity, not necessarily in terms of rights violations, as is Child's wont, but in terms of a denial of fundamental human frailties: (1) Like a torturer, Child's demonic experimenter exploits the human frailty of her victim; (2) by making her intention to exploit that frailty transparent, she deliberately and provocatively humiliates her victim; (3) like a torturer, she wants her victim to be overwhelmed emotionally by the recognition that she deliberately rejects the commonalities of their human condition as a basis for action;[5] and (4) obviously, such actions tend to divert and perhaps permanently impair her victim's quest for meaning in life.[6]

Let us then work from the hypothesis that violence may be problematic because the vulnerabilities violence exploits are common, fundamental human vulnerabilities and because the perpetrator of violence deliberately denies the commonalities as an appropriate basis for respectful treatment. On this hypothesis, what can we infer about responding to violence? Clearly we want to avoid responses that, even in passing, deny the commonalities of aggressor and victim. And clearly we should seek responses that lead the violent to affirm the humanity of their victims. But surely if even this much is clear, the quest for improved practices for responding to violence has considerable point.

Moral Deficiencies of Justified Violence Views

Revenge and Just War

Having established the need for a deeper philosophical justification, I begin to scrutinize and challenge our extant framework for responding to violence. To that end, I present an argument that a practice of revenge is justified. I show how this argument fails, but consider it important because it demonstrates both the strengths and weaknesses of Child's argument for the Justified Violence View.

In many societies, from Homer's Acheans to medieval northern Europeans to twentieth-century South Sea Islanders, revenge has been a well-defined social practice. Its norms have included all of the following: Only specific actions warrant revenge. Only specific, related persons have rights of revenge. Only specific offending persons are acceptable targets of revenge. Only certain means of exacting revenge are acceptable.[7] And the arguments in favor of these means are Child's arguments that, compared to other known means, these means are violence minimizing. With so many norms so clearly defined and so publicly known, various practices of revenge have met many of the formal standards of moral justification. Moreover, the meeting of such standards and the passions of grief and humiliation have doubtless often served as all the justification human beings could want or need for norm-entrenched acts of revenge.

But would you or I be compelled to conclude that any act of revenge in accord with all such a society's standards for the practice of revenge was therefore justified? Of course not. We would argue, contrarily, that by the very logic of the practice, many situations will arise in which the cycle of vengeance will be endless.[8] A practice that perpetuates new instances of deadly conflict wears so much negative value on its face that it has got to be wrong, even if every act of revenge were done strictly within the norms of justification for the practice. And the evolution of punishment, from practices of vengeance to systems of justice under law, strongly suggests that human practices can evolve teleologically toward a greater realization of human value.

I now undertake to transform the following thesis:

> *Thesis.* Properly administered justice under law is a superior alternative to the most orderly practice of revenge.

I want to transform this into an argument against traditional "Just War" views. We have noted that incidents of revenge are subject to moral disapprobation because of the unending violence to which they have led. So it becomes relevant that many historians see almost every war of the twentieth century, including even the violent aggression of Adolf Hitler, as precipitated by the actual conduct of nations ostensibly employing just-war standards. Historians, for example, now treat the Treaty of Versailles as a textbook example of how to sow the seeds of war at the conclusion of what once was declared "the war to end all wars."

Assume, for the sake of argument, that in World War I France was a nation truly and unequivocally aggressed on. Even so, such a nation would surely come to see its future security as a legitimate aim of its response to aggression. And should that nation persevere and triumph in battle, it would see the imposition of treaty terms that foster its future security as a justified precaution.[9] But the regular historical consequence of such thinking has been seeds of resentment used by subsequent adversarial leaders, such as Hitler, to rouse their people to later hostilities.

For such reasons, civilized countries have concluded the unacceptability of practicing revenge. If, therefore, the mere existence of formal norms of morality does not suffice to justify a practice of revenge, then, similarly, the norms of morality implicit in traditional Just War Theory do not suffice to justify just wars. The prospect of a fuller realization of common human goods undercuts the attempted justification.

Gandhi's Teleology

Indeed, it is at exactly this teleological juncture that Mohandas Gandhi based his contribution to our understanding of violence and its abolition. For Gandhi was convinced that our highest obligation is to the greatest long-term reduction of violence. From this teleological premise, Gandhi inferred that any resort to violence, though it may appear to do good, does only temporary good, while the evil in the violence causes later harm. For the resort to violence, he believed, always carries with it the delayed cost of further hostility ready to turn to violence. Whoever may be the immediate beneficiary of an initial resort to violence, and however effectively that resort may achieve its immediate purpose, Gandhi urged that the "beneficiaries" of that violence, molded to it, will see their children destroyed by the very motives they used to save themselves. Certainly the conflict between the Israelis and Palestinians and between the Protestants and Catholics in Northern Ireland lend powerful credence to this view. Gandhi thus believed that violence always creates a social malaise that contributes to the eruption of later violence. This contribution is often wrongly ignored when the "greater good" arising from violent resistance to violence is "proved" by contrast only to the evil that violence immediately averts.[10] And surely, Gandhi's argument here is a strong critique of the Justified Violence View.

Child is correct to assert that a theory of value needs to be supplemented before conclusions about the right will be warranted. But will conclusions follow if we add the premise Child adds, about how the Justified Violence View puts several constraints on persons' justified responsive use of violence? Practices of revenge do as much. But we object to practices of *revenge* with arguments that (1) practices of revenge lead to unterminating and uncontrollable violence; and (2) revenge is not necessary to moral ends.

Following Gandhi, I have argued concerning *warfare* that practices of warfare, even just warfare, tend toward unterminating and uncontrollable violence; and, therefore, conclude the following:

Conclusion: Warfare is no more morally satisfactory than an established, norm-driven practice of revenge.

One might quibble about the degree to which practices of revenge and practices of warfare tend to be unterminating and uncontrollable, but both sets of practices are seriously deficient in those regards. The question thus becomes whether there is a set of social practices that might allow us to replace the alleged necessity of violence, both in war and in civil society, as the rule of law has replaced the practice of revenge.

Deficiencies of Rights Language

In the preceding section I have followed Gandhi, urging that violence tends to be unterminating and uncontrollable. But now I want to deepen this criticism. For I urged in my discussion of the West Africans that both definitions of problems and practices for responding to problems are appropriately evaluated in terms of their fruitfulness in promoting the common goods of human life. Accordingly, I believe that people can define conflict and approach conflict resolution in alternative ways. I have hinted that using an individualistic approach to conflict might intensify alienations and thus be less than optimal. But what deep basis, the reader may ask, might there be for this belief? I now turn to the language of rights, in order to show some of the deficiencies of defining conflict and approaches to conflict resolution in terms of rights.

I begin with what is a mere clue to the weaknesses of thinking that the norms meant to preserve human value, especially in cases of conflict between people, should be expressed as *rights*. The construct of rights focuses on the individual human beings in conflict. (It is they, after all, who have those rights, and it is indisputable that other humans and their institutions are, in modern circumstances, the main infringers on such rights.[11]) So it seems the smallest of steps to think of the individual as needing and being entitled to protection from infringements of those rights.

Observe, then, with a critical eye, as the construct of human rights turns our attention away from a human spirit focused on the *commonalities* of being human toward a *solitary* individual threatened by the frailties of being human. Observe even as it entrenches a perspective of alienation that Chekhov,[12] Ibsen,[13] and Wilder[14] worked so hard to expose.

It has become a commonplace in contemporary moral philosophy that the construct of rights in general and of individuals possessing certain basic rights more specifically has fractured community, atomized society, and led to a crippling alienation of human persons.[15] But that commonplace has special force when we come to address human conflict, both interpersonal and intersocietal. For conflict already has a fracturing, atomizing, alienating effect on community. To attempt to redress those effects with constructs that exacerbate, rather than ameliorate, conflict compounds the wound to community. In criticism of the concept of rights, then, I turn to my argument that the fractured, alienated society we know today has roots in the logic of the concept of rights.

Statements of rights are statements about how persons (rights bearers) are entitled to act and be treated. They are not statements of value, although they are based on value. Thus, while Child and I are at one in our appreciation and endorsement of life, safety, dignity, integrity, and autonomy as *values*, that endorsement does not commit me to Child's views of human rights, especially those of self-defense and the defense of others.

Three Pivotal Presumptions

Both concepts of rights and the Minimal Justified Violence View rely on a particularly problematic use of presumptions. In the context of a theory of violence, rights language contains three rebuttable presumptions, each of which proves problematic. When it is asserted that party, P, has a right against interloper, I, the *disputable presumptions* are these:

1. Conflict exists between P and I.
2. The aggrieved party, P, can be determined not to have initiated conflict.
3. It is right, or at least justified, for outside parties, O, using whatever appropriate force or violence may be necessary, to prevent I from persisting in the pursuit of I's desires.

While these presumptions are so frequently invoked as to appear unobjectionable, I believe we can see that each is problematic. Consider the following difficulties:

1. The mere fact that conflict exists between P and I implies only that if P's wants remain fixed *and* I's wants remain fixed *and both* P and I act to achieve their wants *and* the material and social resources for satisfying wants remain unchanged, then *eventually* it will be impossible that both I and P get *everything* they want.

Not all conflict is irreconcilable. Most of what passes for irreconcilable conflict does so only because persons confuse the ends they seek with the (often culturally enshrined) means they have chosen to those ends and because, when conflict has given rise to some animus, persons amplify their desires to include assurances against the ill will of the other. Thus:

2. That an aggrieved party did not initiate conflict is never more than rebuttably clear from a given set of observations.

For claims of provocation, self-defense and new information may reasonably rebut the claims of the aggrieved. While judicial proceedings within a rule of law can yield solid determinations that an aggrieved party initiated no conflict, most of our judgments within a social order do not invoke the procedures of a rule of law, and in our present time, judgments about international violence have no substantial rule of law to invoke.[16]

Outside such judicial procedures, the determination that the aggrieved initiated no conflict is especially problematic. When we have such knowledge, it surely arises only within the structure provided by some sort of determinate social order, if not only within an established rule of law. For without the structure of such a social order, one could establish no baseline for settling historical disputes. And once we lose the ability to find the status quo ante, we must be troubled about who "initiated" conflict.[17] The simplicity of Child's definition of an aggressor must confront the clarity of his vision of moral ambiguities. Thus:

3. The use of minimum violence by outsiders, O, will do nothing to help the interloper come to see himself or herself as again an appreciated part of a social order. Indeed, the actions of the outsiders are likely to induce a more permanent and more intense alienation between I and both P and O.

I have already cited Chekhov, Ibsen, and Wilder to remind us of the pervasive alienated individualism of our modern culture. And the mass of human population, conjoined in some areas with the mobility of people, makes life more anonymous, thereby reinforcing an alienated individualism. But practices are not justified by their pervasiveness. A practice of invoking the Justified Violence View must be judged against the consequent history of violence. Against that history, it would seem rash to assert anything more than that no superior alternative to the Justified Violence View exists. (I later am concerned to refute that assertion by indicating superior alternatives.[18])

Because of the problems associated with the rebuttable presumptions required for the attribution of rights, it is plausible to develop a pacifist point of view that accepts all the fundamental values a rights theory claims to support, but that makes other rebuttable presumptions. Specifically, we can *presume* the following:

1. Any conflict between P and I is reconcilable.
2. A substantial set of human needs and interests common to P and I can be found.
3. Restoring the community jeopardized by any conflict between P and I is more important than favoring one party over the other in responding to the conflict.

One might ask how the pacifist presumptions I have listed relate to the presumptions I attribute to rights theory. In a strict, logical sense, the three sets of presumptions are not contraries. Consider the following *compatibilities:*

1. A conflict may exist at the same time that it is resolvable.
2. It may be possible to prove that the aggrieved initiated no hostilities, while it is also possible to find a substantial set of needs and interests common to P and I.
3. It may be possible to act so as both to prevent I from harming P and to facilitate the restoration of the community jeopardized by any conflict between P and I.

Even though these presumptions are logically compatible, a practical contrariety may exist between them, and for two reasons. First, time may be of the essence. It may be that, without immediate intervention, conflict will reach a point of inevitability: If time passes without action, the results will be substantially worse than if action is taken. Consequently, we feel entitled to act, even in some ignorance, to prevent things from deteriorating dangerously. Yet the idea that the "results of inaction are worse than the results of action" is ambiguous. For in many instances, *things can become more dangerous in more than one way.* What the alternative presumptions reveal is that people *differently prioritize their fears of outcomes.* But the logical compatibility of the Justified Violence and pacifist presumptions shows that in some adversarial but non-urgent circumstances, it would be possible both to safeguard security and to engender reconciliation.

These divergent priorities lead us to the second source of contrariety between the presumptions. Because the range of scenarios hoped for and feared differs vastly, different people act differently, creating among different of their fellows alliances on the one hand and estrangements on the other. In other words, the different people tend to universalize contrary commitments to and alienations from certain others. Thus the contrariety is practical because it engenders divergent and in many ways contrary histories. In Chapter 4, I return to this pivotal point.

For now, let us see how the teleological character of the pacifism I advocate gives it an advantage in presumptions over a Justified Violence View based in rights language. In general, one presumption can be superior to another in two distinct ways. Both reasons of fact and normative reasons can found the superiority of one presumption over another. We may first consider reasons of fact. Because the presumptions that divide rights language from teleological pacifism are rebuttable, a measure of ignorance exists on each side, and so further evidence is relevant. World War I, for instance, is often cited nowadays as a war nobody wanted, a war that arose out of misinformation and misunderstanding. But is this always true? Is it even usually true, or is it often or almost always true that wars arise out of malicious attempts to advance the self-interest of some at the cost of the vital interests of others? This is an important issue for which evidence might be gathered. Similar evidence might be gathered concerning the social and psychological conditions of crime. We can imagine investigations that would reinforce rights-protection presumptions, and we can imagine evidence that would buttress pacifist presumptions.[19]

Now, if we admit that further evidence might be relevant to the question which of two divergent presumptions to make, we should also note the normative reasons for preferences between presumptions. Following the teleological method suggested earlier, I propose to consider what values both sets of presumptions share in order to infer which presumption is superior. Both presumptions reflect value placed on whatever makes human beings worthy of respect. The ideas of conflict built into rights language imply the impossibility of expressing respect for conflicting persons by affirming their claims to what they want or even need. The ideas of conflict resolution built into teleological pacifism imply the possibility that persons, affirming their common, fundamental human needs, can manipulate the conditions of material resource availability, technological development, and social organization to meet their common needs. Certainly the latter is the happier thought. Indeed it seems hard to dispute that, of two responses to conflict, the one that alone promotes the possibilities of dissolving the conflict is the normatively superior response. The presumptions of pacifism alone lead in that better direction.

Since rights-based theories focus on protecting the victim's rights, they lack momentum toward creating superior situations. In this way, rights-based theories of justified violence freeze social situations. Individuals are separated not only by their conflicting desires but by a socialization that affirms them in making claims of individual rights. Their practices of violent interaction and their theories for justifying violence are sufficiently indeterminate to allow the contrary views of potentially conflicting parties to be "justified." And thus are they covertly moved toward violent confrontation. Teleological pacifism, however, looks to reordered and reconstructed social situations with more attention to community and the community of interests of the erstwhile conflicting parties. In so doing, it evolves teleologically, away from the conflict and toward the creation of harmonies.

It is crucial at this point to remember that in many circumstances one cannot ask whether two parties are in irreconcilable conflict. True, their conflict may become increasingly harder to avoid. But whether a conflict is to become irreconcilable is regularly a matter of human decision and interactive construction. Such questions are not ones of fact but of resolve and complex interaction. As the events centering on Iraq in the fall of 1990 illustrate, only through what parties decide and then only through the way in which their spheres of action come to be constructed does the noose of irreconcilability tighten around them. Accordingly, the presumptions of pacifism alone magnify the attention parties can give to coordinating their actions to mutual advantage.

There are, of course, deep reasons why it is difficult for parties, even perfectly intentioned parties, to coordinate their actions successfully. Nevertheless, if it can be agreed that the presumptions of pacifism lead in a superior direction, and if we can at least entertain the possibility that pursuing that direction need not be foolhardy, then we can reserve to subsequent parts the question of how pacifists might pursue such possibilities.

Child is correct to move from the premise that values sometimes conflict to the conclusion that a theoretical gap exists between the theory of value and the theory of the right. He is wrong, however, to think that such a gap implies that any license for violence has been created. The justification of a kind of action, after all, must be assessed in terms of what kinds of values, what kind of social reality, such actions promote or deter. This is the fundamental teleological point on which pacifists must insist against a static rights-based view, which presupposes that rights of response to perpetrators of violence are sufficient to determine a justified response. Violence tends to perpetuate and intensify itself, and that fact argues for the preferability of patterns of action that reconcile persons and defuse explosive conflict situations. Standing on rights of justified violence exacerbates that very tendency of violence to get out of control.

For now, I conclude that the presumptions of the pacifist are normatively superior to the presumptions of a rights-based theory of the right. Clearly, pacifist presumptions avoid the effects of aggravating conflict implicit in the language of rights as a vehicle for our moral discourse.

I have not, however, explicated the teleological pacifism I propose to take its place (a task for Chapters 4 and 6). Before doing so, we must look more deeply at the concept of violence and find even at so basic a conceptual level how my view differs from Child's. For Child's reference to intention in his definition of violence obscures our typical use of data for understanding conflicts. Those data, I soon argue, underdetermine what, with our socialization, we call the "factual basis" for making one or another presumption.

Violence

A Normative Definition

What, then, is violence? By violence, I mean the doing of irreversible harm to persons. One person harms another when the first does something that causes the second to suffer the loss of some human faculty(ies) or ability(ies). What is morally significant about a human being cannot be separated from everything that allows the being to act, think, feel, and respond in typically human ways. If we consider for a moment a rock, a drop of water, or a grain of sand on a lifeless world, isolated from contact with human beings or from any other form of life, we cannot conceive how that rock, water, or sand could suffer harm.

The wrongness of harm, therefore, is essentially tied to the value of life (and thus to the value of human life) and in the definitional connection that harm destroys this value partially or entirely, temporarily or permanently.[20]

The anathema of violence comes into clearer focus when we explicate its irreversibility. The paradigm of irreversibility is of course death. We cannot bring the dead back to life, and whenever a person is killed without consenting, the death must be regarded as harmful. For death is the total and irreversible termination of all the distinctive capacities of life.

The concept of compensation is intimately related to reversibility. Because compensation makes up for a loss by replacing what was lost with something of comparable worth, we view a replaceable loss as redeemable and thus as not truly irreversible. We may even try to compensate someone who loses an arm in an accident by providing a payment of insurance money. Yet many people will feel that even if a system of insurance and insurance payments is an improvement over no such system, nevertheless, insurance payments are inadequate as compensation because they never replace the substantial loss (of an arm) with anything that restores the victim the lost capacities.

Violence and Intention

Violence has sometimes been defined in terms of intention; indeed, Child so defines it. I find such a definition unsatisfactory for two reasons, the manipulability of the concept and the misfocus of value.

Four Manipulations

Intention and Presumption. At every level, from the personal to the international, agents often act in ways capable of alternative description. For example, refusing to accept a violation of one's rights, providing an efficient and effective defense, responding in a timely fashion, and preventing an offense from gaining a potentially irresistible momentum are all descriptions typically applicable to violent actions. Given that actions are variously describable, how do we decide which of those descriptions captures the *intention* of the action?

In nonconflict situations, we rely heavily on the assertion of the agent. As long as the agent's behavior and statement of intention remain plausibly coherent, the agent's statement stands. Consider how this can work among friends even when behavior diverges sharply from stated intentions. For example, as Child and I discussed writing the third draft of this book, we agreed to exchange objectives for our sections before writing the draft. I sent Child my objectives and waited for his. Some weeks later, he sent me some sections, telling me the others would shortly follow and explaining that he found it impossible to write the objectives without resolving the concrete problems of rewriting the sections. Because of our collegial and friendly relationship, I do not doubt that he first intended to write objectives but changed his intention after encountering problems.

Contrarily to this procedure of mine, in adversarial situations other parties often see their interests as potentially conflicting with an agent's. This perception plays a pivotal role because it typically leads adversaries to doubt the agent's word and to ask, "Does anything about the agent's behavior actually falsify the statement of intention we *fear* is true?" This typically amounts to *reversing* the usual presumption in favor of a person's statement of intention.

Needless to say, cases will continually arise in which since the behavior of the agent is compatible with more than one statement of intention, when the agent states one intention, nothing in the agent's behavior falsifies the statement of a contrary intention that the adversary fears to be true.

Violence often emerges out of such circumstances as these. In them, the data relevant to an agent's intention are crucially underdeterminative. Accordingly, a judgment of intention, in such circumstances, is not a judgment of fact. Where the evidence underdetermines the fact of the matter, one emotion or another may motivate one person, but not another, to conclude what will be *called* the "fact of the matter." One's fear, for example, often fills the gap that the evidence leaves silent. I hear a voice of fear playing such a role in what is therefore, to my mind, Child's partial *construction* of adversarial relations.[21]

Of course, contrarily, the silence of the evidence—even the voice of some negative evidence—need not be interpreted in fear. To see this clearly, let us return to my previous example of Child's intention. I see no point in doubting his statement, even though he wrote four whole sections without telling me of his problem and his changed intention! But if we were talking in any strict way about what "evidence" I have to falsify the "allegation" that Child had other original intentions, the answer is that I have simply his word, which I accept completely. In the light of the evidentially unresolved ambiguity of how he proceeded, however, it becomes obvious how much weight my acceptance (or non-acceptance!) of his stated intention has in the *construction* both of the fact of the matter and of our interaction.

In adversarial international affairs this difficulty of relying on "facts" about one's adversary's intentions is the story of world history. From Vietnam to Afghanistan, from Central America to the Middle East, the message is unanimous. *We* never started anything; *you* always hit us first. From the Philippines to Iraq to Ireland, what *we* did earlier was innocent, defensive, misconstrued, necessary; what *you* did was unprovoked, aggressive, unmistakable, overreactive. *We* know what started it all, despite *your* pretenses to the contrary. When *you* provide *us* with no reliable assurances that the intentions *you* claim are peaceful, *we* know what we see you doing. When *you* deliberately ignore the history *we* have endured, *we* have *our* rights. When *your* so-called preventive defense is nothing but a thinly disguised belligerent offense, *we* must protect ourselves.

Here we see the difference a collegial versus an adversarial relation plays in determining the "facts" of a party's intention: Such is the strength of presumptions about convergent and divergent interests in defining others' intentions! From the schoolyard to international affairs, we hear a universal cry, "I didn't start it; he hit me first." Can one reasonably assume that in each such case there is always exactly one liar? Can one even make the distinctions required for the term "liar" to have application? For we must distinguish between aggression and defense, and between instigation and retaliation. And when these distinctions rest on statements of intentions, the fact that alternate presumptions will often allow adversaries to controvert statements of intentions is dangerous.

Look at the patterning of the thinking: (1) Given different interests, (2) on the basis of which persons find themselves with no basis for trusting each other, (3) and from ambiguous or nonexistent data, (4) people are led to make contrary presumptions, (5) in the light of which they are led to what are called "reasonable" disagreements about intentions. (6) But then, on the bases of contrary presumptions and disagreements about intentions, (7) persons enact contrary courses of actions that concretize commitments and alienations.

The role of presumption in the judgment of another person's intention undermines the naive belief that statements of others' intentions are statements of fact to be read off the evidence. The need to presume in order to construct an account of another's intention from the available evidence thus introduces a danger to understanding violence in terms of intention. For the freedom to presume in accordance with divergent interests moves potential adversaries from nontrust to contrary commitments, from diverging interests to hardening conflicts, from differences of outlook to irreconcilable differences. If we can define violence without resort to the concept of intention, we might avoid the danger of presumption intention introduces.[22]

Intention and "Historical Fact."   Observe, now, how perspectival history turns out to be. *We* claim we never permitted you to act as you did. *You* claim we never prohibited you from acting as you did. *We* claim that if we had foreseen your intentions, we would have issued an explicit prohibition. *You* say that initially you had no such intentions; only our subsequent actions led you to respond in such a way as to make it plausible that you had such intentions. *We* say that within international law, convention, or precedent, it can be argued that your action was unacceptable. *You* say that the cited law, convention, or precedent has validity only within a range of circumstances unlike the present, or that the citation is without validity because of the constrained circumstances in which certain groups were forced to acquiesce in it.

Obviously, within such broad parameters of historical interpretation, the language of rights, because of its reliance on intentions, will prove sufficiently manipulable to support the rhetoric of adversaries as they escalate their disputes to violence. For without the strength a shared legal system provides for establishing an agreeable status quo ante, appeals to history compound the unhappiness created by importing opposite presumptions into statements of intention. For without broadly accepted means for establishing the status quo ante, the available evidence will be too scanty to allow regular distinctions between (unjustifiable) aggression and (justifiable) defense. Yet spokespersons of different adversarial viewpoints, regularly ignoring how the lack of an agreeable status quo ante makes statements of intentions constructions, are oblivious to how manipulable their perspectival histories are.[23]

National Intentions.   The murkiness of the concept of intention only compounds itself when intentions are attributed to nations. Of course, in international conflicts, national leaders frequently claim to know their own intentions, their adversaries' intentions, and the inevitable conflict between them. Is this the kind of thing one can count on knowing? Suppose that my goal, as a head of state, is the security of my nation. What is my intention? That of course depends on how my nation might be threatened. But how my nation will be threatened will differ depending on my country's knowledge of other nations, not to mention the history of my country's relations and perceptions of the needs and intentions of other nations. Moreover, their intentions will be formed in part in the light of their perceptions of my nation and, indeed, of my intentions. But if my intentions are to be related to the threats my nation experiences, and those threats are related to other nations' perceptions of my intentions, my intentions must also be related to my perceptions of the intentions of other nations.[24] In other words, the strategic character of national intentions tends to make them inscrutable.

An important aspect of the difficulty of knowing the intentions of other nations arises from the fact that the people who compose a government are only somewhat like-minded. Even if, contrary to the facts, personnel never changed and individual persons never changed their intentions, the dispositions of the people who form a government continually differ. The position of any organization almost always accommodates the views of many different members, not fully expressing the intentions of any. Even in the most hierarchical of organizations, it is fanciful to believe that the actions of the organization simply reflect the intentions of its chief.

Consider, for example, the account Seymour Hersh provides of events in March and April of 1983:

> The [U.S.] Navy's show of force was but another aspect of its "forward strategy" policy initially enunciated in 1981 by Secretary of the Navy John Lehman, which called for aircraft carriers to move into "high-threat areas" near the Soviet Union. American warships were authorized by the president late in March to operate and exercise closer to Soviet borders than ever before. Three aircraft carrier battle groups . . . sailed defiantly in the icy waters . . . 450 miles

from the Soviet Union's Kamchatka Peninsula. . . . Twenty years before, such activities would have had a good chance of going unnoticed by Moscow for days, but the Soviet Union's intelligence system has been steadily modernized, to the point where, by 1983, as one expert later said, "They know we're there."

That, in fact, was one of the basic purposes of such exercises, so the Navy's most senior admiral subsequently explained to Congress: to show the Soviets who is boss. . . . "Our feeling is that an aggressive defense, if you will, characterized by forward movement, early deployment of forces, aggressiveness on the part of our ships, is the greatest deterrent that we can have. . . ."

The Senate was not informed, however, about another bit of American aggressiveness during the fleet exercise. One night in early April, the *Midway*, after shutting off all electronic equipment whose emissions could be monitored by the Soviets, slipped away from the flotilla and steamed south toward the Kuriles. The Soviets did not track it. "When he [the *Midway*] popped up southeast of Kamchatka," one Navy intelligence officer recalled, "they were clearly surprised." The *Midway's* next act surprised not only the Soviets but also the senior commanders of the U.S. Pacific Fleet. On April 4, a group of at least six Navy planes from the *Midway* and the *Enterprise* violated Soviet borders by overflying the island of Zeleny in the Kurile archipelago. It was a flagrant and yet almost inevitable error, triggered by the aggressive fleet exercise and the demand of senior officers for secret maneuvers and surprise activities.[25]

Assume the facts to be as Hersh states, for they surely represent the kind and complexity of facts typical of international adversarial relationships. Given the facts, we might ask, "What was the intention of the U.S. government?" But how is the question to be answered, given the variety of intentions expressed by different officials of the U.S. government or its navy, and given a degree of consonance and a degree of variance between those statements and the movements of various ships? Surely the Soviet commander who saw the *Midway* when it popped up southeast of Kamchatka was in no position to know the intention of the United States. Indeed, because the statements and actions illustrate a typical lack of coherence, no descriptive basis for ascribing an intention to the U.S. government was clear at all.[26]

Keeping Intentions Deliberately Obscure.   As we have seen, when the concept of intention is applied to nations, both the strategic character of intentions and the variety of agents stating intentions and undertaking actions adds to the murkiness of the concept. But we have still not exhausted the difficulty of knowing an adversarial nation's intention. For these difficulties would occur even under conditions of perfect information (excepting information about intentions). Yet nobody thinks such ideal conditions obtain among adversarial nations. Indeed, let us reconsider the case of the *Midway*. In the midst of all the unclarity discussed above, one thing is clear: To the extent that the U.S. Navy at least had any coherent intentions, it meant to keep them hidden from the Soviets. And everybody must allow that the deliberate obscuring of information about intentions vastly complicates our previously defined problems.

When intentions can be misunderstood in as many ways as this and more, is it ever plausible to guarantee that one nation really knows another's intention? My argument, in summary, is that we cannot know, and for the following reasons:

1. Such "knowledge," reflecting nonmutual presumptions, is not knowledge adversaries can share.
2. Such "knowledge," relying on premises about the status quo ante, lacks the grounding it requires.
3. The concept of a group's intentions presupposes a coherence of understanding, attitudes, and behaviors of its members.
4. Such "knowledge" requires a clarity of data that adversaries will regularly have the desire and ability to hide from each other.

It seems both more honest and more constructive, then, to deny that we can know the intentions of another nation.[27]

We have thus identified four ways in which the inclusion of the concept of intention within the definition of violence will prove problematic.[28] If a theory, like the Justified Violence View, including Just War Theory, is to be useful, then at least regularly, if not always, it must be clear how to apply the distinctions on which the theory depends and be feasible for adversaries to act in accord with knowledge about the meeting of those conditions. But that amounts to a requirement that we know, or believe with high confidence that we know, the intentions of the adversary. Since, as I have argued, such knowledge is exceedingly problematic,[29] it seems unwise to rest conclusions about how nations justifiably act on the intentions of their adversaries.

The Misfocus of Value

The more fundamental problem with defining violence in terms of intention arises from the distortion of focus such a definition includes. Surely the primary focus of a definition of violence should be on the harm of violence to its victim. If, for example, the irreversible harms that automobile accidents regularly cause are almost always unintentional, the violence that victims suffer is not thereby diminished one whit. Some of the causes of automobile accidents lie with factors that drivers of cars can and ought to control; some lie with factors controlled by automotive designers or highway engineers; some perhaps lie outside human control. But the irreversible harms suffered do violence to the lives of the victims, regardless of issues of intention or even responsibility. While a definition of violence in terms of intention might have some usefulness for questions of accountability and punishment (which is not Child's concern), the addition of the concept of intention does nothing to illumine the harm that has befallen the victim of violence.

Indeed, it introduces its own harm. Telling us that whatever is not an intentional action is not an instance of violence leads us to ignore cases where intentions are unclear or the ills arise perhaps regularly but unintentionally. It directs us toward ignoring these cases even if they are ones in which humans could take responsibility to improve the human condition. The desirability of avoiding foreseeable evil works against so limiting a view of responsibility.

Frameworks for Understanding Conflicts: Peace and Rights

Across the world, conflicts over goods make people feel driven to talk about "rights denied" and "honorable intentions misunderstood." But I think it unwise to be driven. For people die at the hands of others who "innocently defend themselves." "Rights" have been invoked to justify centuries of wars. And yet the language of rights has proved loose and slippery enough to have yielded not the elimination of violence but the rhetorical ability of each party to vindicate itself against its adversaries.

My argument has been that the basis of this rhetorical ability lies in the tools of thought supplied us by the liberal tradition: (1) The Minimal Justified Violence View makes three presumptions such that (2) in conjunction with the ambivalent events typically surrounding violent conflict, especially outside an effective rule of law, (3) sometimes compounded by lack of information about the events, (4) often compounded by the conflicts grown out of commitments based on alienating presumptions, (5) often confounded by the opacity of intentions, (6) it is typically possible for conflicting parties to vindicate themselves (7) simply by focusing on certain events and emphasizing particular rights.

The whole of Child's theory of minimal and necessary violence justified by rights of defense rests on the assumption that we can accurately identify an aggressor's aggression. If aggression is an intentional action, as Child assumes, and if violence is intentional, as he explicitly states, then we must be able reliably to discern intentions. We have seen that this can be terribly problematic when conflict wants resolution.

We have also seen that the coherent application of the concept of intention is well nigh impossible when nations come into conflict. Indeed, at this level the very concept of intention threatens to become incoherent. But the result is the ability of adversaries to vindicate themselves rhetorically.

Such universal rhetorical vindication leads away from the resolution of conflict toward greater self-assurance and greater intransigence in the light of the "obviously evil and rights-violative intentions" of the adversary. We can hardly ignore the fact that people around the world profess to love peace but rally to fight wars their leaders call necessary. And leaders persuade with talk about our transgressed rights and their unacceptable intentions, and consequently the justification of our defense. They do not mention the vulnerabilities of all. Theirs are the presumptions of violence justification, not conflict dissolution.

Far better, I should think, to avoid any language derived from the use of alienated presumptions and to focus instead on language derived from the theory of the good. Far better to focus on the common goods of human life than to reinforce an alienation encouraged by an alienated individualism. I therefore urge that the time has come for a deeply pragmatic argument that thinking in terms of intentions, rights, and justified violence has proved a dead-end road. The history of disputes unresolved despite the invocation of rights claims and in the face of contrary attributions of intentions and contrary justifications of violence certainly indicates their inefficacy as peacemaking instruments, as does their exclusive focus on the perspective of one party partially explain their contribution to the intensification of antagonisms.

It is beyond dispute that the rhetoric I criticize has not been the only rhetoric used to incite people to violence. God, History, and the Absolute have all been invoked. But in international contexts the rhetoric I criticize is effectively the same: For in each instance national leaders manipulate the language handily enough to support whatever conclusion they please.[30] Armies are raised, often from volunteers, and if volunteers are not sufficient, then from the common acquiescence to a regime of conscription. In any event, battles are fought, and peace-loving people kill one another. The adoption of a rhetoric of rights in modern times has only helped solidify this age-old pattern.[31] We cannot, then, call our present practices for responding to violence an unqualified success.

A better set of practices would induce adversaries toward agreements. A better rhetoric would help antagonists to focus on shared human needs, not partisan presumption. A better way would focus on common problems posed by circumstances and on the human power to control those circumstances to beneficial ends. Such a social organization would need to be based directly on a theory of good and on identifiable human goods to emerge from emphasis on the common ground of mutual benefit. Hence, if such a set of practices can be characterized with any plausibility, the argument of the history of violence is that such an alternative would be worthy of serious examination. The issue is not so much whether there is a norm-entrenched *right* (under certain circumstances) to resort to violence as whether it could ever be wrong to eliminate or vastly minimize the violence in our world. For if the means to eliminate a great evil can be constructed, precious little can stem the imperative of that construction.

My thesis is that the pacifist tradition, suitably interpreted, contains powerful seeds out of which caring people can construct a new social reality in which violence is avoided or crucially minimized. I believe that this new reality can be reinforcing, in the sense that experiencing it will induce people to want more of it.[32] I believe that it can be stable, roughly in the sense that, when everyone experiences it, no one will want to jeopardize it. And I hold this conviction, reasonably I hope, despite the complications of a world governed by competing ideologies.[33]

Whether there is a better way of talking and thinking and interacting is a complex and deep question. Although we have seen the grave difficulties of a rights-based theory of justified violence, I have only issued a promissory note for its replacement. I begin, in Chapter 4, to explicate that alternative.

PART II

A CRITICAL

EXAMINATION

OF PACIFISM

Introduction

We have examined two views. The first is one that both of us consider aberrant and morally mistaken, namely, that violence is a good thing. We have also examined in much more detail the view (which James Child holds) that while violence is a bad thing, certain conditions can make it a necessary bad thing and therefore not wrong. This is, of course, the Justified Violence View. There is yet one primary position to be examined: the view that violence is not only always bad but, in virtue of its badness, always wrong (i.e., never justified or justifiable). This is a rough and preliminary characterization of pacifism.

Traditional pacifism is characterized primarily by an absolute rejection of violence and coercive threats of violence.[1] Violence or threats of violence are not even tolerable as a necessary evil. But this commitment is not sufficient to define a single fully delineated philosophic position. Indeed, pacifism is not so definitive a position in any case; it is in reality a family of positions.

Let us try to formulate some of the most important members of this family.

Nonresistance to Violence or Threats of Violence

This view is expressed in one strain of Christianity running from a strict interpretation of Jesus' imperative delivered from the Mount, "Resist not evil," through early Christian thinkers like Origen.

The philosopher Robert L. Holmes has characterized nonresistance as "a purely negative, non-coercive attitude which willingly suffers evil without resistance of any sort."[2] Most pacifists reject this very extreme position, holding instead that resistance to evil is permissible, perhaps even morally required, but that such resistance must be nonviolent.

Pacifism as a Strict Prohibition on All Violence

This is the broadest version of traditional pacifism. It bans *all* violence directed at other human beings that realistically could cause injury, disability, or death.

Pacifism as a Strict Prohibition on Lethal Violence

This conception of pacifism is defined as "absolute pacifism" by Jonathan Glover. Glover says: "Absolute pacifism says that it is never right to kill another person, however evil the consequences (including loss of life) of not doing so."[3]

The great Russian novelist and strict pacifist Leo Tolstoy has captured in a poignant story this version of pacifism.

> This spring, at a scripture examination at one of the women's institutes in Moscow, the scripture teacher, and then a bishop who was present, asked the girls about the commandments and particularly the sixth one. When the correct answer was given about the commandment, the bishop usually asked a further question: is killing always and in all cases forbidden by the scriptures, and the unfortunate girls, corrupted by their mentors, had to answer and did answer—not always; that killing is permitted in war and in executing criminals. However, when one of these unfortunate girls (what I am telling you is not fiction but a fact, reported to me by an eyewitness), after giving her answer, was asked the usual ques-

tion: is killing always sinful? She blushed nervously and gave the firm answer that it always was, and she answered all the bishop's usual sophisms with the firm conviction that killing was always forbidden, that killing was forbidden even in the Old Testament and that not only was killing forbidden by Christ but also any evil against one's brother. And despite all his grandeur and art of eloquence, the bishop fell silent and the girl went away victorious.[4]

This version of pacifism turns, most typically, not on an absolute rejection of violence per se, but on an absolute ban on the killing of human beings. This ban is usually rooted in a view that human life is sacred, an ultimate uncompromisable value. The "lethal violence" pacifist must hold that the ultimacy of the value of human life implies a strict limitation on one's own action, ignoring both consequences and the wrongfulness of the actions of others. But, contrarily, one can hold human life to be sacred and reach nonpacifist conclusions. For example, a consequentialist argument based on the ultimate value (or sacredness) of life could instruct one to sacrifice one life to save many others. A rights-based argument with a similar theory of value might differentiate a wrongful taking of life and a rightful use of even lethal resistance, if necessary to such a taking.[5] Thus the connection between the ultimate value (or sacredness) of life and the absolute rejection of killing is not obvious and stands in need of defense.

Pacifism as a Prohibition on Organized Violence between States: War

This is the most familiar form of pacifism. It is also very easy to sympathize with this form of pacifism. War (if we include civil wars and the suppression of rebellions) is by far the most massive producer of human death, injury, and suffering, probably more so than any specific natural cause, let alone than any other human practice or activity. War is so absolutely awful that it perhaps deserves its own special ban. Moreover, war (again including civil war and suppression of rebellion) is *lawless* in a way that violence as practiced under the rule of law (e.g., by police) is not. The capacity for suffering generated and the essentially lawless and thus *unlimited* character of the violence used in war come together in a cataclysmic form in the prospect of nuclear war. There is a chance that many sorts of wars might eventuate in a nuclear holocaust; that alone seems ample reason for a categorical ban on war.

There is a problem, however, for those who do not espouse one of the broader forms of pacifism, but do espouse this form. Someone holding only a prohibition against war would presumably believe that in civil society we are justified in defending ourselves against a violent attack and, even more, that police forces are permitted to use necessary violence to stop civil violence. But exactly what is the difference between those instances and using armed forces to stop violent international aggression? In the simplest possible terms, this version of pacifism would permit violent resistance to an outlaw band if it attacked a town as long as it came from within that polity. But if it came across a national border and claimed to act for another nation, violent resistance would be forbidden. Why? Justifying this distinction on moral (or even rational) grounds is the hardest problem for this version of pacifism. For this and other reasons, our discussion of pacifism does not prejudge the differences between the various forms of pacifism.

Personal and Universal Pacifism

There is another, conceptually distinct taxonomy of pacifism. Pacifism may be defined as a universal moral principle applicable to all human beings, or it may be a moral choice made by individuals, each for himself or herself. Let us call the former *universal pacifism* and the latter *personal pacifism*. Many pacifists espouse personal pacifism, that is, an individual moral choice they make for highly personal reasons, which they do not universalize as necessarily applicable to others. This seems to make personal pacifists much like vegetarians or individuals practicing celibacy. Indeed, we (at least the more open-minded among us) tend to deal with personal pacifists much as we deal with personal vegetarians or celibates. Our sentiment may well be, "It is fine if that's how they feel, but it is certainly not for me." Nevertheless, that disclaimer is uttered with a great deal of tolerance and sometimes genuine respect.

Still, we need to notice that personal pacifism is not like other personal beliefs and attendant lifestyles. It is not a decision affecting only the person making the choice. Pacifism is really about acceptable and unacceptable human relationships and thus is essentially a *social ethic*. It makes two assertions about three-way (triadic) relations:

1. *Universal pacifism.* Everyone has a duty not to interfere violently when one party is attacking another.
2. *Personal pacifism.* It would be morally wrong for me to interfere violently when one party is attacking another.

A pacifist, in other words, holds a view not only about how one might best respond to violence directed at oneself. Instead, the pacifist, even the personal pacifist, makes a moral judgment about responding to violence inflicted on others. As we see in this part, the difficult problems about whether pacifism is an acceptable moral stance tend to cluster around this social character of pacifism.

J.W.C.

D.S.

Problems with Traditional
Forms of Pacifism

Philosophers, theologians, and social thinkers have found a variety of problems in the family of pacifist positions. Many of these problems have to do with definitions of concepts necessary to formulate pacifist positions, such as resistance, violence, and war. Many problems exist only for one or another version of pacifism. But several problems are common to all forms of pacifism, and it is these problems that must be overcome if pacifism is ever to be a philosophically justified position.

The Nature of Evil and the Definition of Peace

Traditionally, pacifists believe that peace is more than the mere absence of war and that nonviolence is more than merely not doing violence. Augustine (himself not a pacifist) believed that peace consisted not only of the absence of war but of justice and tranquility also. Gandhi's notion of *ahimsa* is typical of this pacifist sentiment. Although *ahimsa* can be broken down to the sanskrit roots "noninjury," it was meant by Gandhi to be far more than that. It had a positive, affirmative element. Gandhi told us: "I accept the interpretation of Ahimsa namely that it is not merely a negative state of harmlessness but it is a positive state of love, doing good to the evildoer."[1] This notion is important, for pacifism must present alternatives to violence by offering us other values than merely the negative one of not having violence or not having war. Otherwise, the nonviolent, or "peaceful," world could on other grounds be a living hell.

Yet if we take pacifism to be the view that all violence is categorically wrong, then we can demonstrate that it *is* in fact based on a monistic theory of value, wherein only peace or the absence of violence has value. Needless to say, this is not obvious and is strongly contested by pacifists. Thus it will take an argument to get us there.

We mean here by an *ultimate* value one that cannot be reduced to any other value.[2] Pacifism, in spite of itself, employs a monistic theory of value because, notwithstanding the claims of Gandhi and others, only the absence of violence has value. For if there were other ultimately bad (or good) things, then enough of those values might be sufficient to outweigh at least a small amount of violence. For example, if both the absence of violence and happiness were ultimate values, it might follow that we should be willing to commit a small amount of violence to get a large amount of happiness. If we live in a conquered country where the conquering army treats us very badly and thereby creates a great deal of unhappiness, and if a short battle with few casualties would expel the conquerors and make our whole country much happier (without making the conquerors much less happy), perhaps we should fight the battle. "No," says the pacifist, "because one must never commit violence." Then, no matter how much happiness eventuates, it never overcomes even a little violence. Even a scintilla of violence *trumps* however large an amount of any other value you like. How else is one to understand this but as a single ultimate value?

A related argument makes the same point. Let us ask the pacifist, "What does peace mean to you beyond the mere absence of violence?" Let us say that the answer is as follows:

Pacifist: Peace means $\sim V + A + B + C$

where $\sim V$ means the absence of violence, and A, B, and C might mean, say, justice, tranquility, and happiness. The justified-violence theorist might then respond, "But I am for A, B, and C also. I merely reject nonviolence ($\sim V$) and substitute a rigorously rule-restrained conception of minimal justified violence, so I value restrained violence (here symbolized as RV). Thus:

Justified Violence Proponent: $RV + A + B + C$

The pacifist can only respond that her wolrd is more valuable merely in virtue of nonviolence, even if the world of the justified-violence proponent has much more of A, B, and C. Her only alternative is a factual claim about the world holding that there is something about the nature of violence that makes even a very small, justified, and rule-governed bit of it inconsistent with very much of the good things A, B, and C. That is, allow just a little V and you have no (or radically diminished) A, B, and C. Yet we saw in our example of the conquered country that happiness was quite consistent with a little bit of war waging. The burden is surely on the pacifist to show that justice and tranquility are inconsistent, in the long run, with a little violence. To claim that this is never true, that all the positive values of peace are vitiated by a little violence, is to make a deep metaphysical and moral claim about the universe. Gandhi did just this and worked out his own metaphysics based on Vedic scripture using also Buddhist and Jain trains of thought.[3] But most Western philosophers are not inclined to accept Gandhi's metaphysics or to replace it with a similarly complex one of their own. Without such a view, however, we are safe in holding that a small amount of justified and rule-governed violence is consistent with values, other than nonviolence, typically associated with peace.

One way of formulating pacifism, then, would hold that peace, defined as the absence of violence, is the only ultimately good thing, that is, the only ultimate value. A number of thinkers have taken this point of view alone to be a powerful moral objection to pacifism. Reinhold Niebuhr, the Protestant theologian, believed that one of the problems with pacifism is that it oversimplifies and confuses the nature of evil.[4] Pacifists, Niebuhr believed, tend to reduce all evil (or badness) to violence. There are other forms of evil, Niebuhr believed. A person who deals in malicious lies or blackmail is evil, but not violent. (Remember my urging in Part I: Let us not identify all evil with violence, lest we hopelessly confuse a moral theory of violence with morality altogether.) The sweatshop owner who demands sexual favors of his women employees on threat of termination is evil, but not violent. (They "consent" under threats of nonviolent economic harm, as opposed to being violently raped.) The regime that rules by propaganda featuring hate-filled racist campaigns, brainwashing, and mind control (Orwell's *1984* without the torture chambers) is evil, deeply evil, but not necessarily violent. Slavery as an institution could exist where the slaves were highly socialized in their roles and kept in line only by threats of economic penalties, for example, short rations for themselves and their families. Surely such a system is evil, but not violent.

Violence is not the only bad thing in the world, and it is sometimes not the worst. Niebuhr believed that pacifists are logically constrained to the preference of slavery or tyranny over violence because they counsel surrender to the former if the only resistance to it must be violent. Pacifism, Niebuhr believed, introduces a topsy-turvy moral world where even minimal, defensive violence is rejected, but where tyranny and slavery must sometimes be *accepted*. Surely, believes Niebuhr, this is simply a *moral mistake* about what sorts of things are evil or bad in our world.

Pacifism and Human Nature

It is a venerable truism of moral philosophy that *ought* implies *can*. Thus, if it is indeed the case that we *ought* never commit violence (or commit lethal violence or wage war), then we must be *able* not to do it. Yet, this argument goes, if we understand human beings as they really are, we will see that they simply cannot categorically and unanimously forswear violence. People are simply too egoistic, too indifferent to the pain and suffering of others, and too violent to be able to abide by the extreme strictures of pacifism. Thinkers as diverse as Thomas Hobbes, Niebuhr, and Sigmund Freud have made or would make this argument. And it is terribly persuasive. How can you hold people accountable to a standard that it is simply impossible for them to reach?

Violence does occur, and often. Human beings are capable of the most outrageous acts of violence against their fellow humans. We are all familiar with violence in our communities and across the globe. Anyone espousing an optimistic view of human nature, one that would take pacifism seriously as a social policy, must explain how, if we are capable of never resorting to violence, we have such a violent history and present.

One of the traditional answers to this question is that society makes us violent. We live, we are told, in a bad society, one that encourages violence or is so unfair in how it treats people as to make violence inevitable. This is the argument of many optimists about human nature, and this of necessity includes many pacifists: Humankind is benevolent and good enough to be able to live at peace and in happiness with fellow humans without violence or threat of violence. So it is possible to explain why we are so often violent by pointing to certain social institutions, which make us so violent.

But this "solution" to the problem of the existence of violence only pushes back the problem one step and gives rise to a common circular argument. The institutions of government and sovereignty, the economic system, the institutions of police forces and armies, all are *human institutions*. War itself is a kind of human institution. Human beings act violently because of the perverse influence of human-created institutions. To say that violence-producing institutions lead people to violence is only to push the question further around the circle. Where did those institutions come from? Mary Midgley makes the same point: "But, these cultural causes do not solve our problem because we must ask, how did these bad customs start, how do they spread, and how do they resist counter conditioning? Can people be merely channels? If they are channels, out of what tap do the bad customs originally flow? And, if they are not mere channels, if they contribute something, what is that contribution?"[5] There is no way to eliminate the circularity that will make the optimist about human nature happy. We *are* a violent species. Some of us simply do visit violence on our fellow humans. Something about us causes us to do that. Perhaps such people are in a minority, perhaps even a small minority. Still, there have been enough to provide us with the institutions of slavery, tyranny, violence, and war.

There is a partial answer to this circularity for the optimist. It is that human nature is *not fixed;* it is neither good nor bad. Humans are malleable. They are exclusively products of their environment. There is no "genetic core" of behavior containing a potentially violent nature (or anything else). An environment that is violent or puts a high value on violent behavior makes violent people. An environment that is corrupt, exploitative, and unjust creates resentment, anger, and ultimately violence, or so the argument goes.[6] But an environment that is peaceful, that encourages the art of compromise and cooperative living, that is fair and supportive, will make for peaceful people. Is this correct? Are we such malleable creatures? If this is so, there seems to be an opportunity for perfectibility. An infinitely malleable human seems to be an infinitely perfectible one and certainly one for whom the elimination of violence is a genuine possibility. There remains, however, a curious kind of circularity even in this form of the argument. For if humans are now prone to violence, how can they ever build this less violent world that will be productive of pacifists or, more accurately, people living up to a pacifist standard? It would seem that this argument for the possibility of pacifism based on the possible pacification of a now violent but malleable human creature still begs the question.

In general, we can say that the pacifist must hold that human beings have or can be made to have natures that are surprisingly nonviolent. It is important to realize just how *weak* a claim an antipacifist needs to make about human nature in order to refute pacifism. But before we do so, we must deal with a contrasting point of view expressed by those who abjure the need for ultimate recourse to violence in human social systems. If you think violence or even force is necessary in the affairs of human society, we are told, you must think humans are terrible creatures indeed. For example, Robert L. Holmes tells us that a "root assumption" of many thinkers in this area is to put "a premium upon the use of violence" because "without the constraint of coercive institutions our fellowmen (always others, never ourselves) would immediately fall upon one another, plundering, murdering, and raping at will; that only the threat of force restrains them, hence that the agencies and institutions making good that threat must be maintained at all costs. This assumption provides the basis of our fear of anarchy."[7] As we later see, Holmes is quite wrong, at least in the view that you must accept so dire a premise about human nature to reach the conclusion we do indeed reach. Human beings can be inherently much nicer than Holmes suggests we must assume and still not be nearly nice enough to dispense with the "threat of force" and the "agencies and institutions making good that threat." One does not have to be an extreme pessimist about human nature (as I am not) to believe that such agencies and institutions are absolutely necessary, if not to any society, at least to any society based on the rule of law and its protection of the sanctity of the individual. Let us see how this is so.

*Human Nature and the Impossibility
of Pacifism*

A very strong and very pessimistic claim about human nature e.g., (one that might be made by Lorenz or Freud) would be the following:

1. *All* humans by their very nature are prone to aggression and violence.

To be sure, some of us control it or mask it better than others, but it is there for each of us. A corollary would be this:

2. All of us need to express aggression or violence *for its own sake,* and somehow or other it has to be manifest in our behavior.

That is, aggression and violence are not means to other ends. They are a necessary part of every human personality, and all of us in some important sense *need* to be aggressive; if we are not physically violent against people, then we need some substitute (e.g., verbal aggression) to replace it. Or, with Freud, we need to sublimate it or repress it in some way.

Indeed, one of the sources of pacifism's appeal is that it rejects the extremely pessimistic view of human nature. But this appeal is specious. Just as we saw that one can believe violence is bad without being a pacifist, so one can have a reasonably optimistic view of human nature (as I have) without being sufficiently optimistic to support pacifism. One can refute the pacifist notion of human nature while rejecting both (1) and (2) above. I believe that, in most societies, far fewer than half of all people—perhaps 10 or 15 percent—are inclined to have a quick resort to violence.[8] The tendency to violence is a statistical, not a universal, property of human beings. Second, I do not believe that more than a very few seriously disturbed individuals actually *need* to be violent simply for the sake of being violent. What I do believe is that a significant minority of people in most societies (including all advanced ones) are willing to resort to violence (or threats of violence) to get other things they want. This can be true of them even if being violent is not something they ultimately value for its own sake or are driven deterministically to commit. In short, violence is a *means to an end* for most of those who are quick to use it or to threaten to use it.

Thus, we may reject both (1) and (2) and assume only a much weaker (and more optimistic) claim:

3. A significant minority of human beings, unless deterred by force or threats of force and punishment, are willing to resort to violence or threats of violence to get things they want.

Keep in mind that (3) is a claim *about human beings in all social systems*. To be sure, some social systems might increase or decrease the size of the minority and, much more important, provide more or less *opportunity* to that minority to be violent. Nonetheless, the violence prone will always be among us, at least outside the gates of Eden.

If (3) is true, then what are the consequences for the four versions of universal pacifism considered earlier? Remember that those were a nonresistance to violence, an absolute prohibition on all violence, an absolute prohibition on lethal violence, and an absolute prohibition on all war making by states. (We shall ignore "a nonresistance to violence.")

If (3) is true, then pacifism as a prohibition on all violence *morally requires* that we acquiesce in the inevitable violent attacks from these people without defending ourselves or others so attacked with even minimal violence, if using minimal violence is the only way to resist. In like manner, when we meet with coercive threats of violence from these violent people, we must acquiesce rather than use violence, even if those threats violate our basic rights.

We need add to (3) only the premise that some of those willing to use violence are willing to use lethal violence. If so, then pacifism as a prohibition against lethal violence will require that we submit to lethal attacks or stand by unwilling to use lethal violence in the last resort to stop lethal attacks on others, or submit to threats of lethal violence.

If we add to (3) the assumption that some groups of these violent people will, at least occasionally, capture power in some nation-states and visit violence on the citizens of other states in the form of war, then pacifism does not permit violent resistance (war waging) to attacks by such nation-states.

In relating the truism in moral philosophy that *ought* implies *can* to pacifism, we need not make the deterministic (and very strong) claim that it is *impossible* for any single individual to live up to a pacifist standard. We need only make the statistical (and very weak) claim that *it is not possible for all members of society to live up to the pacifist standard all the time.* That is what is impossible and therefore cannot be asked of a whole society, since a moral theory cannot ask the impossible.

Pacifism and Collective-Choice Problems

Let us look at the consequences of this fact. Suppose a small group of individuals—rather arbitrarily, let us say 15 percent of the population—is willing to use violence if not deterred by violence or threats of violence. Meanwhile, the rest of society valiantly strives to be pacifist. What will happen? The answer is obvious. Those few willing to use violence will rule the society. For they will be both able and willing to use coercion backed by threats of violence to get their way. And the rest of us will be powerless to resist, at least with defensive violence or threats of defensive violence, as sometimes will be necessary.

Another argument against universal pacifism lurks in this set of social conditions, for the pacifist is caught in a collective-choice problem. In other words, what would be rational for all of us to do becomes irrational for almost all of us to do when even a very few refuse to go along.

In order to see this, let us formulate a *General Pacifist Rule* (GPR):

> *GPR:* One ought never use violence or threats of violence against one's fellow human beings regardless of the circumstance.

It is obvious that the world would be a better place if all of us followed GPR all of the time. But we cannot quite rest easy with this Eden. Let us be a little pessimistic about our fellow humans and assume, following claim (3) in the preceding section, that some small but significant minority of the population is willing to use violence or threats of violence to obtain their ends. Let us also assume, as is surely true, that these individuals do not wear signs and are not in any other ways obviously marked as members of this group.

Thus, if you follow the GPR, you will be unable to defend yourself against those who would victimize you using violence or threats of violence. Notice that if you are really serious about the GPR, you will not call the police either, for they will come prepared to use necessary violence in your defense. In short, if you insist on following GPR, regardless of provocation or attack on you, your basic rights will be violated, perhaps fatally. Suddenly, the principle that appeared to be collectively rational, if adhered to by all, becomes individually irrational when we know that some, even if only a few, will not adhere to it. This general problem type is discussed by Thomas Schelling, who calls these "critical mass problems."[9] Here the critical mass necessary to make GPR rational, to keep it from "unraveling," as Schelling says, is nearly 100 percent compliance.

This collective-choice problem arises not only about *self*-defense. For if you happen upon an innocent person being attacked or threatened with attack by an aggressor, it seems rational as well as moral to want to stop the attack, even if violence is the only way. But the GPR will prohibit you. Again, a rule that would be rational (and moral) for all of us to follow is neither rational nor, I argue, moral for any one of us to follow (when we know there will be some few others who will not follow it).

One might respond that this argument is fanciful because most of us are not equipped for self-defense or the defense of others by violence, and our willingness to defend therefore constitutes precious little deterrent to those who would be violent in any event. This may be true, but exactly the same argument can be mounted in favor of our calling for the aid of a specially deputized and trained group (i.e., police forces) to exercise rights to minimal justified violence on our behalf. That is, if no one were violent, we should never call the police (or even *have* police), but as soon as some are violent, we are irrational not to have and use them.

We might develop exactly the same collective-choice problem if we instead limited the pacifist rule to a ban on lethal violence, if only we assume there exists a minority who will use lethal violence if they can be sure of not being restrained by violence (or punished after the fact). Since the effective threat of lethal violence is considerably more coercive, the minority willing to use it can be smaller, with the same effect.[10] Indeed, given the brutal facts about the firepower of modern automatic weapons, the minority willing to use lethal violence can be much, much smaller than the minority willing to use nonlethal violence. Perhaps 1 percent or .1 percent of a population, if they are both willing to use machine guns and plastic explosives and are not readily identifiable, are adequate to violate, murder, or enslave the 99 percent who would scrupulously follow the General Pacifist Rule. Remember, it took far less than 1 percent of armed guards to enslave, brutalize, and murder millions in Nazi death camps (or in Stalin's Gulag).

We can also develop a similar "two person" problem (here a tradiional Prisoners' Dilemma or an assurance game, depending on how the incentives are set out) for two countries, each wanting to follow a pacifist ban on war making, but not being sure the other will do so. Assume that no other countries are involved and that country A and country B are both considering the irrevocable adoption of the *State Pacifist Rule* (SPR):

> *SPR:* Never under any circumstances wage war, even purely defensive war.

If both A and B adopt SPR, a new era of peace will occur, and both countries and their people will be much better off. If one of the countries adopts the SPR and the other does not, however, the country adopting the SPR must be an acquiescing victim for conquest and exploitation by the other. So there is some considerable incentive to bluff and, manifesting apparently pacifist intentions, then violate SPR. Since A cannot trust B (or believes it cannot) to follow the SPR, then it does not dare adopt the SPR itself. B cannot adopt it for mirror-image reasons—that is, B cannot trust A to forgo taking advantage of it and violating SPR. Each country is constrained by rational self-regard from doing what it would clearly be to their collective advantage to do. And it will not do to say, "If only we trusted each other." For simple trust of A in B is not enough. A must also *trust B's trust of A*, and vice versa for B. Thus the trust required here is of a deep and complex kind. It depends not only on your having a good opinion of your adversary, it also depends on your believing your adversary has a good opinion of you. This is the sort of trust that may well be beyond human beings and their institutions.[11]

Perhaps there is a way to overcome these collective-choice problems, although I know of no pacifist strategy for doing so. One thing is certain: Moral exhortation from a position of assumed moral superiority will not suffice. These are real and intractable problems for any society that wants to be nonviolent, and anyone seriously proposing pacifism as a social program must deal with them.

Is the Institutional Capacity for Defensive
Violence Necessary for the Existence
of Organized Society?

The pacifist dilemmas cited in the previous section suggest another problem for pacifism. Most political and legal philosophers agree that organized society would be impossible without some ability for society's government to coerce those who would otherwise break the law or be violent toward their fellow human beings. Indeed, one good definition of *sovereign* government is a set of institutions, and the group of people defined by those institutions, that has a monopoly on morally legitimate coercive force.

This point is not hard to grasp. One way of looking at organized society is as a set of rules for self-governance. Now, outside a pacifist Eden, these rules are not completely self-enforcing. There will be many occasions when it would serve my selfish purposes to steal something or defraud someone. It might even be in my interest to assault and batter someone, or I may be tempted to do so out of anger or hostility. What prevents me from doing these things? Morality may prevent me. Or I may be afraid of the informal social sanctions, such as scorn or ostracism, that my friends, my family, or other members of society might visit on me. Some combination of morality and informal social sanctions goes a very long way toward enforcing society's rules—for most of us, most of the time. But for all of us occasionally and for that small but significant minority of the violence prone often, the rules need formal sanctions if they are to be followed. Formal sanctions are legal penalties; they are fines or prison sentences or both. The view of human nature we articulated earlier makes society's capacity to impose fines and prison sentences a prerequisite for organized social life.

Before drawing the consequences of this seemingly undeniable fact for the social use of violence, let us be very clear about one thing I am *not* saying. I am not claiming that *violent punishment* is a prerequisite of organized social life. This is a position typical of certain conservative thinkers. The French philosopher Joseph de Maistre, for example, believed that the hangman's noose "made social life possible. Without that omnipresent threat of *violent death*, anarchy and chaos would ensue." In the past, torture and whipping were frequently used to enforce societies' rules. Fines and nonviolent prison sentences should suffice in a civilized and enlightened society.

While violent punishment is not necessary to society, we saw that threatened penalties for violations of society's rules are. This simply *is* the coercion on which all but utopian social existence rests. The state must possess this coercive power. A central part of its function is the morally legitimate use of a monopoly over coercive force in the enforcement of its rules.

Yet even though coercion by force is necessary to organized social life, why is violence? If putting someone in prison is not violent, and putting people in prison is sufficient sanction for the requisite coercion society needs to keep order, where is the need for violence? To answer this question, let us look a little deeper at the nature of the coercion necessary to enforce the rules. Coercion is the ability to make credible threats, in this instance threats of fines and jail sentences.[12] For a threat to be credible, however, one must be prepared to use *force* (as distinct from violence) to carry it out. Force is required not only to carry out sentences but to apprehend lawbreakers and restrain them as they go through the trial process.[13] But why must the state be prepared to use force? Let us do a thought experiment: The police have apprehended a burglar and have arrested him, but their job is only half done. They must take him to jail and, if convicted, they (or other law officers) must take him to prison and keep him confined there. Now, imagine that the burglar refuses to cooperate. He says, "I won't fight you, but I won't cooperate either," and he makes himself limp. What do the police do? First, let us note what they do not do. If they are of the right character and are properly trained, they do not use violence because they never use unnecessary violence. Here no violence is necessary. But nonviolent force is necessary. Using their own strength, the police must pick up the burglar and carry him to the police vehicle. Now notice, a very important thing happened here. The burglar chose to *escalate* the situation from one where the police had to move from threats of nonviolent force to the actual application of it, that is, from coercion to nonviolent force. To acquiesce in the burglar's nonviolent resistance and not incarcerate him would be to invite anarchy, for anyone not desiring to obey the law would have only to be willing to practice nonviolent resistance.

We have seen the capacity of an individual on whom society needs to impose a sanction to escalate the measures society must use to do so. But where is the necessity for violence? Let us change the story somewhat. Assume that our burglar is of violent character, as many

burglars certainly are. And imagine only two police officers attempting to arrest him. If the burglar resists with *violence,* the police must
respond with violence or give up on the arrest. Wholesale giving up on
arrests is surrender to anarchy. Now it will not do to say that *every
time* a wrongdoer chooses to resist violently, the police must respond
with violence. If our burglar is unarmed, and the police captain pos-
sessed enough foresight and personnel to send six police officers, his
biggest and strongest, they might be able to restrain the burglar with
nonviolent force, even as he resisted violently.

There are two reasons why we cannot conclude from this case that
police never have to be violent. First, the resources available to the
police usually do not permit it. Second, violent lawbreakers are often
armed, and for any practical purpose, the only way to deal with someone who shoots at you (and endangers innocent bystanders as well as
yourself) is to shoot back. Refusing to grant the police authority to respond violently to violent resistance against their carrying out their
duties is to immunize those willing to use violence. For a police force
restrained from using violence as a last resort is always subject to being
foiled by a criminal who chooses to escalate from the use of nonviolent force to violence. When two adversaries reciprocally escalate
a struggle to a level where one completely controls the conflict and
easily prevails, conflict theorists say that the prevailing adversary possesses *escalation dominance.* Police restrained by categorical bans on
violence give criminals escalation dominance by their recourse to violence. The party who both possesses escalation dominance at a given
level and is willing to escalate to that level will prevail. Thus, police
restrained to nonviolence must let violent criminals prevail. This is to
abrogate their function and their duty.

As we later see, granting such an immunity to violent criminals may
well be immoral. It is surely destructive of organized society, for anyone
so immunized would not be subject to society's rightful and necessary
coercion and would, therefore, be free to flout society's rules. When
others who are violence prone see violent lawbreakers immunized from
necessary violent enforcement of the laws, they will begin to break the
law and react violently if the police interfere.

Obedience to the law is a curious thing. Philosophers have specu-
lated on why people obey the law and have found the answer unclear.
John Austin, the philosopher of law, marked it down to a "habit of obe-

dience." But that explains nothing. Why the habit? Where did it come from? Perhaps, more candidly, the economist and political philosopher James Buchanan says, "It is much easier for our formal models to explain why persons commit crimes than to explain why persons do not do so."[14] But one thing *is* clear: If all the people (or even a large minority number) disobeyed the law at the same time, there would be precious little the police could do to enforce the law. They would be massively outnumbered. The rule of law hangs by a slender thread.

It is made more tenuous by the following conundrum. Obeying the law makes sense as a rational practice only when most others do so as well. If car theft is fairly uncommon, it pays to own a car. But if car theft is so common that the likelihood of having your car stolen if you leave it parked for five minutes is 90 percent, then it will not be worth it to you to own a car. In such a world, if you need a ride somewhere, you will probably do what everybody else does. You will steal a car for your immediate use, abandoning it thereafter. It would, after all, serve you no purpose to keep it. Someone would just steal it from you.[15] Obviously, in such a society, the rules of property completely break down.

Exactly the same analysis can be made for most rights or duties. To use Schelling again, we may call the rule of law a *critical mass phenomenon*. That is, obedience to law makes sense only when a large number of people obey and otherwise faithfully engage in the practice.[16] Without that, the very purpose of the social institutions of property, contract, personal rights, indeed of law altogether, becomes frustrated in the face of wholesale violation. Law is nothing without the reasonable assurance (never a certainty) that it will be obeyed by almost all, that it will be enforced, and that violence will be used to enforce it if criminals who escalate to violent resistance make that violence necessary.

There is a second point. The police are humans too, with all the rights other human persons have. They have a special *duty* for the defense of others, but they have the same *rights* as the rest of us. This includes the right of self-defense. As the police go about enforcing the law, they are the potential subjects of violent attack. For their own protection, they must be empowered to defend themselves, with violence if need be. Imposing on them a special disability (of not using violence in self-defense) would be both morally wrong and destructive of their effectiveness as enforcers of law.

In short, a society ruled by law ultimately depends on the ability and willingness of police officers to use the minimal violence necessary to exert the force and coercion that in turn is necessary to enforce the rules. Without a last but ultimate resort to violence, there can be no organized society as long as even a relatively small minority are willing to use violence to obtain their ends.

Is Pacifism Immoral?

We noted in Part I that Jan Narveson has made an ingenious and famous argument that pacifism is logically inconsistent.[17] It turns on the claim that a right to life does not make sense without an attendant right to defend that life, with violence if necessary. Though Narveson does not directly broach the matter, his analysis opens the way to an even more devastating critique, the demonstration that pacifism is *immoral*.[18] Universal pacifism holds that it is morally wrong for anyone to engage in violence. Personal pacifism holds that it is wrong only for the exponent of pacifism to engage in violence. We argue that each type of pacifism is immoral, although it takes two distinct arguments to get us there.

Personal Pacifists as Free Riders

The personal pacifist's choice of philosophic position, (i.e., to be a personal pacifist) is made against a social background wherein most of us are nonpacifists. One consequence of this is that most of us acknowledge a duty (some only a right) to aid our fellow human beings when they are under violent attack. Note that even many who feel no *duty* but only a *right* to defend another person being attacked will choose to supererogate, and further, since it is not clear who will and who will not defend with violence if necessary (we don't wear signs), the existence of these convictions constitutes a substantial deterrent to those who are prone to violence among us. Thus, many fewer violent attacks occur. Furthermore, when they do occur, they are frustrated or arrested more quickly in virtue of our feeling this duty or believing we have this right and acting accordingly.

Now imagine I am faced with a situation in which a fellow human needs aid against violent attack. I can choose to be a free rider or not. I have in the past benefited from the deterrent effect of the commitment of my fellows in society to aid me if I am attacked. I may have even benefited directly from such aid in the past, when I was attacked. Now it is my turn to ante up and do my bit. If I do not, I am a free rider on the efforts, or willingness to expend efforts, of others, and that is immoral. According to John Rawls, being a free rider is an exercise in egoism and not consistent with a moral point of view. For example, he tells us that "a common sense of justice is a great collective asset which requires the cooperation of many to maintain. The intolerant can be viewed as free riders, as persons who seek the advantages of just institutions while not doing their share to uphold them."[19] Similarly, the rule of law is a collective asset.

This sort of Rawlsian free riderhood seems deeply analogous to my thesis that the personal pacifist is a free rider, for he benefits from the collective asset of a shared willingnes mutually to defend. He benefits, but he does not contribute. But free riderhood in a lawful order is more than analogous to personal pacifism; it is homologous. A consistent pacifist, even a personal pacifist, must believe that calling the police, who will then come and use violent force, is a vicarious exercise of violent force on his own part. This is true because, as we saw earlier, police officers must be empowered to use violence in the last resort. When they do so at the behest of the personal pacifist, they act as the pacifist's agent or deputy. Can a consistent personal pacifist abjure violence for himself, but feel free to have it done for him by others? Thus the pacifist must refrain not only from forceful personal interference in attacks on others but also from inviting in anyone who is likely to interfere with violence.

But we saw that a major constituent of a lawful order is the willingness of many to interfere directly and immediately in a violent attack, violently if needs be. More important is the willingness of many more to call in authorities equipped and trained to use minimal necessary violent force. The pacifist's safety depends even more profoundly on the deterrent effect of the existence of such authorities and on society's maintenance of them. As we saw, the rule of law can be viewed as *being* a system for constituting authorities entitled to make threats of violent force in the enforcement of published or commonly understood rules. So the personal pacifist is in a very real sense a free rider on the whole notion of obedience to law and the existence of a lawful order.

Pacifism as a Universal Moral Claim

We saw that universal pacifism takes the form of a proscribed triadic relation, which holds that no one may visit violent force on a fellow human, even in defense of a third human.

The above claim states, in the Hohfeldian language of rights, a *disability*, rather like "Congress shall make no law" in the Bill of Rights. But, as Hohfeld points out, each disability gives rise to an *immunity*.[20] That is, if I am *disabled* from carrying out some activity in regard to you, you are *immune* from my carrying out that activity in regard to you. Now the universal pacifist position (UPP) has precisely that effect. It immunizes the violence prone among us from violent restraint as they carry out attacks on others. Even more surprising, they are *morally* immune because UPP is a moral claim.

Note, the pacifist will hasten to point out that all violence is evil and thus that what the violent attacker is doing is evil. Of course it is! Nonetheless, for the pacifist, the attacker is morally immune from violent interference with his evildoing.

Most rights theorists hold, and I believe correctly, that important kinds of rights (e.g., the Bill of Rights) are immunities.[21] Thus the universal pacifist must assert that the violent attacker has a *right* to noninterference (at least to not being interfered with by violent force). And since UPP is a moral claim, that right is a moral right. Indeed, conjoined with the claim that we all want to make, that gratuitous violence is evil, the attacker literally has a *right to do evil*.

Rights theorists have considered the possible acceptability of having rights to do what one ought not to do. Indeed, Judith Thompson, among others, has discussed cases where this is meaningful and sometimes even morally acceptable.[22] But such acceptable instances occur only when other legitimate moral constraints are at work. Here we have a right to do positive evil without *any countervailing moral justification* to stop it. This is not inconsistent; it is morally abhorrent.

Ironically then, pacifists, those most gentle and well-intentioned people, seem caught on the horns of a dilemma, each horn of which constrains them to a most unpacifist-like immorality. The first horn is that they are personally disabled by free choice from participating in (and contributing to) an implicit pact that makes civil and lawful society possible, yet they benefit as free riders from it. The second horn is that they hold pacifism as a universal moral claim. In which case, the most violent and brutal among us do what they do by moral right!

If pacifism ends in such a dilemma of immorality, the Justified Violence view should have garnered new substantiation. We clearly have rights to aid our fellow humans, using violent force when necessary. Contrary to what the pacifist holds, gratuitous and justified uses of violence are morally distinguishable, exactly as there is a moral difference between violent aggressors and justified defenders.

Summary

Pacifism is a family of positions, but all the members of the family seem susceptible to the arguments I have developed.

1. The logic of pacifism commits the pacifist to a monistic theory of value, even though pacifists themselves, quite reasonably, want to reject defining peace simply in terms of nonviolence.
2. Pacifism assumes the social feasibility of the pacifist obligation, but the existence of violent persons undercuts that social feasibility.
3. Pacifism is subject to a collective-choice dilemma that what is preferable for all, if the cooperation of others can be assumed, is preferable for none when we cannot guarantee the cooperation of all others.
4. And pacifism, in both its personal and its universal form, is immoral.

This is indeed an overwhelming indictment of pacifism.

DONALD SCHERER

Creating a New Pacifism

Traditional pacifism is, to my mind, a troubled view. Defined in deontological, individualistic terms, it is a deeply flawed position. James Child has skillfully and carefully laid out a large variety of criticisms, many of which seem to me basically correct. Accordingly, I agree that in various ways, many varieties of pacifism are untenable. I do not plan, then, to respond systematically to Child's criticisms. Instead, I silently accept many of them. Yet my acceptance leaves me without anything one could call a full-fledged pacifist position. My goal, therefore, must be to construct a new form of pacifism. This form of pacifism is teleological, not deontological, and social, rather than individualistic. It is a personal, rather than a universal, pacifism. It features a positive, pluralistic conception of peace, as opposed to the monistic, negative conception Child argues the pacifist must hold. And it includes an account of the motivation that leads some to take up this position. I call my view Segmented Teleological Pacifism. Since my primary goal is to expound and show the power of this alternative conception of pacifism, I respond to Child's criticisms largely to the extent that they suggest what the construction of a new, viable pacifism requires.

The Pacifist's Motivation

What kind of person is the teleological pacifist? How are we to understand the motivation that drives the commitment of such a person? Is such a commitment, Child might ask, even consistent with human nature?

Beginning with the last question, I note that Machiavelli, in his attempt to found a science of governance, sought after universal dispositions of human beings that would render them rulable. From this concern of his, it has been argued,[1] arose the modern tendency to discuss political philosophy in terms of human nature. But the time for such thinking, I argue, is past. Rulability does not require universal human dispositions; besides, we know better than to look for them.

For the teaching of modern evolutionary biology is that the concept of human nature is a mistake. Perhaps one can define being human in terms of a capacity for interbreeding, but the study of social primates tells us that we should not expect some strong disposition toward violence, or any similar disposition, to be a universal human trait, for the following reasons:

1. Social animals, being interdependent, need strong dispositions toward cooperation and toward tolerance, else their society will be jeopardized.
2. The rough parity between humans makes violent tendencies dangerous to those who have them.
3. The variety of human offensive and defensive capacities reinforces this danger.
4. The alliance-forming habits of higher primates intensifies the instability of any temporarily dominant clique.
5. The creation of social roles and (in human societies) institutions stabilizes social environments so that niches come to exist in which different dispositions and behaviors become successful.

Accordingly, we should not believe that human beings have a universal and strong disposition toward interpersonal violence.

But (4) and (5) carry further implications. They imply both of the following:

6. Alliance-forming organisms will be more successful if they are suf-

ficiently flexible, attitudinally and behaviorally, to adapt to their (social) environments.

7. The stability of different social environments will lead to the elaboration, inertia, and resilience of different modes of human interaction.

Now (6) and (7) stand in general opposition to universal descriptions of human attitudes. They tell us not to ask the old question of what "human nature" is like. Instead, they lead us to expect both that some people will incline toward complex techniques for inflicting violence on others (especially, but not necessarily exclusively, as a means for dominating those others) and that other people will evolve complex techniques both for resisting such inflictions and for developing stable, nonviolent patterns of interaction.

This biological picture is at odds with Child's earlier discussion of human nature as violent, but it fits well enough with his later idea that a significant minority of humans is willing to threaten and use violence to satisfy its desires. And, for the sake of argument, I grant his (controversial!) further premise that at least some of that minority are "irresistibly" drawn to violence. From these premises, Child concludes that pacifism demands the impossible, and he finds this impossibility to be in conflict with the postulate that *ought* implies *can*.

But notice that if not all persons are irresistibly drawn to violence, then what pacifism demands is an unreasonable moral demand only on those who are irresistibly violent. And this line of reasoning does not touch personal pacifism, whatever its implications for universal pacifism. Indeed, if (7) is true, then some social environments may actually reinforce some people in their pacifist inclinations.

Since we cannot work from postulations of a fictitious "human nature," I think it is clear that the moral psychology of a pacifist view must be empirically oriented. And while I have given a general argument that some persons may have pacifist inclinations, I have not yet provided a motivation for people to focus themselves on the realization of such a peace. Accordingly, I turn to an exposition of the positive concept of peace that I believe has motivated many pacifists.

Peace and the Reconception of Pacifism

The name *pacifism* has stood for a variety of positions. But the conception of pacifism I espouse has two basic aspects. First, it is teleological in the sense that it is motivated by a positive conception of peace toward the progressive realization of the goal of a more peaceful world. I urge that peace should be defined in terms of a conjunction of values. When I advocate a teleological pacifism, I am advocating that (some) persons should commit themselves both to those values in their own lives and to making those values sequentially more real and more significant determinants of human interaction. Second, as I understand it, pacifism is also a program for defusing human tendencies toward aggression and violence, either by neutralizing them or by undermining the conditions that motivate them. (In this part, I discuss neutralizing human tendencies toward violence; in Part IV, I discuss undermining those conditions that motivate human tendencies toward violence.)

*Peace as a Vision of the Good
the Pacifist Moves to Realize*

Philosophers have traditionally defined pacifism as a prohibition of violence. But if a definition of pacifism merely severs it from violence, it is mute about what one should do while abstaining from violence. Pacifism, then, cannot be understood merely as a prohibition against violence. For people want to know what one is to do, besides not being violent, when one's dispositions and perhaps morality itself compel a response to violence. Pacifism must therefore be defined as a commitment to peace, positively conceived, and not merely as an opposition to violence.

*A First Definition of Peace:
Peace as a Pattern of Conduct*

What, then, is peace? Or, to put the question more appropriately, what else has peace meant? For there is little point in merely imagining how marvelous would be a peace that encompassed not only a lack of violence but some fantasized set of ideals. However marvelous such a peace might be, one might wonder whether any precedent might exist for associating those ideals with the absence of war. So let us consider some positive concepts of peace grown out of the experience of historical peoples.

In his *Analects,* Confucius recalls a Golden Age, an age of peace. The glory of the time of the Chou Dynasty up to the eighth century B.C.E. certainly included its lack of hostilities. During that time, China was reputed to have experienced war neither among its various lords nor between itself and its neighbors.[2] We arrive, then, at the first component of our definition:

1. Peace is partially defined in terms of an absence of violent conflict.

Yet the Golden Age is recalled so fondly not simply for its lack of warfare; a widespread lack of hostilities leaves people free for occupations more productive than the making of weapons. If people are so fortunate as to experience a peace in which they are unthreatened, internally and externally, the following is true:

2. They are thereby freed to use more constructively the resources they might otherwise feel compelled to expend on defenses.

With their increased productivity will come an impetus to exchange surpluses with others. Thus:

3. The safety of the transportation routes and the lack of political barriers experienced by trading partners will reduce the overhead of trading, making commerce of greater mutual benefit.

It is a mistake, however, to understand such prosperity merely in economic terms,[3] for this reason:

4. The expansion of trade will reduce the ignorance trading partners have of one another, along with any suspicions grown out of that ignorance.

And what is more important:

5. An expanded relationship grown out of expanded trade will create greater commonalities among the trading partners, to the extent that their lives are shaped by the experiences they share.

As isolation from one another has bred differences and the ingraining of contrary dispositions, so commerce, and more generally, social intercourse, forges interactors toward becoming community. And:

6. Regular social intercourse can lead beyond the identification of recurring problems, induced by the environment or conflicting

traditions, to regularized patterns of resolution growing out of a community of interests and affections.

This is certainly the pattern of development Confucius saw in the Golden Age.

Beyond these economic and social aspects, the blossoming of ancient Chinese commerce led to a flourishing of the arts and exchanges of local culture. For example:

7. As people worked together, their arts and culture became more interwoven, stimulated by the variety of perspectives to which their interactions gave rise.

Thus:

8. The ancient Chinese became appreciative of consideration for one another, for through such consideration each showed to others of various perspective the desire to maintain the relationships of their prosperous life.

And even if expressions of appreciation are introduced for their value in maintaining cordial relationships:

9. A person comes to sense the intrinsic joys of treating others as one is also treated, with kindness.

Philosophically, the nine elements presented here can occur sequentially, becoming a pattern of reinforcing tendencies. Significantly, such elements do tend to reinforce each other. Becuase they are reinforcing, they tend to draw each other in, even if not in the sequence suggested here. I do not know that I have described the elements in the best way. I do not know that any one of them is absolutely necessary nor that any part of the sequence is necessary. I make no such claims. My claim is that peace can mean such a self-reinforcing pattern of well-being.

Peace and Jen: *The Experience of
Humanity in Common*

Rich as this conception of peace may be, an exposition of peace that stopped at this point would be crucially incomplete. And this for two reasons: (1) Conflict is endemic to life, and so any peace must be understood as a peace in the face of conflict; and (2) peace can have an introspective basis at which I have so far only hinted.

I turn, then, to consider these complexities, which were painfully clear to Confucius. For in the course of the Golden Age, the numbers of interacting persons had substantially increased, and different persons had come to engage in increasingly different interactions. Here Confucius sensed the root of a new social problem.[4] For, as the complexity of a society increases to the point where, because of participation in different interactions, the values of different adults diverge, families' differing socialization of their young no longer guarantees a homogeneity of expectations and dispositions that might ensure a broad measure of social tranquillity. The result of differing socializations is bound to be individuals whose dispositions not only diverge but conflict. Thus, when order within society no longer results spontaneously from homogeneous values, that order must come to rest on a new basis. If conflict is not to lead to violence, what might become the new basis?

Confucius proposes the self-conscious virtue of *jen* (human-heartedness). The experiences out of which the concept of *jen* grows are experiences of sensed human community. Such community is probably most deeply sensed in shared moments of human tragedy. For example, somebody dies, suddenly and without warning, as when an accident kills a friend. If we were the Ukrainian friends of a Chernobyl victim, our hearts went out to the most intimately bereaved, for we sensed how an accidental death underlines the ultimate frailty of human life. If we were Swedes experiencing the assassination of Prime Minister Olof Palme, we grieved for the lost opportunity to become the people we had hoped his leadership might have enabled us to be. If we were Americans mourning the *Challenger* crew, we grieved over the loss of national aspirations that their involvement in the American space program symbolized for us.

In such moments, we have a keen awareness of certain aspects of *jen*.

1. We sense the common vulnerabilities of all human beings across the boundaries of personal animosities, divergent socialization, or political ideology.

Also, when, within a society, our identities are tied to the losses of others.

2. We sense irreversible harm to other human beings as a blow to the social projects that shape our identities as a distinctive human community.

And when the violence of human against human creates the harm, we sense what I sensed, ever so dimly, as I walked home from my encounter with the class bully.

3. We sense the human community unhappily broken.

This sympathetic experience of human loss stirs within us an experience of human, not egotistical, value. For the frailties of human life are human, common to us all.

Jen, however, is not simply a deeply human compassion or sympathy. More than a tendency, *jen* is a norm of respect for others and a norm of self-respect. The powerful experiences of recognizing our common human frailty exhort us to care for boundaries that, once crossed, reduce whatever has had human worth to dust. As an ideal, *jen* means that, in recognition of the ultimate common frailty of the human condition, each human being ought to feel and express respect for the potentialities and vulnerabilities of all creatures who share that condition. *Jen*, then, is the virtue of caring, in attitude and in deed, that human action should bring no irreversible harm to the human community.

Our exposition of the virtue of *jen* allows us to state directly what it is that the concept of peace involves:

> *Conjunct 10:* Peace involves respect for the vulnerabilities of
> human community that can motivate affirming
> human persons in all the alienation-reducing ways
> we discussed with reference to the West Africans.
> In other words, peace is not simply a state of
> affairs. It is also an engrained norm of responding
> to conflict respectful of the vulnerabilities of the
> human community.

And the responses are not the rights-based responses I criticized in Chapter 2 for intensifying conflict. They are responses aimed at community restoration and community building.

Must Pacifism Be Monistic?

Confucius thus saw peace as definable, not monistically and negatively, but pluralistically and positively, in terms of a variety of common goods associated with a lack of violence. And, following that pluralistic definition, I define the pacifist as one committed to the realization of peace so defined. Contrarily, Child has argued that pacifism must involve a monistic theory of value. What, then, do I make of his argument?

In agreement with Child, I certainly admit that a pacifist commitment to a monistic theory of value seems absurd for many reasons: (1) Philosophically, it is unclear that the apparent variety of values can be reduced to any unity; (2) even if they could, it is hardly obvious that everything of value can be defined in terms of violence; (3) even if it could, it seems very unpromising to define the value of peace negatively ("no violence"); (4) moreover, a monistic definition of value is foreign to most pacifist traditions. Most pacifists are committed to positive values that are not simply the lack of violence.

Child's criticism is nevertheless telling. If the pacifist is not monistically committed to nonviolence, then in some circumstances the good to be obtained (or the bad to be avoided) by a modicum of violence will suffice to justify some violence. And surely this is incompatible with an absolute ban on violence. How is this criticism to be met?

By the consideration of an analogy. When a married woman bears a child in our society, her husband is presumed to be the father of the child. This is a practice I believe has a solid teleological justification. The justification may be set out roughly as follows:

1. For a developing child, a social father is economically and psycho-developmentally desirable, all other things being equal.
2. When a woman is married, the man best placed to provide that desirable contribution is typically the woman's husband.
3. Thus, children and spouses benefit best from the presumption that husbands are the fathers of any newborn children.

No one, of course, would think that this justification amounts to an argument that no husband has been cuckolded. That conclusion is false and does not follow from the premises. Instead, (3) justifies a set of practices without being a statement of fact. The facts of the matter, in the cases under discussion, include two: A marital and a maternal relation exists. Item (3) does not imply biological paternity, but it urges us to use a concept, *father*, which is commonly understood to be a conjunction of biological and social fatherhood. The justification for using the concept father is not that biological paternity has been proved but that, as (3) says, children and spouses benefit best from the presumption that the husbands are the fathers. And in the course of social development, practices will arise in support of this presumption. Fathers, for example, will have some authority and discretion in the disciplining of their children, as they will also have an obligation of financial support not abrogated by divorce.

Peace, I have urged, like fatherhood, should be understood as a conjunctive concept. The commitment to peace, I have urged, should be understood conjunctively because absence of violence, increased productivity, safer conditions for trade, the expansion of trade, increased commonalities among the trading partners, regularized patterns for resolving conflicts, a flourishing of arts and culture, the appreciation of consideration for one another, for both its instrumental and its intrinsic value, and affirming human persons in all the alienation-reducing ways we discussed with reference to the West Africans promote and reinforce both each other and human well-being. Even as I have mentioned various practices in our society that already support the presumption of fatherhood and as further practices might be developed in its further support, so pacifists are appropriately committed to the development of practices that support and integrate all the conjuncts of peace.

The pacifist is one who thinks it wise to make a commitment to peace, even though the elements of the concept of peace are not necessarily conjoined with each other. It may be wise to presume what is not necessarily true because the practices growing out of the presumption promote human well-being. So I believe it is with fatherhood; so, I argue in this part, it is with peace.

The Pacifist's Commitment to Peace

The first crucial stage of the argument comes out of the recognition that the conjuncts of peace are related only contingently. This contingency implies that, in the course of events, persons will make decisions between alternatives not all of which maximally promote peace.

1. Often, other values will be present in the alternatives that will lead persons not committed to peace to choose an alternative not maximally promotive of peace.
2. Often, the most convenient or usual means of achieving common ends will not maximally promote peace.

Given either eventuality, then, in the light of the alliance formation and niche development of social primates, we can expect that persons not committed to the realization of a full-fledged peace will tend not to choose to promote peace.

The importance of this point can be illustrated by considering its application to the contrast between the teleological pacifist and the liberal. A liberal, surveying my positive concept of peace, might want to express support for prosperity, the flourishing of the arts, and active efforts at conflict resolution. Fair enough. Many nonpacifists, including Child, will find more than palatable many of the elements I enfold within the concept of peace.

The difference between a liberal view and mine is deeper than this: From a liberal perspective, the avoidance of violence is prioritized over the positive elements of peace on the grounds that if violence can be avoided, people can decide for themselves how much of these other values they wish to incorporate into their lives. Thus the priority of liberty and the value of individual autonomy require the deemphasis of the positive elements in my definition. In other words, defining peace as the absence of violence (as is Child's wont) fits with the liberal emphasis on equal liberty of persons, which violence negates. But if the preservation and enhancement of the goods that can arise from human community are given more emphasis, then a negative definition of peace will seem rather empty insofar as it is empty of those goods that arise from human community.

Accordingly, the difference between positive and negative concepts of peace should not be understood simply in terms of commitments consistent with a definition.[5] For when different persons prioritize consistent elements of a definition differently, they will not only be more and less willing to let certain contingent elements of a definition fall by the wayside. They will also encourage and facilitate the development of different practices and social institutions to which the definitions, in conjunction with different priorities, give rise. In contrast to a liberal, a pacifist will focus on how actions can realize the range of values that peace includes.

Peace and the Pacifist's Motivation

For the personal pacifist, then, a merit of a conjunctive concept of peace is that it explicates a range of unrealized or partially realized goods. The realization of these goods becomes the goal to which the teleological pacifist ties his or her moral integrity. And because a teleological pacifist is committed in this self-binding way to the realization of these ideals, the merits of the present social order pale in the pacifist's eyes, as they need not for others.

The Self-Reflective Bent of the Teleological Pacifist

These thoughts lead me to question how there grows in a pacifist the reflective bent from which arises the motivation to initiate and reform peace-promoting practices. Many pacifists are self-reflective people, and one of the motivations that has moved persons to nonviolence is self-reflective. Without wishing to suggest (what is false) that advocates of the Minimum Justified Violence View (including Child) are committed to capital punishment, I think we can see how reflection on a violence-using practice such as capital punishment has moved some people toward pacifism.

For, in contemplating capital punishment, many self-reflective persons feel a repulsion that even if one says one is "executing" the murderer, one is still in fact killing the murderer, just as the murderer killed the victim.[6] If, in one's reflection on an imagined capital punishment, one takes some satisfaction in the execution of a murderer, one may find that satisfaction too much like the base satisfactions of the murderer. "What kind of a person," the self-reflective opponent of capital punishment reflects, "do I make of myself when I endorse not only the practice of capital punishment but the teeth-clenched emotion I (find that I) feel at the 'just deserts' the murderer has received?" When we recognize within ourselves any propensity to take pleasure in the execution of a mass murderer, the very propensity may repulse us. We may shiver that we might share with the murderer a propensity we find depraved.[7] Accordingly, we may want to set up social practices that discourage, rather than cultivate, such feared propensities. Thus, for example, in many jurisdictions that have retained capital punishment, capital punishment is no longer public. This shift to private executions reflects a value prioritization: Better to sacrifice the potential deterrent value of public executions than to encourage despicable tendencies to relish the killing of a human being!

Now we may imagine a person sufficiently repulsed by the base satisfaction in another human's death that the person concludes that the dichotomies between murderer and victim, between aggressor and aggressed upon, must be avoided as the source of vile tendencies of self-degradation. Thus, pacifists may ground their moral integrity on what they perceive to be the belittling effect of doing violence.[8]

It is crucial, at this point, to recall that a pacifist will be committed to a peace defined in terms of its ninth and tenth conjuncts. In accordance with the ninth conjunct, the pacifist will be committed to treating others, as one would also be treated, with kind respect for the common vulnerabilities of human life. In accord with my idea of social niches, the pacifist will in all probability have had some experience and sense of such respectful treatment, and the joy emerging from that experience will tend to motivate the pacifist in a way that others without that experience may not be motivated.[9] In accordance with the tenth conjunct, the pacifist will be inclined to have respect for the vulnerabilities of human community, both the vulnerability of individual humans and the vulnerabilities of human practices and institutions. This respect will motivate pacifists to affirm persons in all the alienation-reducing ways we discussed with reference to the West Africans.

Accordingly, a pacifist will view a merely negative definition of peace ("no violence") as compromising his or her moral integrity. In such a definition, the pacifist will see the goal of avoiding a great evil obscuring the positive values of pursuing a full-blooded peace. Obviously, a pacifist will go to great lengths of imagination, ingenuity, and even self-sacrifice to avoid a perceived compromise of personal moral integrity.

Persons with different motivations and different self-identifications will not be similarly moved. A liberal, for instance, will not feel personally compromised if some course of action involves jettisoning some positive elements of peace. Liberty and autonomy may remain intact even if other aspects of peace are compromised. But a teleological pacifist, asked to accept a merely negative definition of peace, will feel that even if life requires us to compromise our ideals, we should still want our definitions to capture, rather than ignore, our ideals. For if our definitions ignore our ideals, we are perilously close to forgetting them altogether. Accordingly, a pacifist cannot accept defining peace merely as the absence of violence, since the pacifist's moral integrity is itself tied to the ideal of peace as an entire pattern of conduct and a commitment to maintaining a certain self-concept.

The teleological pacifist not only envisions an ideal. For the pacifist is culturally critical in defining that ideal. As I define the teleological pacifist, the following is true of her or him:

1. The pacifist knows that the actual practices of any culture embody many accidents—practices that are not justifiable by any viable moral norms.
2. The pacifist knows that the fundamental common goods and common vulnerabilities of human life underdetermine the norms a given society actually employs.
3. The pacifist knows, therefore, that some other practices are compatible with equal or greater respect for persons and with equal or greater realization of the common goods and safeguarding from the common vulnerabilities.
4. The pacifist knows that practice development and practice modification have been instrumental in the creation and improvement of civil society.
5. The pacifist postulates that what often passes simply for ill will or belligerence is in part the product of what has happened in previous interactions.
6. The pacifist knows that without appropriate practice development, much coordination of persons fails for reasons of inadvertence and misperception.

It will be entirely commonplace for a person of such a critical bent to examine willingly the possibility that the extant practices of one's society will be less than optimal, because of happenstance (see item 1) or inadvertence (2) or a lacking or unhappy history (4 or 6 and 5). Consequently, the teleological pacifist will actively pursue (what will be taken as) the likelihood that superior practices could be envisioned.

Again, the teleological pacifist not only abstractly envisions an evolution toward improved practices. For the pacifist is also concerned to envision and take steps through which the elements of the ideal can be realized. An academic thinker who merely envisioned a feasible evolution of practices would not qualify as a full-fledged teleological pacifist insofar as he or she were disinclined to act on that academic understanding.

Accordingly, a pacifist's respect for human vulnerabilities will be far from the (liberal's) negative respect, which one could enact by not intentionally endangering persons and their present social support systems. A pacifist will be moved by a sense of human well-being and human community to make an active attempt to increase the realization of all that peace can be. The pacifist will not regard peace simply as an abstractly desirable state of affairs. For the pacifist, peace is also an engrained norm of responding to conflict mindful of the possibilities for creating means for reducing the vulnerabilities of the human community.[10]

We can now summarize my view of what a teleological pacifist is.

1. In an alliance-forming society, a niche may develop in which there are supports, in the physical and social environment, for a positive peace to be realized.
2. Some persons in such niches will come to value that peace highly enough to commit themselves to its maintenance and further realization.
3. Some such persons will develop a sense of moral integrity, based on self-reflection, that reinforces them in such a commitment by repulsing them from nonpeaceful alternatives.
4. These bases will motivate some persons to presume that some complex conjunctive concept of peace can be supported by an environment of social practices that will protect and reinforce it.
5. Making that presumption with those motivations, these persons will undertake a commitment not to do violence both as an expression of their own (sense of) moral integrity and as part of their commitment to the realization of a more peaceful world.[11]

While Child is correct in noting that the pacifist is committed to a contingently related set of values, the teleological pacifist will urge the value of extending the environments in which the values are all realized or are realized more fully. So the teleological pacifist is one who makes a commitment to abstaining from violence as part of a commitment to extending the scope and stability of the circumstances in which a fuller peace is realized.

Here a potential conflict arises for any pacifist wedded to a positive concept of peace. Abstaining from violence will be a goal reinforced, as we have seen, by certain feelings about killing. Promoting responsibility will be a goal reinforced, as we have seen, by a vision of peace. These goals may conflict, since they are expressions of the contingently related conjuncts of my definition of peace. Thus, because my pacifist is teleological, the reasons for not committing violence, although very deep, must always be weighed along with the reasons for so acting as to realize (more fully) some other aspects of peace. With deep respect for the motivations of deontological ethics, I make two responses to Child's criticism of my positive definition of peace. First, in many environments there will be no pressure to choose. The conjunction will be maintainable without effort. Moreover, in many other environments, as I later argue, nonviolent force will suffice to maintain the conjunction. Additionally, in still other environments, as I also argue, the moral imagination to create new interests, at least in conjunction with nonviolent force, makes it possible to realize peace more fully. Second, at the most fundamental level, only a deontological pacifism need be monistic. My pacifism is teleological.

Part of the motivation of some pacifists should now be clear: (1) Many pacifists have been concerned to integrate the pursuit of the common values of human life within their own persons so that the manner in which any one value is pursued harmonizes with and reinforces the pursuit of the others; (2) out of a self-reflective concern for integrity can grow a sense of how fundamental are the commonalities of human life; (3) consequently, pacifists come to be motivated away from dichotomized visions toward an inclusive sharing and improvement of the human condition.

The teleological pacifist is thus committed to abstaining from violence not only because it is an evil in itself but also because violence is an instrument for upholding the "right" at the expense of the good of human flourishing. The contradictions within every known social system are recorded by scholars both sympathetic to and critical of those systems. The more shallow one's integrity, the more one must ignore and even deny such scholarship in order to maintain one's outlook. (If I cannot admit the vastness of my ignorance, I must invest a part of my energies to cover up my self-deception.) One must explain away what one cannot explain. One must maintain the appearance of an integrity that one's experience will not confirm. The vision of fundamental human goods all too often compromised by the norms and rhetoric of existing societies, and the terrifying ease with which persons accept the norms and compromises of their own societies, move the pacifist to pursue an improvement of the quality of any peace we currently experience. For the pacifist attempts to criticize and revise the norms and manners of extant societies in the light of what positive peace involves. The pacifist remains committed to the evolution of improved social practices. Unlike people content to conserve whatever value a society currently realizes, pacifists stand ready to criticize established social practices in the light of fundamental common goods of human life.

Pacifism and Collective Choice

Society, Child affirms, would be better off if everybody sincerely forswore the use of violence. But, of course, the pacifist faces the terrible problem that one who forswears the use of violence, when others have not also forsworn, seems only to make herself or himself a more likely victim of violence. And surely it is irrational so to act that one puts oneself at a unique disadvantage in relation to others.

I find no difficulty with Child's premise that some people tend to be violent.[12] But does it follow, as Child says, that "if you follow the GPR [General Pacifist Rule], you will be unable to defend yourself against those who would victimize you using violence or threats of violence"?[13] If we use our imaginations, we can see why it does not follow.

A Historical Parallel

To stimulate our imaginations, we will again do well to study Chinese society during the decline of the Chou Dynasty. The thinkers of that era were proud of their *jen*, their human-heartedness, and, as self-reflective people, they were equally proud of the developed system of ethical precepts of the *chun-tzu*, the human-hearted. Thus, while they were ready to accept the necessity of fighting, they took themselves to be civilized in virtue of their allegiance to the precepts of the *chun-tzu*, including the concept of a fair fight. No good man, for example, would attack another from behind or when the other lay sleeping. And yet, these thinkers realized, what no good man would do, a barbarian might. Here lurks exactly the collective-choice problem Child discusses. For these thinkers sensed that one's allegiance to a "higher standard of morality" may put one at a decided strategic disadvantage against an adversary not similarly restrained.

Indeed, this collective-choice problem seems to me a central root of what is commonly called political realism. The European tradition extending from Machiavelli to Clausewitz echoes the Moists who sneered at Confucius in China. This tradition includes the arguments that morality is baggage and that altruism is evolutionarily self-defeating, since it is irrational to impose unilateral disadvantages on oneself in one's relations with enemies or even potential adversaries.

The thinkers of the declining Chou Dynasty pondered such views. Because they regarded themselves as civilized persons, they faced a tension between their moral integrity and their survival in the face of enemies who did not recognize their norms of action. Must those who would be committed to moral integrity finally admit that might makes right?

Many people, I suppose, including many present-day adversaries, would find the ancient Chinese concern with integrity chimerical. For we recognize that much of our lives is not of our making and is indeed beyond our control. And so we base our self-esteem on that for which we are responsible, not on what is beyond our control. In circumstances defined by a barbarian's initiation of barbarous action, how we "must" act, we are inclined to think, does not threaten our moral integrity. Child's endorsement of Minimal Justified Violence rests on this same appeal to necessity. Without at all condoning barbarity, defenders of Minimal Justified Violence see a recourse to violence as sometimes having been necessitated.

But the intuitions of the ancient Chinese had a different foundation. They started from the premise that maintaining one's integrity requires not responding barbarously to barbarians. And I would concur with the premise Child has added: Not responding at all to barbarians is not only self-defeating and irrational but also in conflict with legitimate moral demands to aid the weak against their oppressors. These two premises yield the conclusion that any ethic compromises fundamental values unless it is built on a preparedness for repulsing those who might do what one must well understand but never do. I conclude, therefore, that a pacifism entailing nonresistance to violence, most notably violence to others, is immoral.

I therefore reject any pacifism defined in terms of nonresistance to violence and threats of violence. Pacifism must countenance resistance in order to meet the legitimate requirements of morality. Resistance will include all manner of nonviolent force used to deter and prevent violence. Thus the demands of morality constrain the pacifist to investigate what powerful resistance to violence force, in its various nonviolent forms, may include. But if this is so, we must carefully consider what force is, and how it may differ from violence.

Force

Although a pacifist will disdain violence, that disdain should not be construed as a prohibition against the use of force. For force is far too broad a concept to be confined within the walls of violence. Consider, for example, some ways we use the concept of force: The force of an argument may lead us inexorably to its conclusion. The force one uses to open a stuck window will typically involve no violence, since one's goal is to make the window work, not destroy it. Force is used by parents when, without resort to physical compulsion, they evoke their children's desire for their approval to make the children obey them. At an intersection, a traffic signal en*forces* a coordination pattern without which traffic would snarl and everyone would move more slowly. A police officer secures a parade route by forcing drivers to detour in response to a *Street Closed* sign. When we care for people, we force ourselves to ignore the little ways in which they irritate us, for the sake of the relationships we aspire to maintain. If all these examples involve some use of force, then we should not automatically equate force with the armed robber who uses a gun to force the bank teller to hand over the money. We should not visualize in our mind's eye the show of force of a nation's military maneuvers and conclude that a pacifist must disdain all use of force. The force that Hitler commanded was used to execute six million Jews, but the resistance of Danish Christians who wore Stars of David on their arm forced Hitler to set aside the imposition of the Final Solution in Denmark.[14]

If, then, we are to keep clearly in our minds how separable force and violence are, we must conclude that force is best defined as the use of power to effect a result. The value of the result and the character and the consequences of the power remain unspecified. Keeping the definition so broad thus clarifies that any general evaluation of force will belie the variety and complexity of what force is. When a precise philosophical definition gains its clarity by modeling itself on a narrow range of cases, one all too easily accepts the implications of the definition, even though they ignore the realities the narrowed range of cases also ignores.

By showing how I believe this happens to Child, let me also indicate why I find it valuable to define force more broadly than he does. After introducing the concept of an aggressor, Child argues that aggressors have the power to coerce those who resist their aggression into an escalation of forceful means. Eventually, he urges, their means may need to reach violent force in order to be effective. Because Child accepts this argument, he sees little point in displaying the varieties of force I have mentioned. But, conversely, by displaying the varieties of force, I lay the groundwork for rejecting the argument that aggressors have the power to coerce defenders into the use of violent force.

How unfortunate, then, would be the characterization of the pacifist as one who disdains all use of force. As innocent and effective as the use of force may be, the conclusion must follow easily that only foolishness, or a terrible lack of careful thought, could lead a person of pacifist tendencies to abjure all force. Did Mohandas Gandhi not force the English to grant independence to India? Did the Montgomery bus boycott not force the people of the United States to reexamine their consciences, even as it forced the Montgomery Transit Authority to integrate its service? Surely, passive resistance and civil disobedience have been powerful forces for effecting nonviolent change. They have dramatized the rightness of their causes. They have revealed the plight of the oppressed. They have manifested an initial expression of an alternative social reality, thereby empowering others to continue the cause. They have symbolized the achievability of the good unadulterated by the evil of violence. Indeed, and this is most important, they have manifested the power of persons to magnify that most important of all distances, the distance between force and violence.

The distance between force and violence is crucial to pacifism because the pacifist abjures the use of violence. In a world of people who share the perspective that violence and the threat of violence are indispensable means of protecting oneself and one's rights, the renunciation of violence is likely to look like the renunciation of the linchpin of civilization. But surely this is a mistake. People defend themselves by teasing, joking, arguing, avoiding aggressors, making commercial alliances, negotiating differences, and coordinating interests. Our uses of force can be as ingenious and creative as they are many.

A sophisticated pacifist, then, impressed by Mohandas Gandhi and Martin Luther King, Jr., as well as by numerous other forceful leaders, will want to investigate what powerful force is available to those who disdain violence. For pacifism, after all, prohibits violence, not force.

The Moral Significance of Aikido

An interesting historical fact is that the entire tradition of the martial arts was born in response to the problem of the barbarian attack.[15] The ancient training included repulsing attacks from behind and attacks when one lay sleeping, but the training was focused as much on the maintenance of one's moral integrity as on the repulsion of an unfair attack.

In the course of time, the tradition of the martial arts has undeniably been corrupted from those original goals. Today in the United States, for example, thousands of people enroll in karate or kung-fu classes without ever hearing that they are learning an ancient discipline built on principles of self-knowledge and moral integrity. Indeed, only a few masters seem to teach their most advanced students the self-transformative character of the discipline of a martial art. And judges have interpreted legal prohibitions against the use of violent weapons to apply to the hands of practitioners of various martial arts. Consequently, the martial arts are widely perceived as being dangerous and potentially lethal methods of attack, rather than as means of self-defense founded on a concern for self-reflective moral integrity.

All the corruption of the martial arts from their original defensive and self-transformative goals notwithstanding, the ancient motivation for the development of the arts remains perceptible in contemporary *aikido*[16] with its special emphasis on defense. While in other martial arts one may learn of more subtle offenses, which will allow a somewhat smaller opponent to defend herself against a somewhat larger aggressor, in *aikido* one does not learn to mobilize a more subtle or a stronger force than one's opponent. Instead, one learns to concentrate on the opponent's aggression. For the teaching of *aikido* is that the opponent's aggression will always imbalance the opponent, so a sure and adequate defense will consist of guiding one's unbalanced opponent, thereby making his unbalanced, aggressive force work against him.[17] The instability that the opponent's aggression inevitably introduces into his position, one learns in *aikido*, can be exploited to turn the aggressor's force into a sufficient weapon against him. A small woman, properly trained, can ward off the aggression of a much larger man.[18]

From the practical teaching of *aikido*, we can abstract a logical lesson of the greatest importance. *Aikido* illustrates that resistance to violence does not imply the use of violence, nor does effective resistance to violence imply the use of greater violence. Effective resistance to violence does not even imply the initiation of any further force! Here we grasp a fundamental insight: Neither a commitment to one's own moral integrity nor a commitment to the innocent victim need give way in order to achieve effective resistance to violence.

Aikido, I want to say, can be a metaphor for all nonviolent force. To understand this metaphor, let us compare *aikido* to the other martial arts. What *aikido* and other martial arts have in common is their emphasis on the balance that the practitioner of the martial arts should maintain. All martial arts agree that maintaining balance is central to self-defense. To some extent, all martial arts include training designed to take advantage of one's opponent's imbalance. But most martial arts, like karate, involve offensive weapons. That is, the student learns how to initiate effective (and perhaps violent) force against the opponent. In *aikido*, contrarily, one does not learn to initiate force. The teaching of *aikido* is that the by-product of maintaining balance and deflecting the force of the aggressor can be that the aggressor's force defeats him.

How is this so? *Aikido* is based on three premises:

1. One's opponent will use aggressive force.
2. The opponent's aggressive blow takes time to strike.
3. The opponent's position in the striking of the blow is imbalanced.

The required time for striking the blow becomes the time for preparing to defend against the blow. The imbalance of the striking opponent becomes the powerlessness of the attacker to prevent the force of the attack from becoming self-destructive. And the swift and forceful movement of the opponent's aggression is subverted by the *aikido* master, thereby disabling the opponent.

The practice of *aikido* aims to stabilize the currently fragile circumstances under which it is unnecessary to choose between a life under attack and a moral integrity to be maintained. From the perspective of *aikido*, it is admissible that some conflicts are, at least practically speaking, irreconcilable. But the practice of *aikido* allows one to argue that the premises (1) irreconcilable conflict exists, and (2) unilateral violence has been undertaken do not together yield the conclusion that (3) responsive violence is justified.

Even in the face of violence (which we can postulate to be totally unprovoked), responsive violence is justified only if it has been made necessary. This is the teaching of Minimal Justified Violence. The historical practice of *aikido* shows that aggressive violence does not necessitate responsive violence. Responsive violence and surrender do not stand alone against initiated violence. Thus, the "necessity" of using a minimal justified violence should not blind us to developing patterns of interaction that obviate choosing between inflicted violence and inflicting violence.

Nonviolent Force and the Criminal

Let us apply this insight to another example, that of police work. In most countries, police are armed with guns and live bullets. The argument for arming police is that arming them is necessary in order to provide the minimum force required to protect citizens and defend themselves.[19] But the *aikido* metaphor raises the question whether a police force must use violent force to fulfill its duties. *Aikido* suggests the value of looking for a means of neutralizing an aggressor's attack without introducing new violence into a situation.

Consider Kitty Genovese, attacked on the streets of New York City over twenty years ago by a man with a knife.[20] If half of the thirty-seven people who later admitted having heard her screaming for help had entered the street when she was first attacked, her attacker, having initially left the scene, would have been forestalled from returning. If one of the thirty-seven had opened a door to her, or if another had simply called the police when the attack began, her attacker would have been unable to kill her on returning. And if people so easily miss these possibilities of resisting violence nonviolently, what more complex possibilities are even more obscured from us? We must consciously ask, as I do in Parts III and IV, "What options can we create for responding to violence nonviolently?"

But Child objects that a thoroughgoing pacifist does not have the option of calling the police. For a call to the police is a call to those committed to using violent force if necessary to subdue the assailant. I admit that most police are so organized, but must they be? This is not obvious, since English "bobbies" carried no guns for centuries. Police are simply a group of people authorized to protect the citizenry and empowered through training and equipment to enforce their will.

Since enforcement does not imply violence, we can infer abstractly that calling properly equipped police need not involve invoking violence.

Moreover, the lesson of *aikido* is that initiators of violence do not necessarily have the power Child asserts of them, the power to force defenders against violence to intensify force in order to subdue the violence. The alleged power of the initiator of violence is not really a fact about the initiator, but a question about what cultivated means of defense the attacked person may have available. It is a question about the power of the social environment to resist violence nonviolently.[21]

The limitation of *aikido* is that it relies on bodily contact between the aggressor and the practitioner of *aikido*. In *aikido*, one deflects the violence of the aggressor through physical contact. But an armed criminal need not be physically proximate in order to cause irreversible harm. *Aikido*, then, although suggesting a distinction of the greatest moral importance, is itself a means of exploiting that distinction, a means tied to mutable premises about the physical methods of particular attacks. Accordingly, the question arises of how to neutralize an armed assailant's violent potential without relying on the assailant to initiate a corporeal, proximate force. Suppose, then, that one developed a gun, such that its "bullets" would paralyze its victims for twenty minutes. Such weapons, called stun guns, disable the violent without imposing any irreversible harm.[22] Without relying on an aggressor for a proximate attack, then, these guns accomplish the nonviolent undoing of incipient violence.

The Generalized Argument

But suppose it is objected that I admit too much in allowing the ineffectiveness of *aikido* against *certain* forms of aggression! Suppose someone points out the obvious ineffectiveness of a stun gun against a nuclear attack! The logical point implicit in this objection is that the vulnerability that some method of attack creates is relative to that method of attack. Thus, the concept of an effective nonviolent defense must be defined relatively. An effective nonviolent defense against some kind of aggression does not assure us that all defense can be effective and nonviolent.[23]

But let us reconsider this contingency from a positive perspective. A contingent fact is a mutable fact. Mutable, then, is the contingent fact that every defense against a particular form of aggression is violent. If every form of the initiation of violence carries within itself the creation of a set of attacker vulnerabilities, then it is always plausible to seek to develop the "*aikido* remedy" for any particular method of attack. And since, as the Minimal Justified Violence View acknowledges, violence is never better than a regrettable "necessity," human beings have a responsibility to change the fact, whenever it is such, that no nonviolent form of defense exists against a particular possible form of aggression. Only an irresponsible fatalism moves us to duck that responsibility and resort to the rationalization of a violent defense, the rationalization that sometimes violence is necessary. For the Minimal Justified Violence View itself justifies no more violence than is necessary. From this it follows that if no violence need be necessary tomorrow (provided we invent a stun-gun analogue today), then we have an obligation today to make violence superfluous tomorrow.

Let me make this argument explicit: Traditional applications of the Just War Theory focus on whether, in a concrete set of historical circumstances, it is justifiable for a particular nation to go to war. Instead of facing that question directly, I am focusing on an earlier moment, a moment at which the technology for repulsing an aggressor's attack nonviolently could have been developed. The responsibility to use minimal necessary violence, already mandated within the Minimal Justified Violence View, must include the responsibility to minimize the violence a future defense will require. When one has not taken the responsibility to invent the stun-gun analogue, one's hands are no longer morally clean, even if one later truly claims that purely defensive responses require a degree of violence.

The gloss of contemporary morality is that the circumstances of one's responsive actions are often sufficiently determined by others that one cannot be responsible for having to defend oneself or others through violent means. Yet this gloss is not quite thick enough to obscure the fact that the ability to respond forcefully, yet nonviolently, can be cultivated mightily.

The goal of a nonviolent world, then, is that for every form of aggression, its *aikido* remedy is known. For in such a world violence is rendered futile. How disarming for one's violent initiatives to magnify one's vulnerabilities! It is a cultural legacy—one might say curse—of many people to have chosen such little cultivation of nonviolent responses that, as we read Child's argument, we may fail to discern that nonviolence does not imply acquiescence, even in the face of violence.

The Minimal Justified Violence View, admirable and restrained as it sounds in theory, works in practice on the presumption that no one should ever jeopardize one's safety while checking out whether a violent defense is really necessary. Contrarily, the *aikido* metaphor teaches us that we should be learning how to minimize effective response time and make a violent defense always unnecessary.

The Pacifist Vision

One upshot of our extended discussion is that political realists are wrong: Premising our own behavior on ethical norms does not imply assuming naively that others will base their own behavior similarly. The moral insight that originally motivated the development of the martial arts is that moral integrity does not require folly; nor need battle strength rest on treachery. So, we may say, it is unnecessary to accept a lowest-common-denominator view of human relations, which presupposes (falsely, as I have argued) that morality rests on the assumption that one's adversaries will not do unto one as one would not do unto one's adversaries. Clausewitz's argument, that in the face of violence morality is self-defeating, is itself defeated.

In response to the Minimal Justified Violence View, I concede that protecting one's life (or the life of others) and maintaining one's pacifist convictions are potentially conflicting goals. But individual skills and social practices can be developed that create possibilities for the reconciliation of potentially conflicting values. Whenever the nonviolent means can be discovered to make aggression disadvantage the aggressor, the nonviolent reconciliation of value becomes realistic. A pacifist morality rests not on the assumption of a reciprocity of standards among one's associates but on the ability of responsible parties so to construct social circumstances that the defense of the innocent does not require violence against the aggressor.

The Moral Vindication of Personal Teleological Pacifism

Because peace is so much more than the absence of war, we know that examining the justifiability of violence will not by itself suffice as an evaluation of the pacifist program. For the program rests not simply on the judgment that violence is both bad in itself and morally avoidable but also on the judgment that violence interferes with the development of a reign of peace. Thus, even as I devote the remainder of this chapter and Chapter 6 to the justifiability of violence and the morality of abstaining from violence, so I focus my work in Chapter 8 on the efficacy of the pursuit of peace and the morality of peacemaking.

Pacifism as Inconsistent

In arguing that pacifism is inconsistent, Jan Narveson defines pacifism in terms of the duty not to do violence to others, which he infers rests on a right of the others not to be a victim of violence.[24] From the right of a potential victim of violence, it seems to Narveson to follow that others have a duty to defend the potential victim, if necessary, violently.[25] But from the premise that pacifism rests on the *right* of persons not to be victims of violence, the only acceptable conclusion would be that one has a *duty* to defend the potential victim. Surely the *manner* of the defense would not follow from the duty to defend. Suppose by analogy that a police officer has a duty to apprehend an escaping felon. But the felon runs down a crowded street, and so the police officer must shoot several innocent bystanders to apprehend the felon. Here law affirms what moral sense would also say, that the police officer is not duty bound to do *whatever* apprehension requires. Indeed the officer is duty bound to refrain from firing. Therefore, a duty to do something is not a duty to do *whatever* proves necessary to that end. Certainly the thesis that a pacifist has a duty not to defend the potential victim *through the use of violence* will not yield the conclusion that the pacifist has no duty whatever to defend the victim.[26]

And suppose it is objected that if the right of persons not to be the victims of violence does not imply a duty of others to prevent that violence, then the would-be perpetrator of violence has a de facto immunity. But the case of the felon in the crowd shows that this immunity is circumstantial, not general, and tied to moral constraints quite independent of pacifism. One's duty to protect victims of violence, like any other duties, is to be discharged within the boundaries of morality. No duty implies that one ought to act immorally. Indeed, the idea that the duty carries this implication is obviously contrary to the proportionality clause of the Minimum Justified Violence View. Being moral disables one from many unscrupulous responses to life's ugliness. Thus such immunity as the unscrupulous may have lies, not at the doorstep of pacifism, but of morality.

The Morality of Pacifism and
Duties to the Helpless

Although I began by recounting my run-in with the class bully, many who question the morality of pacifism are content to raise no questions about such one-to-one situations. No doubt, a pacifist's reflective moral integrity might lead the pacifist to view (even "responsive") violence as self-demeaning, but the usual focus of moral objections to pacifism has allowed, in effect, that if a pacifist so chooses, it is permissible for the pacifist to forgo violent self-defenses.

Instead, the charge that pacifism is immoral, as Child makes most explicit, focuses on the rights of innocent but defenseless others: Even if the pacifist need not insist on his own right to be defended from attack, some nonpacifists may want to be defended. So how can the combination of their want plus their right be ignored?

At the heart of the moral argument against pacifism stands the pacifist observer of the innocent victim attacked by an overpowering aggressor. The pacifist must face, not the emotional question whether to stand by and allow his mother to be raped, but the moral question whether, given the moral innocence of his mother, he has a duty to defend her.

Nor should we think that aid for the week is a peripheral concern of morality. Even in the age of which Homer writes, an era whose moral code was much simpler than almost any known today, the importance of concern for the vulnerable is perceptible in the *virtue* that hospitality for travelers was recognized to be. Similarly, concern for the widow and the orphan is admonished from the code of Hammurabi onward,[27] and the ancient Israelites are enjoined to "oppress not a stranger; you know the heart of a stranger, for you were strangers in the land of Egypt."[28] The duty parents owe their children, to protect and nurture them, is itself an instance of the obligation to care for the helpless. Surely no one should quibble with the assertion, and no pacifist should dissent from the affirmation, that an obligation to aid those who cannot fend for themselves is at the heart of morality. When an innocent individual is violently attacked, the fact that proving the innocence of the victim is sometimes difficult is both moot and irrelevant, and the protection of the victim may be urgent, lest a life be jeopardized. Doubts about the concept of rights notwithstanding, the question of the obligation of the pacifist to protect the victim of aggressive violence cannot be shunted aside. We must, instead, stretch our moral imaginations and adjust our moral intuitions accordingly.

The Responsibility a Pacifist Takes

I begin with a concession. Even if an *aikido* defense against every offense is possible, it is not real. Against some offense, no *aikido* defense may be known. Against another, no expert defenders may be available. Thus I have not argued that all violence will prove nonviolently controllable. So I do indeed concede that violence will continue and that in practice some of that violence will be controllable only violently. Are pacifists, then, free riders, enjoying the benefits of civilization, peace, and civil society only because others recognize the value of resisting violence violently?[29] Although the suspicion lurks, I nevertheless think pacifists are not free riders, and I now argue, contrarily, that pacifists are responsible members of a community in moral transition.

Any modern society, I observe, is premised on a specialization of roles. The worldwide movement away from agricultural societies is a movement toward the diversification of labor. In a diversified society, almost nobody is self-sufficient; most people meet many needs through exchanges. We avoid the conclusion that we each free-ride with regard to what we do not produce for ourselves by the argument that we use what we have earned to procure what others have produced.

Now suppose a surgeon refuses to perform some needful task (park maintenance, for example) for fear of injuring her hands and thus her ability to operate. Surely the needfulness of the task does not make her a free rider. Quite possibly, she better serves society by refusing to endanger her hands. Of course it may be true that if everyone refused the needful task, as did our physician, some morally abhorrent or catastrophic consequences would occur. Yet this result need not affect the appropriateness of the physician's refusing the task. The pervasive specialization of society makes it quite clear that the conclusion of the immorality of the behavior of an individual will not follow either from the social needfulness of a specific task or from the fact that everyone's acting as the individual acts would be unacceptable.

So let me now generalize my argument to the volunteer services on which communities (and individuals) regularly rely. Am I a free rider if I go to the hospital never having done volunteer work at a hospital? If I accept blood without donating? If I enjoy the trees that Arbor Club members have planted in the city park? Surely not, if in my turn I have organized a chess club for the town's youngsters, teaching them the glories of the game, from Murphy to Casablanca, from Alekine to Kasporov. "What would happen if everybody did that?" is hardly a decisive moral rejoinder in a society of specialized labors.[30]

What, then, might be the specialized work of the pacifist? The pacifist's role, I argue, is teleological; it is the promotion of peace. To show this role, I imagine, again, a society without institutions of punishment under law but with an established practice of revenge. Such a practice, of course, implies the social recognition of a duty of a slain person's relatives to kill the person responsible for the relative's death. And the need for the rectification of the perceived injustice in the original slaying has regularly led persons in such societies to see the particular occasions for revenge as determined by those who cause the harms to which revenge is the only (socially available) answer. Many persons in such a society may, in less hostile moments, decry the need for practicing revenge. Many will note that the passions of the avenger repeatedly aggravate and compound violence, rather than restore comity. Many may bewail that the cycles of revenge, once started, threaten to be endless. Still, in that moment of history when another killing is fresh, the majority of persons will argue that when the occasion for revenge arises, it is good that people are willing to practice revenge. This argument will rest both on the need for justice and on the desire to forestall giving de facto license to others to practice violence with immunity. (This is of course a close analogue of the argument that leads citizens of every country to follow their leaders into war.)

Thus, in a revenge society, a person who, when wronged, proposed the development of procedures of trials, sentencing, and punishment might be accused of free riding. Others, after all, do their bit to enact justice and deter violence by practicing revenge as appropriate. Yet I do not see why the proposer of institutions of punishment is a free rider.

Most obviously, the proposer of institutions of punishment creates a disadvantage for himself or herself because of foregoing the opportunity for revenge. If a loved one has been killed, and if in the eyes of the victim's relatives the death was undeserved, then revenge will in

some societies provide the only extant practice for rectifying the injustice the original death created. The relative who disdains revenge,
therefore, effectively nullifies the only socially established means of
attaining justice. Certainly in this light the disdainer of violence is not
taking unfair advantage of the work others have done to establish a
practice of revenge.

Indeed, the pacifist goes beyond the call of duty even further than the
human-hearted who commit themselves to the use of the martial arts,
but who do not forswear the use of violence as a matter of principle.
For, out of commitment to an ideal of respect for persons and for community, the pacifist forswears the use of violence as a legitimate tool
for combating violence without obtaining any immunity from even the
most violent of conflicts. The pacifist alone gives up the socially sanc-
tioned opportunities to resist violently any violence he or she suffers,
judging that the maintenance of the principle of nonviolence is worthwhile in the light of the greater realization of common human values
and the maintenance of one's moral integrity.

But what about charging the disdainer of revenge with failure to
maintain the only socially established means of restoring justice in the
face of violence? Certainly the lapsing of a practice of revenge could em-
bolden one's enemies to increased, unprovoked violence. And is there
no obligation to maintain the (best available) means of maintaining
justice?

The promoter of the rule of law, however, does not disdain the value
of the social fabric. An increase in unprovoked attacks inspired by the
disdaining of revenge might strain the social fabric in the short term.
And if the society divides over the feasibility of shifting from a practice
of revenge to a rule of law, the social fabric may suffer short-term strain
even if further attacks are not forthcoming. But the eventual adoption of patterns that minimize the violence done in restoring justice
strengthens the social fabric in the long term.

One may well have an obligation to contribute to making justice
possible. But one does this either by maintaining current practices of
attaining justice or by contributing to making one's society's practices
for doing "the right" practices that maximize the good. The pacifist
chooses the latter path. In this light we grasp the importance of defining pacifism not only negatively but, teleologically, in terms of the
promotion of peace. A pacifist who opposed killing but did nothing to
make violence unnecessary might be accused of free riding; a pacifist

devoted to the replacement of violent social practices with nonviolent practices is not similarly irresponsible.

True enough, whenever the *aikido* remedy for some forms of violence is unknown, the individual pacifist has no share in providing the minimal justified violence required to defend some innocent victims of violence. But, of course, the specialization of social roles makes almost everybody a "free rider" in this sense, inasmuch as few of us vaccinate dogs for rabies, few of us collect charitable contributions for cancer research, and few of us are police officers.

What work, then, does the pacifist accomplish by focusing on the positive content of peace? Pacifists voluntarily accept the obligation of actively promoting the conditions of social intercourse under which persons would not incline toward violence. Although others may feel they have done their duties by not harming anyone, by paying taxes to underwrite a police force, and, perhaps, by coming to the aid of a victim of violence, pacifists will see the use of violence against the violent (perhaps even by a police force) as a dangerous moral compromise, reflecting a social fabric that itself undermines the higher standard of right action implicit in learning how to respond nonviolently but effectively to the violent. Even though it is generally conceded that the pursuit of ideals goes beyond the call of duty, pacifists will accept the obligation of working to create practices and institutions that reduce society's reliance on violence and make violence more containable.

If, then, pacifists can be more effective in the evolution of peace, it is surely because they are motivated purely by a desire for social harmony. In an antagonistic situation, even the adversaries of one's people can perceive such a motivation to be in their own interests. Removing motivations toward violence and making nonviolent coordination mutually beneficial thus defends the innocent as surely as guns and bullets.[31]

Even the partial realization of such pacifist dreams protects the innocent as surely as the movement from a practice of revenge to a rule of law. The supererogatory voluntary service of the pacifist committed to the realization of a positive ideal of peace makes the pacifist a contributor to the social good, not a free rider. For the pacifist program answers the West African question of how to develop social practices and institutions through which the maintenance of justice coheres with the restoration of community.

Scarcity and Irreconcilable Conflict

"But surely it is naive to dismiss irreconcilable conflicts?" will be the retort to the line presented above. The objector apparently believes that while the organization of improved coordinations will yield beneficial results, it is naive to adopt a pacifist approach to irreconcilably conflicts. Suppose, then, that seven people want to go to a basketball game for which only five seats are available. Must not someone's interest be negatively affected? That is, does not scarcity imply unavoidable conflict? This, to my mind, is the important question. Accidental and inadvertent conflicts will surely be as enduring as human life. But if, in a peace-loving world, steps toward a positive peace are numerous and mutual, the accidental and the inadvertent will be forgivable; such acts are not intended, they will not continually recur, and steps of conciliation and compensation can follow. Contrarily, scarcity seems to imply inevitable conflict, perhaps escalating to violence.

But does scarcity really imply inevitable conflict? Of course not. A market example occurred recently in the United States when airlines (which overbook flights, thereby creating potential shortages) adopted the practice of bidding to buy back the seats of persons.[32] What the bidding does is to introduce a new interest on the part of passengers (in getting money) into a situation in which their previously sole interest (in airline transportation) could not be satisfied. While it may be true *relative to a specific interest* that scarcity implies conflict, interests need not remain constant. Even when an unchangeable scarcity implies that existent interests must conflict, practices that bring new interests into play require persons to reprioritize their interests. Then nobody's (reconstituted) interests need be negatively affected, even though original interests "irreconcilably" conflicted.[33] "Irreconcilable conflicts" are, we must grasp, interest relative.

But suppose it is objected that the airline example differs crucially from the basketball example. For the airlines created the obligation to respond to the shortage by selling enough tickets (and thereby making enough contracts) to create the shortage. The basketball team did not overbook the basketball arena. Consequently, in the airline case alone does one party have the responsibility for creating a solution to the shortage problem.

When situations are not structured so as to create a responsibility for creating a solution to a scarcity problem, everyone may think, "It would be more to my advantage if somebody else initiated the solution to the scarcity problem," with the result that nobody initiates the solution. No doubt some of the people who did not help Kitty Genovese shared this thought. No doubt many members of revenge societies have shared this thought.

The role of the pacifist, in such social circumstances, is to accept the responsibility for initiating a solution to the problem. Even when violence is not anticipated (as when seven friends receive only five seats for a basketball game they all want to attend), a pacifist will want to initiate something like a straw-drawing procedure to minimize later acrimony within the friendship. The future course of the friendship may be smoother if the five who attend the game acknowledge that they "owe one" to the two left behind. Thus, as long as the society would benefit from replacing practices of violence with structures that develop reliability and obviate mistrust, the pacifist is a visionary. For the pacifist accepts a responsibility not clearly assigned to anyone because of the greater positive value to be realized through the development of peacemaking practices.

Instituting the Peacemaker

In Chapter 2, I urged that the presumptions of pacifism, although logically consistent with the presumptions of rights-based Minimal Justified Violence, have in practice been inconsistent. Part of the practical inconsistency arises because a given person is often temperamentally suited to one presumption or the other. Part of the practical inconsistency is that, in a limited time, it may be impossible to enact all the deeds both presumptions involve. Part of the inconsistency is that those who act on one set of presumptions become less credible agents of acts based on the alternative. For all these reasons, a nation with a Secretary of Defense needs a Secretary of Peacemaking. Instituting the quest for a positive peace is, in an age of specialized labor, simply a virtually costless step, a step that can only advantage nations to take. And as pairs of nations take the step, they create a salience, an obvious means through which to facilitate reciprocating whatever sincere steps each wants to take toward a peaceful world. (I elaborate these peacemaking themes in Parts III and IV.)

The problem of developing a higher morality thus becomes the problem of developing means that both allow established groups to maintain the security they currently enjoy and foster the development of the kind of harmonious integration of lives and societies that promote a greater flourishing of individuals and encourage a greater stability of relations. How does one flesh out a plan for developing the practices and institutions of peace? The contours of such a program are the topic of Part IV.

Of the Morality of Pacifism

But if pacifism is not immoral, does it follow that it is moral? Here we must be very careful to understand what I have said. When I considered the question whether pacifism is immoral, the argument I made was that a person who lives by pacifist principles does not thereby act immorally. I even argued that a person may act morally in living by pacifist principles. Persons who devote themselves to the establishment of less violent means of responding to violence may achieve some good without causing any evil. This is a justification of personal pacifism. But we should not conclude from this argument that, however many persons in however many societies are inclined to pacifism, the world would be a better place if a few more persons would join the pacifist's ranks. Certainly, if no persons are pacifists, the world will be a better place if a few people begin to devote their energies to the establishment of a more peaceful order. Certainly, if only a very few persons are pacifists in any given society, then the world will be a better place if their numbers increase to the point that, in every nation, in every cohesive group, persons inclined to pacifism are widely and openly known and accepted for their efforts to create a less fragile structure for realizing the positive values of peace. And, at the other extreme, certainly if every person save one or save a very few is a pacifist, not only would the world be a better place but, indeed, then the few nonpacifists would be morally obliged to become pacifists.

It is not at all obvious, however, in a world full of societies each with a few prominent pacifists, that individual persons, knowing that many persons are sometimes ready to act violently, have a moral obligation to become pacifists. When such persons know the pacifist means of resisting (all) violence nonviolently, they should become pacifists; that much is clear. But I have presented no argument concerning the case when *aikido* remedies of pacific resistance are unknown. I have urged, however, that especially when the lives of the innocent are put on the line, the society is morally deficient that does not pursue the pacifist goals of discovering a nonviolent means of effectively resisting violence and creating the interests through which to reconcile "irreconcilable" conflicts.

Summary

I have argued that pacifism is neither inconsistent nor iimmoral. Bearing the *aikido* metaphor in mind, we can clearly see that pacifism is not inconsistent. Acknowledging the rights of others not to be treated violently does not require a violent response from the pacifist. Certainly, one who recognizes a duty to help others in distress will recognize a duty to resist violence against them, but the force–violence distinction implies that a duty to resist violence is not a duty to resist violently.

Since pacifism is not identical with nonresistance, the pacifist's problem is one of inventing and disseminating the means of resisting violence without recourse to violence. This is not a logical problem, but a problem about the moral deficiency of a social order that has accounted neither for the *aikido* metaphor nor for the insight that "irreconcilable conflict" is interest relative. This is not the alleged pacifist failure of moral duty, but a social failure of moral imagination, a social failure the pacifist supererogates to address.

From the earliest days of states, the value of a military organization for the security of the state has been understood. Yet in the late twentieth century, the value of creating practices that help to realize peace, both for the well-being of people and, therefore, for the security of states, is yet to be appreciated.

In summary, then, because I acknowledge duties to victims of violence, I reject any pacifism based on nonresistance. Because I envision the teleological pacifist relying on the present-day restraints of violence, I accept only a personal pacifism. Because the pacifist I describe is motivated by the pursuit of peace, the pacifism rejects the categorical duties of deontological thinking in the name of feasible action to create improved social environments. Because the roles I describe for the teleological pacifist will exist within a society relying on diverse, specialized labors, I urge only that a segment of populations should be teleological pacifists. Hence I call my view Segmented Teleological Pacifism.

PART III

THE MORAL AND METAPHYSICAL FOUNDATIONS OF PACIFISM AND THE JUSTIFIED VIOLENCE VIEW

5 *JAMES W. CHILD*

On Justifying Violence

The Deep Structure

The crux of the difference between Donald Scherer and me can be found in our respective definitions of violence against persons. Let us examine them.

Scherer's Definition: By violence I mean the doing of irreversible harm to persons. One person harms another when the first does something that causes the second to suffer the loss of some human faculty(ies) or ability(ies).

Child's Definition: Violence is an intentional *human action* that (1) is itself capable of causing great pain to and/or injuring or killing, the person acted on; (2) is done with the *intent* of causing great pain to, and/or injuring or killing, the person acted upon; and (3) involves great force or vigor.

I begin by applying these definitions to violence committed by individual human agents, extending my discussion only later to violence between states considered as legal persons.

The most obvious difference between our definitions is that I insist that violence "involves great force or vigor." This is important, particularly in the consideration of nonviolent options, and we consider this issue later in this chapter. There is, however, a less obvious but deeper difference. I require that violence be a human *action* done with *intent* to cause pain, injury, or death.[1] Scherer does not make intention a requirement. His emphasis is on the *harm* consequent on the violence, not the *intent* to cause the harm. Scherer sees violence as a "doing," but not necessarily an action. But doings generally, and actions more narrowly, are substantially different. As one action theorist has put it, "actions are only a subclass of doings. People hiccup, bleed, tremble, shudder, stumble, and fall. They give birth, grow taller, fall asleep, catch cold, recuperate, faint and die. Each of these is something people may be said to 'do,' yet none is an action."[2] I am sure that Scherer would agree that the subset of *intentional violent acts* is in principle distinguishable from the more general class of *irreversibly harmful doings* that he defines as violent. Yet, this subset plays no particular role in his definition of violence, a fact that illustrates the lack of emphasis intentionality receives in his view of violence.

Distinguishing intentional violent acts from irreversibly harmful doings is not just a philosopher's verbal quibble; it is of considerable moral moment. For one is not responsible or accountable for all one's doings. After all, you cannot help a hiccup or a stumbling. In contrast, you can *choose* not to commit an intentional act, and my definition of violence is that it is an intentional action and therefore subject to choice. Even more narrowly, violence is not merely an action done with some intention or other. It is an action done with the specific intention of causing pain, injury, or death.[3]

I originally defined our enterprise as an analysis of the moral propriety of rules, both moral and legal, governing violence and how, if at all, violence is properly used. This has led us to two moral theories about violence, Scherer's Segmented Teleological Pacifism and my Justified Violence View. Now ask yourself this: What sense does our analysis make if violence is not deemed to be the intentional action of rational agents? Unintentional violence (to the extent such a thing might exist) is by definition regrettable, but discouraging its existence has more to do with safety procedures than it has to do with rules directly governing intentional acts of violence. Moral and legal rules presuppose rational agents who can follow them (or can choose not to) and who are, consequently, accountable for following them.

"Law" the philosopher of law Lon Fuller says, "is the enterprise of subjecting human conduct to the governance of rules."[4] He might as well have said this of morals. But Fuller went on in a way most instructive for what we are doing here: "To embark on the enterprise of subjecting human conduct to the governance of rules involves of necessity a commitment to a view that man is, or can become, a responsible agent, capable of understanding and following rules and answerable for his defaults."[5] Thus I would argue that the focus of our concern *must be* on violence as the object of the intentional acts of rational agents, else a moral theory about violence would be in vain, at least as a way of guiding our action. And what else is a moral theory for?

This is not to say that other acts or omissions are not morally relevant to the issue of violence. If one through negligence contributes to a circumstance that will, with high probability, cause violence, that contribution may create moral culpability. If one knowingly or through negligence omits to do something that will forestall violence, the omission may create moral culpability. A candidate for moral culpability in this area might be the failure to conduct a sufficient search for nonviolent measures to prevent violence. Still, by my lights, violent acts are by definition intentional with all the consequences for responsibility and culpability that such a definition implies. The primary moral focus must be on the intentional act of violence, particularly the series of intentions and acts that *initiates* violence.

What might we conclude about the definition of violence? We might dub the harmful consequences of negligence or other unintentional harmings caused by human conduct as violence. To that extent we may agree with Scherer's definition. But the paradigm case of violence is the *intentional infliction or use* of violence. It is the intentional action that moral rules governing violence must be primarily directed toward.

The Happening Theory or the Agency Theory?

The source of the emphasis Scherer puts on harm and that I put on intention comes from our respective reliance on two theories, each one much deeper than Segmented Teleological Pacifism and the Justified

Violence View, respectively. These two theories, which I call the Happening Theory and the Agency Theory, respectively, are about what violence is and how it fits into our moral world. The two theories are not necessarily in direct contradiction. Instead, they emphasize the moral relevance of different aspects of violence. While I believe Scherer holds a version of the Happening Theory, I begin by a generic description of the theory before applying it to his views.

The Happening Theory holds that violence is something that simply happens in interpersonal and international interactions. It is *caused* by a variety of things over which those involved in the violence, even those who are perpetrators, often have little control. Violence is frequently caused by misunderstanding, miscommunication, and misperception. It often grows out of prejudice, ignorance, and social injustice, particularly out of a morally bad or unfair distribution of resources, all of which ought to be remedied regardless of whether they produce violence.

The Agency Theory is similarly a matter of emphasis. For no one can deny that violence has *causes*. But the Agency Theory lays stress on violence that is the intentional, voluntary action of rational agents. Such violence fits at the foundation of the Justified Violence View because it posits that each of us has a prima facie moral duty not to commit violent acts on our fellow humans. Only moral agents capable of rational choice and of bearing responsibility for that choice can be charged with such duties to others. From this fundamental notion of moral agency come all the basic rights of persons we discussed in Part I, as well as the second-order rights of self-defense and the defense of others.

It is fairly easy to extend the Happening Theory and the Agency Theory from violence to the more general notion of conflict situations. We can define *conflict situations,* as we did in Chapter 1, as situations where two or more parties want and intend to bring about inconsistent states of affairs. The Happening Theory is inclined, as its name implies, to treat a conflict situation as something that simply occurs, rather than something that somebody intentionally brings about. The Agency Theory holds that a conflict situation often arises when one person intentionally sets about creating it through aggression, also as defined in Part I.

Let us illustrate these different emphases with an example. Suppose a mugger accosts you on a lonely street at night and while leveling a pistol at you, says, "Give me your wallet or I'll shoot you."[6] The two theories would pick out different features of the situation to emphasize in a moral account of what is occurring. The advocate of the Happening Theory might well point out that the mugger had a deprived childhood, was out of work, and was a member of a minority group that had been denied social justice. It is simply a statistical truth, the advocate of the Happening Theory would say, that when a group of people experience such deprivations, some of them will commit such crimes; that is, such occurrences simply *will happen.*

The partisan of the Agency Theory will stress an entirely different set of facts. This mugger, the Agency Theorist will say, is perfectly in charge of his faculties. He intentionally chose to accost you in this way. He was under no duress. (Let us assume that the mugger, while poor, is not starving. Starvation might give rise to a defense of necessity. This we do not want our example to do.) We are all under general moral duties to obey the law and not to be aggressors. This mugger's act is a violation of those duties, and he was not acting under any recognized justification (such as self-defense) or under any excusing condition (such as insanity or mistake or necessity). Therefore, he is morally, and thus legally, accountable for his duty-violating action.

The Agency Theory focuses on *specific individual cases.* It asks about the rights and wrongs of the actions of specific parties in those cases, not about the causes of violence in sets of cases. The Agency Theory alone provides an appropriate description when we are concerned about the individual moral responsibility and accountability of the mugger or the rights, including self-defense, of the victim.

The Agency Theory is applicable from either of two perspectives. It is employed by a judge from an *adjudicative perspective.* The judge looks at a single case that occurred in the past and tries to determine who was right and who was wrong for the purposes of assessing claims for reparation (in tort) or imposing punishment (in crime) or issuing the appropriate orders to keep the same conflict between the parties from arising again (in equity).

As an advocate of the Justified Violence View, I am less interested in the adjudicative perspective than in the issues of self-defense and the defense of others (the rights that pertain in situ). Therefore I shall assume the other perspective from which the Agency Theory is appropriate, the specific perspective of a party to the violence. The *party perspective* differs from the adjudicative perspective in focusing on contemporaneous, not past, cases.[7] Thus, I shall ask what behavior is morally and legally appropriate *for the parties* in the midst of some conflicting interaction.

Both the Happening Theory and the Agency Theory contain important insights. Indeed, some of the most important new facts we have learned about violence in the past several decades come under the Happening Theory. One of these facts is that violent conflict can escalate out of the control of any of the participants. It can get beyond intentions, anybody's intentions. Another fact is that certain kinds of violent conflicts are not "started by someone" in any simple way. In some situations there may be *two aggressors,* and in other situations there may be *no aggressors.* Situations in which there are no aggressors are more prevalent and more important in international conflict, but they exist in domestic contexts as well. They are often caused by misperception, deep suspicion, or miscommunication in situations involving a high state of readiness for attack. Scherer has emphasized these facts. He is correct to do so.

The Happening Theory is indispensable if we are making social policy to reduce crime and, one hopes, to increase social justice. Accordingly, the Happening Theory assumes a *policy perspective.* The policy perspective is prospective; it looks to the future in an effort to alter long-term societal problems. Oriented statistically to finding causes of cases of violence, it asks what we are to do *as a society* to reduce the frequency of such cases in the future.

Now, no one who is at all sensible can deny that there is a very great deal to the Happening Theory of conflict and violence. Indeed, *exclusive* reliance on the Agency Theory in policy contexts, especially in international cases (or in any instances of collective or organizational conflict), can result in moral abominations. It can lead to a paranoid search for scapegoats or attributions of collective guilt and consequent acts of revenge. As we often hear in such claims as "the Palestinian's are responsible!" "No, the Israelies are responsible!" My only argument is with an equally *exclusive* claim by the Happening Theory that it is *the* singularly appropriate moral account of all violence or conflict. As we later see, a misplaced exclusive application of the Happening Theory can lead to egregious moral mistakes as easily as can the misplaced application of the Agency Theory.

This is clearly true in international conflict, when one is faced with an obdurate aggressor, like Adolf Hitler. His extortive threats and, later, unprovoked attacks are models of the sort of action I maintain must be morally identifiable as irredeemably wrong. Actions like his justify violent defense in the last resort.

Notice, however, that one can give a Happening Theory account of how it *happened* that Hitler came into a position to make the threats he did. Scherer reminds us[8] that the Treaty of Versailles sowed "the seeds of war," and no doubt it did. The causes of World War II and the rise of the Nazis in Germany are very interesting from a policy perspective. If one is concerned to make long-term international policy, especially to decide how to treat a conquered foreign country, the Happening Theory provides the appropriate account. If we put ourselves in General Mac-Arthur's place in 1945, trying to work out a policy for the occupation of Japan, the Happening Theory of Hitler's rise would be the morally and prudentially appropriate theory to study. Surely the Treaty of Versailles is completely irrelevant, however, in assessing the morality of Hitler's (and derivatively Germany's) behavior at Munich in 1938.[9] For this we need the Agency Theory, which condemns threats of violence and attendant extortion as immoral and counsels both morally and prudentially that we resist. Moreover, if we are concerned, as a party to the conflict over the Sudetenland, to *deter* Hitler, the Agency Theory will show the strategic way toward morally appropriate incentives and disincentives. For Neville Chamberlain and Edouard Daladier, only the Agency Theory and the party perspective were relevant.

Viewed from the perspective of a party, the Happening Theory is an irrelevancy and a blind alley for issues of moral appraisal and prudential and strategic assessment. Indeed, the worst kind of appeasement of aggressors, a kind that gives pacifism a bad name (fairly or unfairly), arises out of a conflation of these two theories. To say that what the mugger is doing is excusable or ought not to be resisted because he had a deprived childhood is such a conflation. To say that the people of Czechoslovakia ought to have been handed over to Hitler because the Treaty of Versailles was unfair to Germany is also such a conflation. To use the Happening Theory to exculpate aggression morally or to mandate acquiescence is a profound *moral mistake*. Indeed, it is a mistake as potentially terrible in its moral consequences as some typical abuses of the Agency Theory, such as seeking scapegoats or attributing collective guilt.

Who Started it? Fault, Intention,
and Moral Responsibility

Scherer does allow that judicial proceedings within a system of the rule of law can do a fairly good job of distinguishing the aggressor from the aggressed upon. Accordingly, rights of self-defense and the defense of others might be taken to arise derivatively, after the fact in the *adjudicative perspective*. But, of course, that is not sufficient for our strong claim of moral distinguishability of aggressor and aggressed upon, even in civil society. The Justified Violence View holds (and I believe truly) that we can regularly (though not always) distinguish unprovoked attack and legitimate defense in context, that is, from the *party perspective*, while they are going on and even immediately before they take place. Thus the righteous defender or the passerby or (and this is especially important) the police officer who arrives at the scene can make these determinations then and there and, acting within one's own rights or on behalf of the victim's, prevent or stop the aggression.

Even so, Scherer reasonably urges the epistemic dimension of the issue of violent intentions. Can we *know* what we need to know about a violent conflict? Can we *always* pick out an aggressor and a defender in cases of violent conflict? Can we *ever* do it? Can we do it often enough to make moral sense of the distinction? A great deal turns on the possibility of this distinction, for what we are discussing is the very basic notion in law and morals of *fault*. The Justified Violence View and its more basic foundation, the Agency Theory of violence and conflict, both assume that crimes of physical aggression or attack, such as murder, kidnapping, assault and battery, and rape, are crimes of fault, and that fault is in principle determinable.

Yet the answer to Scherer's question is not clear. Let us sort out precisely what we must find out if we are to be able to distinguish the party at fault. First, we must be able to take any conflict situation and determine *who the parties are*. In most instances, this is very easy. Of course, in mob violence, gang violence, clashes between opposing crowds of demonstrators, and the like, just distinguishing the parties from the bystanders is difficult. But most often, in interpersonal conflict (versus interstate conflict, which we consider later), we can determine the parties without too much difficulty.

The next question is, "Who, among the parties, is at fault?" Crimes and torts of violence are intentional acts. Thus, the answer is, conceptually at least, not too difficult. Who intends to initiate violence? Intentions are sometimes difficult things to infer, but usually they are not. The law and more broadly civil society require that we make inferences to intentions all the time. Intentions, like other mental events (or entities) such as beliefs or desires or fears, are not directly visible. We must infer them from behavior, including verbal behavior. But often, in fact overwhelmingly often, those inferences are so easy that we do not even think of them as inferences. Your friend says, "I'm going to the store," and you infer that she intends to go to the store. Other behaviors, actions, and preparations similarly indicate intention. If the baseball pitcher winds up, we infer that he will pitch the ball. Of course, all these inferences are subject to error. Your friend might be deceiving you. The pitcher might throw to first base. But these inferences are far more often right than wrong. It is, then, from verbal and other behavior that we infer who intends to initiate violence and who only intends to respond. Sometimes it is difficult, but usually it is not.

One must always grant that the application of any rule in the real world will produce fuzzy cases. For example, John McEnroe and the tennis umpire will argue about whether the ball was in or out. But everybody agrees on most of the calls in tennis (even McEnroe), or there could be no game. In like manner, a civil society based on law depends on the overwhelming majority of clear cases of aggression and accepts the expenditures of vast energy and controversy on only a few "hard cases."[10] Thus we cannot allow some hard cases to vitiate a conceptual framework that enables us to deal successfully with the vast majority of easy cases. Thus I take the easy cases as my paradigm of intention, fault, and responsibility.

Following this procedure in instances of interpersonal attack and violence, we usually know pretty well what we mean by "Green started it" or "Green is at fault" or "Green is responsible." There are a variety of reasons for this, but the most important is probably that rules governing civil society (i.e., our laws of self-defense or the defense of others) are fairly well understood by attackers, victims, defenders, bystanders and witnesses, police, judges, juries, and society as a whole. Intuitively, the notion of violence is fairly clear. Cursing is not violence, throwing rocks is. Menacing someone with threats of immediate violence is assault, while making long-term or conditional threats are not. Legally we understand the application of these rules quite well. Modern society has a fairly good record to demonstrate that the rules and definitions of the Justified Violence View do work, most of the time, in most circumstances, to the extent that any rules or other means of social control of behavior can ever be said to work. (And it is worth noting that the system of *rights* on which those rules are based also has a good record.)

Now comes the moral conclusion. The party initiating aggression (understood as intention plus overt acts in pursuit of the intention) is at fault.[11] Even if the wrongful attack is not carried through to fruition, the law often designates such initial steps by themselves as *attempts* (or if done with others, *conspiracies*) and treats them as crimes.[12]

Fault, Intention, and Moral Responsibility in International Relations

As Scherer clearly realizes, his skepticism about picking out attacker and victim cuts deepest in the sphere of international relations. For three reasons, it is in this context often difficult to tell who is the aggressor and who the defender. First, what people and countries *say*, as we later see, is not always a good index of whether we can know who started what. Second, and more important, as Scherer says, the countries themselves often do not *know* who really started a conflict. Third, there are problems in philosophically analyzing claims about nations' (and other collective entities, such as corporations) knowing, intending, and deciding anything. Much philosophical ink has been used in discussing this. Yet there has been no convincing analysis of it. But there is no doubt that we do use these notions with reasonable sense and precision in spite of that. So we will proceed as if this is not a problem.

To ferret out how universally the Justified Violence View can be applied, we need to ask two crucial questions: In any violent conflict situation, is there always an aggressor? Is there always only one aggressor (in a two-party conflict)? However difficult these questions may be, one thing can be agreed on at the outset: In any potential two-party conflict, there are four logical possibilities (see Figure 1). The Justified Violence View supplies a fruitful moral analysis in the common-sense cases, cells 2 and 3 in the figure; we have an aggressor and a presumptively innocent victim. One of the most interesting things we can learn from modern conflict theory, however, is that cells 1 and 4 are not

Party   A

Aggressor   Nonaggressor

		Aggressor	Nonaggressor
P a r t y B	Aggressor	1	2
	Nonaggressor	3	4

Figure 1

empty. Conflict can break out between two powers, both of whom wanted the conflict. Some historians have argued that this was true between France and Germany twice—in the Franco-Prussian War in 1875 and again at the beginning of World War I in 1914. Such conflict is, at least, possible in principle. If both sides wanted war because they wanted to commit aggression on each other or on innocent third-party countries, and both countries commence such aggression more or less simultaneously, then neither country's action could be justified under the Justified Violence View.

What about cell 4? Can a war break out in which both sides are innocent? Before the 1950s, most authorities would have said "clearly not." After all, war is not a happening; waging war is the intentional act (or series of acts or a policy) of a nation-state or its leaders. As contemporary conflict theory has learned more about how war starts, however, we have learned that this is not so. Wars can happen when neither party engaged really wants war or has pursued it as policy. The regnant theory about the inception of World War I holds that it started in this way.[13] Moreover, there is no question that a nuclear war between the United States and the Soviet Union *could* begin in this way.[14] In fact, most experts agree that is how a nuclear war *would* start, if one ever did.

What is the answer to Scherer's question about a nation's claims to be nonaggressive: "Can one reasonably assume that in each . . . case there is always exactly one liar?"[15] The answer is clearly no. Sometimes there are two, sometimes there is none, and sometimes the combatants themselves do not even know. Consider a brief list of examples where knowing who the aggressor was might well have been impossible:

- The United States, Nicaragua, and El Salvador, 1982–1989.
- The Sino-Soviet border disputes, 1968–1969.
- All the original combatants, except Britain, in World War I.

Here Scherer's concerns about the inherent fuzziness of claims of original aggression and legitimate defense are well founded.

In the most intractable of these cases the issue becomes what the truth is, not merely who is telling it. Both the United States and North Vietnam lied in crucial ways during the Vietnam war.[16] They lied not only about their intentions; they lied about what they had done and were doing. They lied about what they perceived was being done to them. They told different lies to different constituencies, to each other, to their own people, to the international press, and to their allies. Indeed, in the United States there was so much dissembling and public relations posturing within the chain of command that one could say with regard to many matters that the top leaders in the United States literally did not know what they were doing.[17] Moreover, the allies of both powers and the neutrals—the Soviets, the Chinese, the Cambodians, the South Vietnamese, and so on—all lied.

Indeed, the further we analyze the Vietnam war, the more confusing things become. For we have not only limitations of knowledge here; we have limitations of brute fact. It is easy to reconstruct the history of the Vietnam war, while being relatively faithful to the known facts, in such a way that either party was the aggressor or that both parties had aggressive designs (cell 1) or that neither party did and that each sincerely believed itself to be acting in good faith in defense of its (and its allies) "legitimate interests" (cell 4).

Indeed, the Vietnam war is a tailor-made example for Scherer. Personally, I despair of making moral sense out of that tragedy. In this regard, the Vietnam war was very like World War I. Such apparently purposeless struggles, entered through inadvertence and confusion under various illusions and misperceptions, promote moral ambivalence and ambiguity, and pacifism gains new credence in the light of such debacles.

But our point now is that cells 1 and 4 do not exhaust all cases. In many instances throughout history, one nation was clearly guilty of aggression and the other nation was a genuinely innocent victim of aggression. In the real world, all four types exist.

One important reason why historians sometimes have difficulties picking out the aggressor is that the concept of aggression (or aggressor) is difficult to define in international law.[18] At times, it may be impossible to determine who the aggressor was. Yet, as we have seen, we must regularly deal in concepts that are fuzzy at the boundaries. I do not have to have a precise definition of baldness to pick out obviously bald or obviously hirsute men.

Sometimes, in fact often in international conflicts, the identity of the aggressor and the defender is equally obvious. Examples would include the American invasion of Mexico in 1848, British aggression against China in the Opium War, Japan's invasion of China in 1937, and the Soviet Union's invasions of Czechoslovakia and Afghanistan. And consider Hitler's invasion of Russia, Mussolini's invasion of Ethiopia in 1937, Hitler's invasion of the Low Countries and France in 1940, Hitler's air war against Britain in 1940, the Soviet invasion of Finland in 1937, and Japan's attack on the United States in 1941. In these and many other instances, the aggressor did not even pretend innocence.

Certainly we must be chastened by the consequences of quick and ill-considered resort to international violence. Some wars do erupt between countries neither of which intended aggression; that is, cell 4 is not empty. But Hitler reminds us that other wars are the result of overt aggression; cells 2 and 3 are also not empty.

What is more important, the mere fact that one nation lies about its aggression does not make it impossible to tell who really is the aggressor. In 1939, Hitler said Poland invaded Germany. In 1949, North Korea said South Korea invaded it. On both occasions, the lie was transparent, offered pro forma, without a serious intent that it be believed. Germany and North Korea were clearly aggressors, an issue about which historians never have entertained even the most transient doubt.

As a practical matter, working out actual applications of the Justified Violence View can be very difficult. But the fact that cells 2 and 3 are not empty makes clear that the theory refers to some straightforward cases of aggression, in which equally clear rights of self-defense exist. For a philosophical defense of the view, we need only show that distinctions are sometimes clear and therefore that they can be applied in principle. The fact that they can be applied in a large number of important real-world cases indicates the distinction is not only philosophically but practically important.

The Possibility of Knowing States' Intentions

Scherer points out that we cannot know the intention of a nation-state with certainty. He is correct. It is often difficult to know the intentions of states, but they are clearly *knowable*. Moreover, we can, and often do, have rationally warranted beliefs about such intentions. Just as we can know (within normal bounds of assurance) that your friend intends to go to the store (when she says she does) or that the pitcher intends to throw the ball (when he winds up), so we can know (within the same sorts of limits) that when the Soviet Union vetoes a resolution before the UN Security Council, it intends that it not pass, or that when the United States declared war on Japan, it intended to wage war. Some actions and intentions of nations have *legal* significance and enter into the legal assessment of what has occurred.

"Is it ever plausible to guarantee that one nation really knows another's intention," Scherer asks doubtfully.[19] The answer is indubitably yes. States surely can be said to *act* and can and do *have intentions*, and we can build a perfectly meaningful moral theory of state fault and responsibility on such a foundation. The Justified Violence View, as applied to states, has its feet firmly planted in the Agency Theory. Although practical problems of application may be worse, the notion of holding a state morally responsible and of being justified in taking action, including violent action, to prevent its violent wrongdoing is as acceptable as the corresponding notion and justification in the case of human individuals.

Remember why we took this detour into the action theory of states. If we cannot know states' *intentions* (as a matter of course, most of the time), then they cannot be said to engage in action for which we can determine their responsibility. That in turn makes the injuries and injustices people experience at the hands of states, especially when they engage in military invasions, conquests, and so on, more like happenings than like *acts* a person performs. Your rights are not violated if a rock falls on your head as you make your way along a mountain trail. It makes no sense to attribute intention to a rock, or to other rocks that might follow it, tumbling down the hill toward you. But we must resist any theories that tend to push rights violations by states toward this happening-like end of the spectrum of occurrences. States act, often intentionally and often wrongfully. Moreover, when they harm or threaten to harm people by their intentional action, they are responsible for the rights violations they commit. The victims of such state action have all the same rights to defend themselves that they would have if their fellow humans in civil society similarly threatened them.

There is, however, great force in Scherer's point. For often, within the confines of certain contexts, we cannot know intentions, even of individual human persons. And state intentions are usually more difficult to know than individual intentions. Yet, I insist, state intentions are in principle knowable. In fact, the wonderful example Scherer draws from Seymour Hersh's book is very telling. Did the United States *intend* to violate Soviet airspace? Obviously, this is a terribly complex question, but two important points can be drawn from it, only one of which Scherer makes. First, to any Soviet general of the air defense forces trying to decide on the spot (in situ, so to speak) whether the American incursion was intentional or accidental, the problem is almost unsolvable. Remember that this general is the international analogue of the police officer defending a citizen in the domestic case. "What are the Americans doing?" he asks himself. "Is this a hostile action or a mistake in navigation?" That is what Scherer wants us to see, and he is correct.

But there is a second point, not so obvious but philosophically as interesting. It is quite possible (indeed probable) that an international tribunal (the World Court, for example) could reach a reasoned conclusion on the question of the intentionality of the U.S. infringement of Soviet airspace. That is, the pertinent intentions, rights, and duties could have been determined from what I have called the adjudicative perspective. To be sure, an adjudicative tribunal's determination of a state's intention would require the fairly complicated conceptual machinery of international law. Moreover, the tribunal would have to gather reams of factual information. But, adjudicatively, state intentions are clearly knowable. Such intentions are, after all, on the same conceptual footing as corporate intentions. If Ford Motor Company can have intentions (say, to ignore its knowledge of faults of the Pinto, as in the famous case), then a country, another legal person, can also have intentions. If we can know the one, we can know the other. And if state intentions are knowable, then so are the rights and duties based on them. Thus, at least adjudicatively, state intentions, rights, and duties are knowable.

To be sure, neither the reams of factual information nor the conceptual apparatus of international law would have been available to the Soviet general. So surely this is a case where the Justified Violence View would not yield a definitive guide to action for him. And so much the worse for it. Yet I do not claim either universality or irrefragability for the Justified Violence View about the intentions of states. What this case does *not* show is that national intentions are *unknowable*, precisely because a post hoc analysis and investigation *could* well have reached a completely determinate answer as to what U.S. intentions were.

We have learned something interesting here: Intentions, rights, and duties that can be determined from an adjudicative perspective are *in principle* discernible from the party perspective. Thus intentions, rights, and duties must exist in situ, and it is only a contingent matter if, as with the Soviet general, the situation is so confusing that they are unknowable.

So far in this section, my argument has relied on (1) citing official acts of nations (Security Council votes, declarations of war, and treaty makings) as intentional; and (2) arguing that post hoc knowledge of national intentions is possible through judicial proceedings. Yet, if our knowledge of international intentions is confined to official acts and possible post hoc analyses, Scherer would remind us, we will be engulfed by epistemic difficulties in instances of relations between fairly equal adversaries. He has noted that in such cases, keeping intentions unclear will be regularly advantageous. Thus, when we are, outside the realm of official acts, in situ knowledge of states' intentions will often be difficult.

Nevertheless, I believe there are cases in which the empirical evidence makes the intention of a state clear in situ. When the United Kingdom, for example, launches an armada of warships weighted down with amphibious assault troops toward the recently fallen Falkland Islands, it is not difficult to infer its intention to invade. Of course, the launching might be a bluff, and the inference, like any other, is fallible. Still, such an inference is not terribly problematic.

In order to reaffirm how problematic knowledge of national intentions is, Scherer, in discussion with me, has compared the allegation of aggression and the attribution of fault in international affairs to similar allegations and attributions among elementary school children in a schoolyard, where ascriptions of intention can also be problematic. "Johnny started it. He pushed me," Jane shouts at the teacher. "No, Jane pushed me first," Johnny responds. And so it goes. These are often unresolvable conflicts, and often because of the very murky facts Scherer fears will obfuscate international attributions of fault. This is both a pregnant and a problematic analogy. Let us investigate it. I find three important ways in which international incidents are like incidents that take place on an elementary school playground. We may thus ask why it might be difficult for an elementary school teacher to ascertain what really happened on the playground when each student blames the other. One reason is that the practices of reporting and disseminating information that go with a free press, practices of careful, impartial observation and description taken for granted at the level of national policy, are only in embryonic development among the young schoolchildren actually on the playground when the incident occurs.

By comparison, the information about what went on leading up to and during an aggressive attack within an open society is often easy to discover. This is clearly not true in international affairs where some of the parties (nation-states) are closed societies, having no tradition of search for objective truth, and lacking both institutions that perform such searches and institutions that preserve the truth, once discovered. (To some extent, this difficulty arises even in open societies if, being hostile to each other, their governments frustrate impartial reporting.) The lack (or nonfunctioning) of such institutions at the international level impairs the efficacy of the rule of law among nations, for it impairs the capacity to discern what really occurred.

There is a second reason why international disputes can be like schoolyard disputes. Which child's behavior constitutes the aggression is typically less clear than it is in adult affairs. Indistinctness exists because young children do not know the customs and mores by which adults publicly legitimate the courses of action on which they embark.[20] In civil society, those practices rely on all manner of conventional demarcations—from a driver's use of turn signals to the written ascertainment of consent in a contract. These practices often establish presumptions or define a status quo ante. Thus the rule of law tends to deescalate tendencies toward violence through practices that explain and legitimate courses of behavior.

Such conventional and legal practices are not totally lacking in international affairs. There are procedures for a jet interceptor to use in identifying and communicating with an intruding aircraft and for escorting it to a forced landing. In international relations, however, such procedures and conventions are rudimentary at best. Accordingly, the international community sorely needs to develop a variety of procedures and mechanisms for signaling and thereby clarifying intentions, especially when violence might be an outcome. Hotlines, notices of military maneuvers, and on-site inspection rights exemplify such practices.

Third, the international community resembles the schoolyard in operating outside effective juridical proceedings. Juridical proceedings, when complete with enforcement powers, have a profound deterrent capacity. They especially deter parties that recognize they are going to have to continue to interact with others whom they do not dominate and whose rights a court with effective jurisdiction will protect.

The logic of intention, then, relies on practices of observation and description, practices of demarcation and legitimation, and practices of adjudication and enforcement. The further development and maturation of such practices would increase the usefulness of the concept of intention in international contexts, as it would also increase the efficacy of international law, which depends on it. I take this, rather than the strict unknowability of national intentions, to be the constructive thrust of Scherer's critique.

This discussion, however, suggests another lesson in favor of Scherer's position. Consider, especially, the many times when there is incentive for one state to deceive another about its intentions. In such instances, the *actions* of states are often *hard to anticipate* and sometimes even *difficult to interpret* as they are occurring, precisely because they are meant to be so. In these all too frequent cases the possibility of misperception and inadvertent war is great. We further investigate such problems in Part IV. For now, suffice it to say that such cases argue for great care in arriving at moral judgments about the actions of states and in determining appropriate violent countermeasures. Both are fraught with problems. But so is a categorical refusal of defense.

Answering the Challenge of Pacifism

Does Violence Beget Violence?

One way in which the Happening Theory of violence and conflict is clearly true is that violence sometimes creates more violence.[21] Scherer cites with apparent approval the views of Gandhi, who urged that it is the very nature of violence to escalate. Scherer could easily have in mind the following sequence of events:

1. A attacks B, using violence.
2. B (following Child's Justified Violence View) resists with violence.

Then what happens? As an exponent of the Justified Violence View, I would like to say, nothing. Realizing her attack will be frustrated or prove too costly to her, A withdraws her attack, and the violence is over. But, says Scherer, this is often not how events go. There exists a "fact" about violence; it tends to produce more violence. For example:

3. A gets even more violent as she presses the attack.
4. B gets even more violent in defense.

And what began as a shoving match ends up as a gunfight. Or consider a further course of action in the escalating rounds of violent conflict:

5. A, seeing she cannot defeat B using only her own capacity for violence, calls for her friends' help.
6. B, realizing he is soon to be outnumbered, calls for his friends.

Very quickly, we are off on the road to mob violence or civil war. Or, if A and B are nations, we go from a minor border incident to a world war (the World War I model).

Scherer is correct that such a tendency exists in many violent conflicts. It is a danger in using violence, sometimes a terrible danger. But Scherer apparently follows Gandhi in locating the tendency in the very *nature* of violence, and I believe this is a mistake. Conflict theorists have spent much time looking at systems where violence or threats of violence "escalate." This is precisely what Scherer has in mind, a kind of negative feedback system that very quickly gets out of control.

But it is not a general truth that all violence must escalate or even that it must *tend* to do so. Escalation is one path that violence might take, and it is simple prudence that great care should be given to such possible outcomes *before* violence is undertaken and while it is being used. Our question, however, must be this: Will violence *always* tend in this escalating direction, just by its nature? Empirically, the answer is clear: Even as some conflict situations tend toward escalation, some tend toward deescalation. These situations follow a course where considered and well-managed doses of defensive violence, or even nonviolent force combined with a threat of violence, will dampen violence and control it. The best example of this is the way well-trained, competent police forces quell barroom brawls or even more widespread outbreaks of violence at athletic events.

Thus the tendency of violence to escalate depends heavily on the kind of violence used and the context in which it is used. Some uses of violence pose a great risk of increasing violence, and others almost none. But if violence by itself does not cause escalation and if its tendency to escalate is context dependent, what is it about a particular context that causes it? Many books and papers have been written on escalation, and we can give only the briefest overview, but we can glimpse some causes of escalation.

Escalation

One can escalate during at least three stages in a conflict situation. The first is at the stage of *threats*. "I'll beat you up," says Mr. Jones. "Oh, yeah?" responds Mr. Smith. "I'll go home and get my shotgun." "We have a preponderance of conventional forces in the area and could prevail in any conflict there," says a spokesman for Country X. "We could carry any conflict to other theaters where we have supremacy," answers a spokeswoman for Country Y.[22]

The second stage is in actual physical *preparations* for a conflict, both real and for show. This could go on during, after, or completely independently of explicit threats. Preparations might include fleet maneuvers, a call-up of reserves, massing troops and armor on the border, or putting strategic nuclear forces on alert. In more mundane cases of interpersonal violence, the "preparations" for a fist fight often include the almost ritualistic removal of the coat or rolling up of the sleeves. Many analysts treat these gestures as implicit threats, which they are. But they often prepare the way for real violence as well.[23]

Finally there is actual *escalation* of the level of violence *once hostilities have been joined*. This might include more of the same—more troops, more tanks, and so forth. Or it could mean different kinds of weapons and targets. What started as a border incident escalates to air strikes against bridges and roads a long way behind the front, then to air strikes on cities, and ultimately perhaps even to the use of nuclear weapons.

One is inclined to think of escalation at any of these three levels as the conscious decision of an actor, very much in accord with the Agency Theory. People choose to threaten or to fight, so this view would go, and they equally well choose to escalate those threats or that fighting. This is certainly true. But that truth is not the whole story. Richard Smoke, a conflict theorist who has written extensively on both deterrence and escalation, puts it very well:

> Let us begin with two simple images of escalation that are especially frequent in general discourse about escalation and war. I shall call them the *actor image* [our Agency Theory] and the *phenomenal image* [our Happening Theory] of escalation. The actor image presents escalation as being a unilateral *act* of specifiable individuals and institutions, an independent and conscious decision to commit a certain kind of action and the deliberate execution of that decision. The phenomenal image presents escalation as being a natural *phenomenon* of war, a process that seems to get started and keep going on its own, partly outside the control of any participant. In other words, wars "naturally" tend to expand.[24]

He goes on to say:

> The phenomenal model includes the concepts that escalation tends to happen automatically in war; that it is almost a kind of force; that this tendency or force is constantly present; and that it may get out of control and is likely to do so.[25]

And further:

> In the phenomenal model escalation is something that *happens*, in which the participants are caught up. In the actor model, escalation is something that some government unilaterally *does*.[26]

What sorts of mechanisms could cause a conflict to get out of control in the way Smoke describes? One of the most common is the Security Dilemma and the many variants of it. In its most basic form the Security Dilemma is this: I have made you less secure by making myself more secure. If I arm, I feel more secure because I can use those arms to protect myself should you attack me. But you feel that I can attack you with my new arms, so you feel less secure. You then arm so as to feel as secure as you did before I armed, but now your arms make me feel less secure again, so I arm some more, but then you feel less secure.[27]

Escalation based on the Security Dilemma is at least partially intentional. Though we are motivated by our adversary's last move, the decision to build arms, or to put our air force on alert, is simply that—a decision—and is thus intentional. To be sure, it is made in *constrained* circumstances, and those circumstances are mutual, and thus the dilemma. Still, decision is by definition ultimately intentional. Nonetheless, it is the hallmark of the Prisoners' Dilemma, of which the Security Dilemma is an iterated version, that one's intentional decisions do not produce desired outcomes. This is because the decision of the agent in question has an additional effect of influencing the outcome of the other player (adversary). Together these two interdependent decisions yield an outcome desired by neither. So, is escalation based on the security dilemma intentional in the way the Agency Theory requires? Not clearly!

Perhaps a deeper and more frightening mechanism of instability and escalation is sometimes called the "spiral of misperception." Here we deal, not with a decision, but with the preintentional process of *perception*.[28] What escalates is the mutual and reciprocal picture each party has of the hostile intent of the other.

Let us say that the ruling party of county A adopts a platform calling for vigilant defense against its unnamed "enemies." The ruling party of country B interprets "enemies" to mean itself, and it interprets "vigilant defense" to mean preparations for attacks. It then incorporates in its platform a plank calling for vigilance *against* A. Now the more suspicious and bellicose members of A's government are vindicated in their suspicions of B. So A calls for war plans to defend against possible aggression by B. B, knowing it has no intention of attacking A, sees A's plans as a disguised plan of conquest. And so it goes.[29] At some point an arms race will ensue, perhaps simultaneously with the escalated hostile perceptions, perhaps sequentially. At a further point or points, temptations to attack preemptively will arise, and so on.

Here we have a good example of potential violence that exists only for lack of proper information. We have escalation neither party wants, and we risk violence neither party wants. Both A and B believe themselves to be acting under a right of self-defense. Neither is the intentional aggressor. If either party can succeed in communicating its true intentions, or if both parties can somehow be convinced to stop their escalation for a cooling-off period, then needless violence can be averted.

This spiraling set of misperceptions is made worse by the tendency of each side to engage in *worst-case thinking*. That is a natural thing for each side to do if they want to be conservative and cautious. Napoleon once said, "Don't tell me about my enemies' intentions. Tell me about their capabilities." What he meant was that no one can know intentions for certain and that if he knew his enemies' capabilities, he could assume the worst about their intentions and make provisions for that. Assume the worst; "it's better to be safe than sorry." Despite criticism by pacifists and members of the peace movement, worst-case thinking makes perfect sense *for one party*. Often it really is better to be safe than sorry. Yet, as in Prisoners' Dilemmas, worst-case thinking as a rule for action, while perfectly rational for *each* potential adversary to follow, gives an irrational result when *both* do it. We have really only scratched the surface of mechanisms of escalation. But we have said enough to conclude that on top of all its other thoroughly undesirable qualities (studied in Part I), threats of violence, preparations for violence, and violence itself can frequently get out of control in ways no one desired or intended. Such cases teach deep lessons about how *strong* the presumption against violence should be and how dispositive the evidence for its needed use must be.

These cases, however, are not a very good argument for pacifism. Nor are they even a good argument for the exclusive truth of the Happening Theory of violence. But they do tell us a great deal about how agents must be very careful in their intentional use of violence if they are to be both rational and moral. The newly understood nature of violence as unstable and possibly escalating does tell us a lot about what rational and moral strictures the Justified Violence View must consequently impose on the use of violence by rational, morally responsible agents.

Escalating Violence and the Principle of Controllability

The tendency of violence to escalate, although context dependent, does carry with it an important implication for the revision of the Justified Violence View. As we have seen, the view hedges in the morally proper use of violence on all sides. The new lesson is that these rules must do more than prohibit the *intentional* misuse of violence. Anyone who would use defensive violence must be morally responsible for using it in a *non-escalating* way, for there are uses of violence or threats of violence that can have a deescalating, dampening effect.

This moral requirement is not part of traditional Just War Theory. One can assume that until this aspect of violence was understood, there could be no rules governing it. In the late 1950s, however, one of the leading Just War theorists of that period, John Courtney Murray, formulated a *Principle of Controllability* that he believed followed from the notion of proportionality.[30] According to it, one must choose military means that produce *controllable consequences*. Although Murray did not follow the consequences of his principle to the end, it seems clear that the Principle of Controllability requires leaders to adhere to what the law calls a *negligence standard*. That is, government leaders must carry out their duties in a reasonable, prudent, knowledgeable way, showing due care for the power and potential unintentional misuse of their office, especially in how they use violence or threats of it. The game theorist Stephen Brams has written about "non-myopic rationality" as the rationality to foresee the danger of these cycles of negative feedback and avoid them.[31] Being "non-myopically rational" is a minimal moral standard to which the Justified Violence View must hold our leaders. To fail this standard is a kind of negligence, a kind of unintentional immorality.

We must then add the Principle of Controllability to the principles of necessity, minimality, and proportionality considered in Part I, making a complete list of the moral restraints on the justified use of violence.

Ways of Controlling Escalation: A One-Sided Commitment to Nonviolence

Certainly one way to deal with the dangerous, unstable situations of potentially spiraling violence is a kind of instrumental or tactical pacifism. That is, make a publicly stated commitment not to use violence. Sometimes this tactical pacifism works very well. Both Gandhi and Martin Luther King, Jr., used it in this way with enormous effect. Imagine you represent a militarily very weak group of people. This group is treated in a bad way by their society, with great injustice. Imagine further that there is substantial support in the society at large for the removal of injustice against this group. This support extends not only to the ruling majority but to the highest reaches within the elites of that ruling group. Moreover, imagine that the society in which this group operates is inherently decent, committed to justice. To be sure, there will be distance in any such society between their ideal and real norms; that is, hypocrisy will exist. Still, many of the society's citizens believe that the kind of oppression practiced against these people is "not what this society stands for." Thus, many are repelled by the violence visited on this undeserving group. Perhaps this society has strong, free media, which can be counted on to depict both the original injustice and any violence the society may use on the group militating against the injustice. Perhaps also it possesses free political institutions in which those supporting the group being treated unjustly can lobby for better treatment.

Here is an obviously great opportunity for nonviolent protest. If the police forces of the society are stupid enough to be violent in response, then the political reaction in favor of the protestors will be even greater. In some contexts, such tactical pacifism is enormously successful, and a tool for justice to be applauded. It worked brilliantly in gaining Indian independence from Britain and in the early days of the American civil rights movement. Its leaders were both moral giants and brilliant tacticians. But moral and effective means in one context can be pathetically ineffective and morally negligent when applied in the wrong context. Tactical pacifism had significant efficacy in Manila in 1986, but nonviolent resistance was ineffective against tanks in Tiananmen Square in 1989.

Unfortunately, there are many contexts in which such techniques will not work. Perhaps the Danes had some marginal success using nonviolent protest against Hitler. The Nazis, however, considered the Danes brother Aryans, and the occupation of Denmark was the most mild in the Nazi empire. What if Jews or Poles or Ukrainians had tried nonviolent protest against the Nazis? They would have been slaughtered summarily, as many were. When an aggressor aims to exterminate or enslave a people, their nonviolent protest only facilitates the aggressor's achievement of its heinous goal. Ask an inmate of Dachau or Buchenwald why she did not engage in nonviolent protest, and she will think you either insane or tasteless in your jokes.

Nonviolent Force

A central point for Scherer is that nonviolent force is often a powerful substitute for violence. Indeed, the use of *aikido* is almost a metaphor for Scherer's conception of pacifism. *Aikido*, as I understand it, is a mode of defense in which only nonviolent force is used.[32] If we explore

Scherer's *aikido* metaphor a bit further, it will tell us a great deal, not merely about the martial arts, but about the offensive and defensive use of both force and violence in general. I believe the metaphor to be a very rich one. Many of the most basic characteristics of force and violence can be described using it.

Now let us imagine combat between two masters of martial arts. Master A is a specialist in nonviolent *aikido*. He engages in combat with Master B, who is a specialist in the most violent form of karate, including kicks and chops that can cripple or kill. Master B is also skilled in defensive techniques. Assume each knows the other's strengths and skills. Master B has an inherent advantage, for he can do everything Master A can do plus all the crippling and killing blows.

Scherer holds that the use of offensive force always creates exploitable vulnerabilities on the part of the user. This is probably true. A good example comes from an elementary point in military strategy. A frontal assault always exposes the flanks of the attacking army as it penetrates deeper and deeper into enemy territory. But there are two crucial points, both of which tell against the brand of pacifism illustrated by *aikido*.

First, the offensive force knows how it will strike, where it will strike, and when. This is a tremendous advantage. A carefully planned and opportunistic seizure of the offensive intiative can almost always overcome the vulnerabilities its attack creates, at least between roughly equal forces and sometimes even against a much larger force. An attack always creates some vulnerabilities that in *some* logically possible case could be exploited by *someone* (e.g., flanks are exposed). But a skillful attack will not create vulnerabilities exploitable by *this* enemy in *this* situation (e.g., the defending force is too surprised, too confused, too shattered to take advantage of the exposed flanks).

Second, the *aikido* master (Master A) has handicapped himself even further, for he has publicly forsworn offensive blows, and thus Master B knows this. (We assume that Master A is sincere, and Master B also knows this.) It clearly follows that there are no necessary vulnerabilities created for Master A to exploit by Master B's attack, given A's voluntarily assumed handicap. This is not merely a point about the martial arts but a general truth about the uses of violence in conflict. The advantage A has given B is this: Master A can only turn and parry blows. As a result, he can terminate the conflict only in the unlikely event that he can cause Master B to injure *himself* as he carries out his offensive blows.[33] This might be easy to do against an untrained opponent, but not a trained one. Failing this, Master A must continue as long as Master B wants, or has the endurance, to continue. Of course, Master A will very quickly be able to disarm an unskilled combatant and subdue him without violence. I believe that this is Scherer's idea. But with a combatant of equal skill (as Master B, by hypothesis, is), this is a vain hope indeed. Compare this to Master B, who needs only to land one crippling blow on Master A to win outright. If Master A parries ten blows (or a hundred), and Master B lands only one, Master B wins. In short, the capacity and willingness to initiate offensive violence (as opposed to merely parry and deflect it) gives one of two otherwise equally matched opponents a huge advantage.

Thus, our conclusion is this: The use of nonviolent force, where it is conjoined with a public commitment never to escalate to violent force, is of highly limited usefulness against a party willing to use great force and violence.

Ways of Controlling Violence:
Deterrence as Escalation Dominance

There are instances where even the instrumental or tactical use of pacifism is less effective than are potentially violent efforts to change the situation from one prone to escalate to one where violence can have a self-limiting and dampening effect.[34] Indeed, I hold that it is actually the willingness and ability of well-trained and disciplined police forces to use *as much violence as is necessary* that so often makes it possible for them to avoid violence. This may sound inconsistent with the Justified Violence View. "As much violence as necessary" sounds like a desertion of the notions of minimality and proportionality. But it is not. Let us assume for the moment we are talking about police forces, although the principle also applies to personal self-defense and interstate military instances. The police can so situate themselves that they can (implicitly) say to a potential lawbreaker:

We will not initiate violence as we go about our job of keeping the peace and arresting lawbreakers. We will use nonviolent force only. But if particular lawbreakers use violence, we will mass a capability to impose so much violence that we will be able to prevail and reestablish peace, taking the perpetrators into custody. We will never use more than the minimal, proportional, violence necessary but that will be enough regardless of how much that takes and however much the lawbreaker(s) escalate.

For many years (and perhaps to this day), the Federal Bureau of Investigation (FBI) had a rule that whenever they were making an arrest of a violent criminal, or were otherwise likely to meet violence, they would have the potential perpetrators of violence outnumbered at least six to one. Furthermore, they did not hesitate to arm themselves with shotguns and submachine guns when they felt the need. Television shows and movies to the contrary, the FBI almost never had to use violence.[35] Now imagine that, instead, the FBI went about, trained in *aikido,* carrying stun guns and publicly committed to pacifism. The chances of vastly more violence being visited on them and those they protect would be dramatically increased.

It is the responsive (i.e., noninitiating) and measured, but ultimately *unlimited,* capacity for violence that causes a criminal to say to himself or his confederates, "We can't win." That is the heart of what conflict theorists call *escalation dominance.* Optimally, it causes most would-be criminals and other perpetrators of violence to say "We can't win" before they ever start down the road to violence. In that event, *deterrence* and escalation dominance are the same thing. Does it work? Not always, obviously. But often. Indeed, it must work often for, as we saw in Part II, *it and nothing less makes civil society possible.*

One can look at the effective deterrence of violence by military or police forces as escalation dominance at the first stage of escalation, that is, the decision to use violence or not. The FBI makes sure it possesses escalation dominance so completely that it minimizes the need for actual violence almost to the vanishing point. From this we can generalize to something profound about violence and escalation. Escalation dominance dampens and deescalates violence. It is the primary and most effective way of dealing with the potential uncontrollability of violence. Escalation dominance works not only in controlling actual outbreaks of violent conflict once they begin but also, in the case of the deterrence of violence, before it begins. For often the most effective way to stop escalation is to be able to escalate with vast use of both nonviolent and, where necessary, violent force.

Many Sorts of Spirals and
Many Sorts of Outcomes

We have seen some deep and dangerous characteristics in the use of violence. No proponent of the Justified Violence View can ignore the dangers of uncontrolled and unintended escalation. Violence cannot be undertaken, no matter how otherwise morally justifiable, without a conscientious effort to take its potential instability into account. But there are analogous problems with pacifism. Surprising as it may seem, pacifism too can get out of control both psychologically and strategically.

To illustrate this point, let us take Munich and the string of moves, meant to propitiate Hitler, that preceded and followed it. Each time Hitler made a new demand or threat, first over the Rhineland, then over Austria, then over the Sudetenland, then over the rest of Czechoslovakia, then over Danzig, the timid Allies sought to give him this last demand, sure that the demands would stop. This was certainly a misperception, one that grew out of denial, wish fulfillment, and naive optimism. Each time, in fact, Hitler grew stronger, and his appetite for conquest more voracious. Each time, the Allies dealt from greater weakness. We have seen that we can misperceive the intentions and actions of our neighbors through misplaced suspicions and worst-case thinking. But one of the most dangerous products of a pacifist outlook is that we fall victim to misperceptions borne of denial, wish fulfillment and misplaced optimism. Few of us wish to believe the worst of our fellow humans or the other nations with which we share the planet, and most desire to live in a peaceful world. But by systematically thinking the best of our neighbors and selectively interpreting events and actions as evidence of benign or even benevolent motives, we can come to expect only the best and set ourselves up for great disappointments or, worse, disastrous consequences for our country and our way of life.

Eventually, even Chamberlain and Daladier saw they must take a stand, even if it was one much disadvantaged by their earlier temporizing. Once Hitler invaded Poland, war was necessary; it probably would not have been in 1936 had the Allies vigorously opposed Hitler's reoccupation of the Rhineland. Moreover, the war was much longer and bloodier in virtue of that disadvantaged position. This was the cost to the Allies. The cost to the Czech people was far worse: slavery, nothing less. So, a cycle of demand, then appeasement, then greater demand is also a spiral. The outcome of this spiral can be surrender to the violation of a people's most basic rights, or it can be war or a worse war, fought on even more disadvantageous terms.[36]

I am not saying that we always face Hitlers. I am not saying that we never suffer paranoia, especially mutual paranoia, and invent enemies. Scherer is concerned that we might invent an enemy. I respect that concern because such invention is possible. Mutual misperception, miscommunication, and misunderstanding can make adversaries where there need be none. But, although we do not always face Hitlers, we *may* face an obdurate enemy determined to violate our most basic rights as a people. I ask only that we not deny the enemy who is there. We cannot rule out this last possibility merely because it is so unpleasant and undesirable.

Contrast and Summary

We have seen two ways of controlling the escalation of violence. One is making commitments to nonviolence; the other is escalation dominance. It is an ironic but very deep truth about human social life that a willingness and capacity to wage effective defensive violence can be one of the most powerful ways of avoiding and preventing violent conflict. Conversely, the adoption of pacifism, even by many, can easily increase the amount of violence in society and ensure that the victims will be the innocent and undeserving. For only the forces of law and justice, and those citizens forswearing defensive violence, will be self-disarmed in this way. Violent criminals will be the last to join the ranks of the pacifists. Thus, of the two paths of controlling the escalation of violence, which is the most effective is context dependent, but I have argued that often it is escalation dominance.

Nonviolent Force, Passive Defenses, and the History of Warfare

Scherer stresses the necessity of our investigating nonviolent uses of force with which to control violence. This ought not to be dismissed too quickly, for there is much in it. Indeed, as we have seen, the Justified Violence View, as much as pacifism, requires this, for it mandates a search for nonviolent solutions, especially violence-foreclosing solutions occurring before attacks take place. Well-lighted streets and Block Watch programs, as Scherer notes, are powerful deterrents to crime (violent and otherwise) and ought to be strongly promoted, by the dedication of significant resources, perhaps even at the sacrifice of some of the police department's latest high-tech weaponry. Still, the history of armaments and warfare give little credence to Scherer's belief that this approach offers a significant, general alternative to the defensive use of violence and violent weapons.

It is the most tired of tired clichés to say that the best defense is a good offense, but like many clichés, it has usually been true, at least in warfare. It may be, as Scherer implies, that this is merely because we have not worked hard enough to come up with truly defensive techniques. A little reflection, however, renders this hypothesis implausible. Let us take a particular development in weapons technology, the tank, as an example. Here is an offensive weapon if there ever was one: a heavily armored, highly mobile fortified bunker carrying a cannon and several machine guns. It is tailor made to smash infantry formations, crush fortified lines of defense, and charge into enemy rear areas destroying supply lines, cutting communication, and sowing havoc and panic. Imagine that you are in charge of weapons development and deployment for a nation facing an adversary heavily armed with tanks (e.g., France in 1940 or Egypt in the 1960s or NATO throughout the cold war). If you are rational, you will be willing to use any countermeasure that works. You will not favor the offensive over the defensive weapons or the violent ones over the passive ones. All you want is something to render your enemy's tanks impotent. You will use what works best, pure and simple. You might consider clearly offensive weapons (e.g., attack aircraft or your own tank force), or you might consider defensive but still violent weapons (e.g., antitank artillery and missiles or land mines), or you might consider the sort of defenses Scherer would approve of (e.g., tanks traps or impassable obstacles).[37] The point is that technology follows its own course with efficacy as its only criterion. When passive defenses work, they will be used. If this is true, then passive, nonviolent systems are relatively neglected, not because of an innate prejudice toward killing or a lack of "moral imagination," but because they seldom work very well.

In general, defensive weapons have been dominant for only very short periods throughout the history of warfare. World War I was one such time. But the defensive weapons that dominated battle then were hardly passive (nonviolent) ones. Primary among them was the machine gun, backed up by barbed wire and the breach-loading, repeating rifle. It is instructive for our purposes that together these "defensive" weapons conspired to create some of the most bloody and horrific battles ever fought in human history. Obviously, these are not the defensive weapons a pacifist would wish to recommend.

The only instance of which I am aware in which truly passive defense was ever dominant occurred in the high Middle Ages. Briefly (circa 1200–1350), the medieval castle stood invulnerable against any weapon save protracted siege and starvation. But in less than a century, gunpowder and siege artillery ended forever the security of fortifications.

We must ask why this is so. We must satisfy ourselves that this is not merely a failure of "moral imagination." I think honesty requires us to admit we do not know all the reasons why offensive weapons and tactics are so dominant. One thing we do know is that offensive weapons tend to be more mobile than defensive ones and active weapons much more mobile than passive ones. Impassable tank traps and fortifications by definition cannot be moved. Mobility in turn allows for seizure of the initiative, flexibility of maneuver, and concentration of forces. Indeed, Clausewitz is still the definitive authority on this issue, and he gives a good account of it.[38]

Nevertheless, I suspect even deeper reasons, physical reasons, for this bias toward the offensive and destructive, at least since the invention of chemical explosives. It is easier to blow things up than to keep them together in the face of explosives. It is easier to kill living creatures than to keep them alive against earnest efforts to kill them. These seem to be special (admittedly very special) instances of the Second Law of Thermodynamics. It tells us, in very rough terms, that highly organized states of matter (e.g., human bodies or human cities) tend to move toward disorganization, and that when "disorganized," the process back toward organization is either impossible (a human being) or very difficult and expensive (a city). But it does help explain the usual dominance of the offensive weapon over the defensive one and the nearly total dominance of the violently active weapon over the passive one.

Pacifist Dangers, Pacifist Temptations

Pacifism as an Empirical Claim
about the Nature of Conflict

One popular version of pacifism, very close to that espoused by Scherer, goes like this: "Of course I don't approve of people stoically resigning themselves to being passive victims of violence, nor do I believe people should choose slavery or tyranny in preference to using violence to resist it. I simply don't believe that we are ever faced with such choice. Since conflict and especially the violence that often issues from it, are happenings, we can, with foresight, avoid them." Notice that the emphasis in this position is on conflict brought on by inadvertence, not conflict and violence that somebody *wants* and *intends* to bring about.

Now our examination of the nature of violence has taught us several things:

1. Conflict can come about (or be escalated) by inadvertence.
2. Conflict can be brought about (or escalated) by noncommunication or miscommunication.
3. Conflict can eventuate because parties fail to avail themselves of possible preexistent nonviolent resolutions of their differences.

These are empirical claims about conflict. Like Scherer, many pacifists, impressed by these claims, need not and do not insist that persons must be passive victims of violence because they believe that violent conflict *always* comes about from (1) through (3). This is an important clue to understanding such pacifism. For this kind of pacifism is a claim about the *world*, about people and the nature of conflict situations that obtain between them. Since this form of pacifism is more about the way our world is than about moral claims, we might call it "empirical pacifism."

Against this form of pacifism, we need to be very clear that *aggressive* violence is all too common and real. Think of an ordinary criminal case. A approaches B, who is alone without recourse to the aid of others. Thereupon, A demands of B something violative of B's most basic rights. He wants to kill B or injure B grievously, or to enslave B or forcefully to use B for his sexual purposes. And A backs up the demand with a threat of extreme violence. B rejects the threat. Clearly, we have a conflict situation, for A wants whatever it is that will violate B's most basic rights, and B does not want A to have it. These two states, each wanted by one, are irrefutably inconsistent. This conflict was intentionally created by A. He was acting under no moral right when he created it. He was under no dire exigency; he was not starving, for example. No common-law excuse such as necessity or duress of circumstance was present. B has only two choices. Either she must use violence in her own defense or she must acquiesce in the violation of her basic right. Try as she might, she can discover no other alternative.

Here we have reached the essence of an irreconcilable violent conflict, which we can define as a situation where a determined aggressor manifestly and imminently intends to invade one or more basic rights of another person using violence and has undertaken concrete steps to that end.

Irreconcilable conflict occurs when an aggressor is determined to bring about a state of affairs that includes the violation of one or more of the victim's basic rights. Irreconcilable conflict does not always depend on scarcity or any other "defense of necessity" motivating the aggressor. Thus the issues of scarcity that bother Scherer do not represent the only case he must consider. Independent of scarcity, the aggressor may proceed with a *rights violation* for any reason, for example, his own perceived "need" or his selfish will to impose himself on another. The apparently unavoidable rights violation, caused by the aggressor's will, is the heart of irreconcilable conflict.

The empirical pacifist is here on the horns of a dilemma. On the first horn, he must advocate acquiescence in the rights invasion. One can usually avoid violence by surrender, but there are occasions when one can avoid using violence in self-defense only by surrendering to the violation of very basic and important rights.[39]

On the second horn, the empirical pacifist must deny that victims of irreconcilable conflict ever face only the alternatives of acquiescence in basic rights violation and responsive violence. Indeed, it is from this denial of certain possible factual situations that the "empirical pacifist" gets his name. Thus empirical pacifism simply refuses to admit that instances of aggressor-initiated irreconcilable conflict exist. But, put this way, it is obvious that they do: Every day, the criminal courts are jammed with violent criminals who imposed themselves on their victims. Thousands of persons—battered wives and battered children, mugging victims, and police officers shot while going to the aid of defenseless innocents—testify annually to the falsity of empirical pacifism.

Perspectives on Irreconcilable Conflict

The empirical pacifist claims that there is always a preferable nonviolent solution to a conflict. Scherer has an especially ingenious way of putting the claim. He tells us that while interests may irreconcilably conflict, conflict is *interest relative*.[40] If we realize that interests are not fixed, and we can bring new interests into play, what appeared to be an irreconcilable conflict dissolves. Witness Scherer's airline-ticket example. Of course, he is quite correct. Many conflicts can and should be reconciled in this way.

But some interests are so morally important that we give them special moral protection; we call such morally important interests *rights*. My interest in not being involuntarily put in pain or not having my personal and bodily integrity violated are "inalienable" in precisely the sense that it is immoral to force me into a situation where I must bargain about them (and with them) and therefore make them "interest relative." Yet clearly an aggressor, intent on dominating his victim, may precisely intend to violate his victim's rights.

Scherer's discussion of the reconcilability of apparently irreconcilable conflict is also flawed by a subtle equivocation between the *policy perspective* and the *party perspective*. As a policymaker addressing a problem "from above," as it were, I can dispassionately and sagaciously decide that we can shift the interests involved in a conflict so as to avoid conflict. This role might be played in Scherer's airline-ticket case by the airline itself or the Federal Aviation Administration (FAA). But that does not speak to the problem of the individual (or individual nation) when that individual (nation) faces an aggressor intentionally creating an irreconcilable conflict.

Scherer misses the way in which an aggressor consciously manipulates those very interests for his own ends. "Give me your wallet or I will shoot you," the mugger says. He has "created a new interest," your interest in not being shot. What, in situations like this, is the victim supposed to do by way of "creating new interests" with which to compromise? "Here, take only half my money?" What, if a woman is actually under attack by a rapist, ought she do by way of creating alternatives for the rapist? As a *party* to a violent conflict, this is a singularly impractical solution, precisely because it is looking at the situation from a *policy perspective*.

We can now see why I insisted that the definition of violence should include the delivery condition that it be done with "great force and vigor." Facing an imminent or occurrent attack implies that one's time of reaction is tightly constrained. A party cannot be expected to treat the situation with the same calm deliberation that a policymaker can.

Yet there is an even deeper problem with Scherer's notion of new interest creation. Why ought the victim of an attack have this burden of new interest creation heaped on her, constraining her options for defense? By definition, the aggressor has refused to undertake such a burden. Why should the victim have it imposed on her, making her already difficult defense of her rights even more difficult?

And yet a clear examination of this question requires us to divide the chronology of any violent attack into three phases: preattack, attack, and postattack. Postattack bears on issues of reparation, punishment, and deterrence of similar acts in the future. It views the attack either from an adjudicative or policy perspective, retrospectively in either case. It is not immediately relevant to the Justified Violence–pacifist argument. In the preattack phase, the Justified Violence theorist and the pacifist abstractly agree on the nature of the duty to seek nonviolent options. The preattack phase can be confusing, however. It can be understood as referring to a *particular aggressor,* beginning when one first has evidence that a particular person intends to undertake a particular attack and running until some time when that attack seems imminent. Note that this treatment of the preattack phase is very much from the party perspective. Our concern is strictly with what this potential victim can do that will prevent this aggressor's aggressions. Here it would seem my Justified Violence View and Scherer's pacifism would be in agreement. If Mr. Green calls Mr. Blue on the phone in a tavern and tells Mr. Blue he is coming to attack him, the common law insists that Mr. Blue leave the area (since it is not his home) and call the authorities or otherwise take measures to avoid a violent conflict.

But this agreement is only partial. For the Justified Violence View recognizes that we are in a *strategic* situation in the preattack phase. On the one hand, leaving the area where the aggressor expects to find you avoids conflict by modifying your own situation, perhaps even to your detriment, if you had a reason to stay there. And such measures are important and sometimes appropriate, even though this particular measure significantly limits one's liberty.

But the burden of avoiding conflict must not be placed exclusively on the potential victim and especially not on his willingness to compromise his interests or even sacrifice his rights. Forcing changes in the potential aggressor's behavior is equally legitimate (often, I would argue, *more* legitimate). Thus we have deterrent threats of force or violence as a means for avoiding conflict. That is, we may do things like calling the police, which discourage the potential aggressor from committing aggression.

Deterrence can certainly be a legitimate alternative to more passive responses, such as compromises or sacrificing one's interests. For deterrence, if successful, is nonviolent, although it often involves having the capacity credibly to threaten violence. Implicit in Scherer's argument against pacifism as nonresistance is the presupposition that morality requires deterrence of violence. We agree on that. Moreover, Scherer and I agree in one more step: Morality permits deterrent threats of nonviolent force. But, building on that admission, I have argued the following:

1. Nonviolent defenses tend to be less effective than (potentially) violent defenses.
2. The possession of violent escalation dominance can deescalate violence.

From these additional premises, I draw a further conclusion, one that Scherer might find uncomfortable.

3. One important nonviolent option to violent conflict is to possess the capacity for violent resistance, as much as is necessary, and to be willing credibly and sincerely to threaten its use.

Scherer makes further comments that seem directed toward the pre-attack phase. For in discussing revenge, he details how we must not merely pursue a practice but must also stand back and examine "the teleology of the practice itself." What are its results? Ought we to change it? Might modifications of it, or even new practices, work better?

We reach here an important point in the argument because we have learned another important thing from Scherer's pacifist position: Each of us as a citizen and all of us as representing organized societies must try very hard to develop new procedures, practices, and institutions to make violence less a threat in our lives. To the extent that this is Scherer's pacifist message, we are all pacifists. And we must not merely pay lip service, for the question is far too serious for that. Violence, after all, is ubiquitous in our society (and in most other societies as well). It is an omnipresent threat in the international arena: Terrorism, guerrilla war, and all sorts of civil and regional wars abound. It looms, in the form of nuclear war, over modern life as what John Kennedy called a nuclear Sword of Damocles, conditioning the very terms of human existence.

An exhortation to consider the teleology of a practice, however, can readily become yet another conflation of descriptions from the Happening Theory with descriptions from the Agency Theory or another conflation of the *policy perspective* with the *party perspective*. In its most extreme form this conflation yields results that are absurd. Remember Mr. Green, who called a local tavern to inform Mr. Blue that he was coming right over to kill Mr. Blue. Surely Scherer does not seriously propose that Mr. Blue should promptly engage in a dispassionate sociological and philosophical analysis of the general practice of calling the police versus leaving the scene, versus some new and as yet untried practice for avoiding violence. This is just a confusion. There is a place for considering "the teleology of the practice," namely, policy issues, and all of us as citizens, believing that violence is bad, should work hard on these issues. But that is a different question from what poor Mr. Blue should do as a party in a potentially violent situation.

This conflation is not simply a philosopher's difficulty. In the past, I often spoke to peace groups about the importance of military preparedness and maintaining adequate deterrent forces. On almost every occasion, I get the following question: "Instead of all this money we are spending on defense, don't you think we should be working on developing nonviolent measures of conflict resolution?" This question (certainly not Scherer's) commits the same conflation. We must stay well armed, as a party in a specific potential conflict situation, in order to deter conflict. That is the party perspective. At the policy perspective, we should also work to develop such nonviolent measures of conflict resolution. Maintaining a strong defense and developing means of nonviolent conflict resolution do not conflict. They complement each other because they address *different* questions.

In the attack phase—when the attacker is present and the attack is imminent or under way—a major difference between the Justified Violence and pacifist theories arises. Even here, the Justified Violence View holds that you have a duty to search for nonviolent options. But in the attack phase that duty is highly limited. For Scherer's pacifist, this duty to search for such nonviolent options throughout the attack phase seems open-ended. In fact, it seems open-ended along several dimensions.

First, in the common law, one is not required to consider options that involve acquiescing in violations of basic rights. You do not have to avail yourself of any of the following options: let him kill me, let him rape me, let him drive me from my home, let him enslave me, let him assault and batter me, without violent resistance on my part. Indeed, it is precisely these options that your right of self-defense (or the defense of others) is meant to protect, that is, to preclude the unresisted violation of these rights.

Second, there is apparently no natural temporal limit to the search Scherer enjoins. Yet it is critical to realize that a defender, when under attack, is under great time pressure. One only has a given amount of time to consider alternatives, before the attack is joined. So our would-be defender must consider options hastily.

Third, our defender is bound to be under a good deal of psychological pressure, for violent attacks make the best of us nervous, to say the least. So allowance must be made for both physical and psychological limitations on the *ability* of the would-be defender to consider options.

It is clearly impossible for the law to give us a checklist for nonviolent options we may have and must exhaust when an attack is imminent or under way in whatever our circumstances. So it has recourse to a familiar standard. One must exhaust all nonviolent options a *reasonable person in those circumstances* would consider and try.

Contra Scherer, one is not required to be especially creative or ingenious in coming up with nonviolent solutions. One does not have to embark on an indefinitely long examination of options. In short, a cursory common-sense examination of ways of avoiding violence is enough. More than that is supererogation; it might be praiseworthy, but it is not morally or legally required.

Summary

We have learned several things about the Justified Violence View from Scherer's pacifist critique.

1. Wars (and related things like arms races) can occur when there is no self-conscious and dedicated aggressor, and violence can escalate out of anyone's control with potentially catastrophic consequences intended by no one.

2. The intentions of states (and other political actors on the international stage) are sometimes very difficult to know, especially in situ, and misperception and confusion are always a grave risk.

3. The Principle of Controllability, because of such dangers as delineated in (1) and (2), morally requires that leaders of states use violence when justified only in deescalating and dampening ways and by so doing control future reciprocal uses of violence.

4. Each of us has a duty to encourage and aid in the pursuit of the development of practices and institutions that will encourage peace and especially prevent escalated and uncontrolled violence. This duty is not only the long-recognized duty to search for nonviolent options when as attack is imminent. It is also the duty to be engaged now and in an ongoing way in this process of institution building.

But we can admit (1) through (4) without adopting pacifism in any recognizable form. Indeed, the most valuable part of Scherer's message seems only unnecessarily encumbered by his pacifism. For we cannot accede to an absolute duty to refrain from violence. We must recognize and acknowledge that we must use violence, albeit morally and responsibly. But that *is* the Justified Violence Theory.

6 *DONALD SCHERER*

A Viable Pacifism

Taking Stock of the Dialogue

Child's criticisms of my view seem to me in some ways wanting, in other ways impressive. My first two tasks, then, are to expose a basic deficiency I find in the Justified Violence View and to concede some of the retrenchment I find necessary to a pacifist orientation.

Assessing the Coherence of Theories

In the light of my criticism, Child recasts the Justified Violence View to take account of the fact that violence sometimes leads to further violence in an escalating cycle. He commendably amends the Justified Violence View to include a controllability clause. The traditional Justified Violence View is certainly troubled when world history includes such prolonged altercations as those between Israelis and Palestinians. The world would be much better off if national leaders undertook only such defenses as would dominate the aggression they faced.

The addition of a controllability clause, however, highlights a problem already implicit in the Justified Violence View. To set the case, let us imagine a circumstance in which somebody's immediate action is required to prevent some grave harm from being violently imposed. Even in that circumstance, I now show, the Justified Violence View does not clearly justify the presumption of intervention. For Child argues that a person justified in introducing violence is one who can dominate the escalation of that violence. Thus we can imagine that I am about to be gravely harmed and that only the introduction of *nondominating* violence has any real chance of preventing that harm. If to say I have a right (to defense against this harm) is to say that others are to presume themselves justified in interfering, while, following Child and Murray, their interference is justified only if they can dominate the escalation of the violence, then it follows, as a matter of strict logic, that I have no right in such circumstances.

In other words, the Justified Violence View, as Child reasonably amends it to include views about controllability, is not clearly a coherent position. Violence that may be justified as *the minimum violence necessary to the defense of the most basic of "human rights"* may be unjustified because it may or does *yield an uncontrolled spiral of violence.*

Here we reach the root of a strong critical line, which helps explain the failure of the prevalently accepted Just War view to minimize the violence of war. For the problem of coherence I have now raised is indeed broad: The structure of the objection I have raised to Child's controllability principle implies objections to the theory even without the addition of the controllability principle.

To see this fundamental problem, suppose one sincerely insists that violence should never exceed what is minimally necessary to resist the aggressive violence of others (Child's conditions 3 and 4). Suppose that adversary nation A takes (what nation B regards as) aggressive action against B. And B vows to follow every canon of Just War Theory. But the minimum of necessary violence that might plausibly be predicted to arrest A's aggression is not at all certain to be effective. Is it now B's duty to employ as little violence as it is plausible to believe may be effective in arresting the aggression? This amounts to reading the minimality condition as having priority over the necessity condition. Or is B entitled to do everything necessary to provide the greatest possible assurance that A's violence is arrested? This amounts to reading the necessity condition as having priority over the minimality condition.[1] But the theory does not tell one to prioritize minimality over necessity, or necessity over minimality.

The same problem re-presents itself as one considers the relation-ship of the proportionality principle to the minimality and necessity principles. For we can imagine that without using violence out of pro-portion to the violence used in an attack, no response will be effec-tive against some aggression. Shall we then say that when the mini-mum necessary violence is disproportionate, acquiescence is always the proper course of action? Neither common law nor Just War Theory has ever so generally prioritized proportionality over necessity. What, then, shall we say? That when the stakes are dire, proportionality ceases to be a requirement of the Justified Violence View? But surely this amounts to saying that when the stakes are sufficiently high, any violence reasonably perceived to be necessary is justified. Surely, ac-cepting such a priority of "necessity" amounts to abandoning moral constraints!

The theoretical problem underlying the three above arguments is that the Justified Violence View does not prioritize its conditions.[2] Without prioritizations, the Justified Violence View apparently entitles one to argue in ways so divergent as to be contrary, undermining the coherence of the theory.

This theoretical problem has severe practical consequences, which we can see by recurring to nation B, which vowed to follow every canon of Just War Theory in its response to A. Suppose B, its vow strong, encounters a situation in which the principles diverge in the way the arguments detail. Suppose B chooses, for example, to do what is necessary and even proportional, but not minimal and perhaps not controllable. The result is that nation B's failure to follow two of the principles of Just War give nation A justification for taking defensive action against B. For clearly, relative to those two principles, B has not stayed within the realm of defensive violence that is alone acceptable within the Justified Violence View. And now an amazing result occurs: Whereas presumably only one nation to a two-nation conflict would be justified by Just War standards, the lack of prioritization in the prin-ciples of the theory, in conjunction with the complexity of the facts, will frequently support arguments that both parties to a war may be justified in defending against the aggression of the other!

Nor is there anything significant to be gained if we make it explicit that nation A attacked nation B. For even if nation A first resorted to armed force, it does not follow that nation A initiated the aggression. As we have seen in our discussions of the Justified Violence View and intention, the presumptions involved, before hostilities broke out, may have made it unclear who the aggressor was.

Yet it should not seem surprising that Child does not prioritize, for two reasons: (1) His fellow philosophers in the Just War tradition do not prioritize; and (2) if they did, their thinking would undermine the usefulness for local heads of state of justifying violence by means of the theory. That is, heads of state regularly proclaim the justifications of their nation's course of action. The plausibility of their assertions is valuable for the stability and success of their government. Having a theory of unprioritized principles suits this purpose admirably. When they apply to that theory data that incorporate presumptions and statements of intention that suit their purposes,[3] they have enormous power to justify whatever courses of action they are wont to justify.

Nor need such political behavior be terribly unscrupulous. Most heads of state love their nations, and most feel very strongly a duty to protect the land and its people. If a theory composed of unprioritized principles can be interpreted in several ways, and if only an interpretation that, for example, prioritizes necessity over proportionality and controllability allows the fullest and surest discharge of one's heartfelt duty, then it will be no surprise if the implementation of the Just War Theory often amounts to no more than "we'll do what we must and 'justify' as we can." But surely it is a devastating criticism of the Justified Violence View that says that the play allowed in the application of the theory often converts the "theory" into "rhetoric in support of a favorite ideology."

Powerful as I believe this criticism is, I hasten to agree[4] that, within many societies, institutions of observation and reportage and effective adjudication, along with a host of conventions for demarcation and coordination, set many boundaries and give concrete meaning to otherwise unprioritized principles. My criticism, in other words, underlines the importance of the development and broad acceptance of practices for applying a set of abstract, unprioritized principles. As Child has indicated, international relationships are troubled by the large degree to which such principles of the right have no standard meaning. For without such meaning, nation A cannot prove (and nation B cannot ascertain) nation A's compliance with such abstract principles as the Justified Violence View provides.

But if, following Wayne Sumner, we call a theory "intuitionistic" whenever its principles are unprioritized, will not my pacifism be as intuitionistic and as troublesome as Child's Justified Violence View? Contrarily, I believe the Justified Violence View is distinctly more troublesome. In the first place,[5] the practical orientation of the teleological pacifist alone is toward the "supererogatory" development of practices for smoothing out the wrinkles to which intuitionistic views can give rise. Accordingly, making the Justified Violence presumptions often provides conflicting nations with rational tools for proving themselves "justified in their defensive reactions to the aggressive enemy." In contrast to such alienation, the results of making the pacifist presumptions are typically inventive means for keeping the components of peace mutually coherent.

Yet, important as it is to avoid the escalation of alienation that violence tends to involve, the superiority of the presumptions of pacifism is not so easy to establish as this reason suggests. For, as Child would rightly point out, this reason ignores the possibility that making the pacifist's presumption would lead to terrible harms to persons, violations of their rights at the hands of aggressors. Thus, before completing this line of argument, I must pursue the line that although the Justified Violence View has significant flaws, the pacifist line I have been developing, with its affinity for some of Gandhi's views, also has significant problems. I turn to assessing them.

Escalation Dominance and the Future of Pacifism

Some prominent pacifists employ the premise that a superior option to violence always exists. Strict nonviolence, they claim, is the only path to peace. Certainly the models of *aikido* and stun guns give some plausibility to this premise, a premise, as I have argued, that exploits the conceptual distance between force and violence.

Like Child, however, many nonpacifists have said that, in whatever quarter pacifism might find success, a pacifist response to Hitler would have been simply suicidal. Shall I resist this line by following Gene Sharp's argument for the potential of any nation to resist its military conquerors through the passive resistance of its citizenry? In many books he argues that the munitions of a few hundred thousand soldiers could never enforce anything on hundreds of millions of people who ignored the dictates of the soldiers.[6] Even as it is well known that no law that is widely broken can be enforced, so he urges that no would-be dictator can issue dictates to a population that will not heed what it hears. A passively resisting population, he claims, will nonviolently overcome tyrannic invaders.[7]

I believe that passive resistance has wrought immense social change in our own century and that it slowed even the terror of Hitler. But this belief does not make me forget that traditional passive resistance requires a mass of people so large, so united, and so visible as to overwhelm the power of an army. Faced with tyrannical power, a pacifist simply acts as she or he thinks right, in the calm conviction that either she or he will be killed or will persist as appropriate to the situation. And impressive is the witness of individual pacifists, from Anabaptist history[8] to the American abolitionist movement,[9] from Gandhi's drive for Indian independence to the American civil rights movement. But it is dubious that such courage is sufficiently widespread to ground a universally effective pacifist movement. Strong, for instance, as the Chinese student movement may have been in the spring of 1989, it did not withstand the armed occupation of Tiananmen Square. Violent force prevailed when members of the People's Army opened fire on their own unarmed people, however traumatic the soldiers may have found such action.

Suppose, then, that the arguments of the pacifist shall all finally rest on a premise of moral courage that personal histories and individual dispositions often prevent people from exhibiting. Or suppose they shall rest on the consciences attributed, rightly or wrongly, to soldiers. If so, any truth in the pacifist position shall profit humankind only sporadically or, to speak more precisely, only when a dominatingly dynamic proportion of a victimized population displays the moral courage of a Gandhi.

Even here, the issue is not perfectly clear. Gandhi's successful drive for Indian independence was against the British, whose self-concepts and national character, Child has urged, made them incapable of the brutal suppression that might have defeated Gandhi. For Child believes that the Poles would not have succeeded to the degree that the Danes did in passively resisting Hitler, given the kinship Hitler felt toward the Danes but not toward the Poles. And Ferdinand Marcos claimed that it was his Christian conscience that made him forbear from massacring his compatriots. (Or maybe it was the squeamishness of his

American allies!) Accordingly, for all the impressive victories of passive resistance, the explanation of those victories, and thus the reliability of passive resistance as a pacifist method, is unclear.

But if I set aside the pacifist premise that a superior option to violence always exists, how does one reply to Gandhi when he concludes the superiority of a nonviolent response by arguing that the resentment created in those treated violently will become the seed of further, later violence.

Child replies by counterpoising the FBI model: The use of potentially (and, sometimes, actually) violent force does not inevitably lead to increased violence. It can instead result in escalation dominance and a declining spiral of violence. And although a tyrant may also practice escalation dominance, Child has in mind the important possibility that an appropriate social environment will foster a nontyrannical escalation dominance. In addition to police powers, such a social environment (as Child and I have now emphasized) will include suitably developed independent practices of observation and reportage, established procedures for defining the status quo ante, suitable conventions for clarifying and coordinating intentions, and enforceable practices of judicial review.[10] I interpret Child to mean that *in such an environment* violence-dominating practices can be instituted that, although potentially violent, clearly decrease the total violence among human beings.[11]

When those developed practices regularly decrease violence, one could complain only if their development led to complacency and the conviction that the introduction of a rule of law sufficiently minimizes violence. But this complaint is not about the development of genuinely violence-deescalating strategies. It is merely the insistence that since violence is bad, substantial strides toward its deescalation justify ignoring neither the goal of its elimination nor the importance of continued evolution thereto.

In the light of Child's arguments, buttressed by the above considerations, I infer that the Gandhian argument is overdrawn: Who would seriously propose, even in countries where the law takes considerable care to protect civil liberties, that the sometime violence of the police officer creates violence greater than the alternative violence of revenge practices or of tyrannical states? When a substantial reduction in violence is achievable, it becomes incredible that the social response to the remaining violence must be a malaise prompting increased violence. It is much more likely that citizens will gratefully pay the price of the remaining violence in exchange for a greater, previous violence. Thus, when it is possible to move to a rule of law in which civil liberties are protected, it is implausible to reject the move because of the violence of police work. I therefore accept Child's argument that violence does not always escalate. Some uses of violence deescalate violence.[12]

Moreover, Child strengthens his argument for the use of violent defenses by noting how scarce are the successes of nonviolent defenses in the history of warfare. And here, too, I must begin with a concession: In many situations where violence is about to be initiated, no *aikido* remedy is available. Perhaps there is no known *aikido*-style remedy for some offensive weapon; perhaps no practitioners of *aikido* are available to ward off the violence and make it redound against its initiator. However effective mace may be against a male assailant, some woman may have none at hand at the moment of an attempted rape.[13]

Thus the question to which I now turn is how to redevelop a pacifist position in the light of these important concessions. What defense of the morally vulnerable is appropriate if and when no *aikido* remedy is available? What pacifist view is possible if violence sometimes substantially reduces violence?

In response to these questions, the conclusion for which I argue in the remainder of this part is that if societies can provide for their own defenses through specialization of labor, then a pacifist segment of the population can be committed to the development and improvement of practices through which peace will be realized as it otherwise would not. I thus obviate the charge that a pacifist ignores the duty to defend those innocents on whom violence is imposed by postulating pacifists living in a society that makes provision for the effective discharge of this duty.

The Responsibility for Improving the Status Quo

*Responsibility and the Happening
and Agency Theories*

Child and I both view responsibility as a postulate of practical life. Since people are social, they by definition regularly interact. But the interactions that characterize human society are not instinctually co-ordinated (as they seem with the social insects), and, as a matter of fact, some interactions have deep and quite undesirable effects. Thus we should have to imagine the social order of human life to be no more complex than that of chimpanzees or the psychology of humans to be as simple as that of a bee in order to obviate the need for social practices of responsibility.

And how can we expect the Happening Theory to provide us with a satisfactory account of responsibility? Insofar as an advocate of the theory simply describes what *happens*, no responsibility is ascribed. Indeed, the assertion that events, including acts of violence, merely happen forecloses any obvious basis for attributing responsibilities. Thus, however descriptively adequate a determinist might argue the Happening Theory to be, its exclusion of practices of responsibility makes it at best an incomplete and thus inadequate view of human practical life.[14]

This consideration, however, does not lead me to endorse the Agency Theory of violence. And at bottom, paradoxically, I withhold endorsement for the same reason I reject the Happening Theory, namely, its narrow concept of responsibility. Consider how narrowly Child himself, an avowed champion of the Agency Theory, draws the bounds of responsibility: Having pointed out that, on my view, violence is a doing but not necessarily an action, Child says, "For one is not responsible or accountable for all one's doings. After all, you cannot help a hiccup or a stumbling."[15]

I agree with the assertion that one is not responsible for *all* one's doings. But how far Child overdraws this truth is suggested by my wife's experience with stumbling. Over several years she repeatedly stumbled, fell, and sprained her left ankle. Because of this, the muscles in her foot became increasingly less flexible, and she progressively lost sensation on the ball of her foot. Consequently, smaller and smaller stones under her foot became large enough to imbalance her, causing her to fall and resulting in further injury to her weakened ankle.

According to Child, my wife was not responsible for her stumblings. But nevertheless she undertook physical therapy, strengthening her muscles and making the foot actually more flexible than her healthy foot. She still steps on stones, as we all do occasionally, and consequently her foot is thrown on an angle. But no longer does she fall and sprain her ankle as she once did. Thus, although hiccups and stumbles are things for which Child says one is not responsible, compulsive hiccuppers, through training, stop hiccupping, as my wife, through strengthening and flexibility training, gained the power not to stumble.

When one is unaware of the extent to which stumbling is a controllable interaction between foreign objects around one's foot and one's strengths and flexibilities, one likely sees stumbling as an uncontrollable fact of human life: a doing for which one is not responsible. When one has developed the strength and flexibility of one's foot muscles—when, that is, one has learned how not to stumble—not stumbling will be a doing for which one has taken responsibility. Before my wife went to see the physical therapist, she came to believe that if continued stumbling eventually crippled her or put her in a wheelchair, it would be her fault. In other words, *she would bear the responsibility for not going to the therapist.* Her judgment seems to me correct in this matter, even though none of her stumbling had ever been intentional. On each occasion, her stumbling was an unintentional doing. Yet for taking responsibility for seeing a therapist, she deserves the credit for having ensured the existence of many unintentional nonstumbles!

To my mind, Child's comments about stumbling need to be considered along with his comment that the policy considerations he sees me emphasizing are matters of safety or prudence, but not morality. Clearly, as Child would agree, my wife was responsible for her decision to see the therapist. Child would emphasize that decisions are intentional actions, not mere doings. What I must emphasize is that by taking this action (for which she is responsible), she converted what had been an unintentional harm-producing tendency into an ability through which she now habitually and without conscious consideration avoids the harm. The fact that stumbling is typically a doing for which one is not responsible is compatible with the fact that improving the strength and flexibility of one's ankle is often a goal one responsibly adopts in order to overcome one's harmful tendency to stumble.

Responsibility and the Development of Practices

The example of my wife's taking responsibility for ending a series of incidents of harm none of which was her fault is analogous to the way in which a society, by developing a social practice, may take responsibility for avoiding violence no incident of which is anyone's fault. As there are important relations between intention, habit, and responsibility in the life of an individual, so are there similar relations between intentions, social practices, and responsibility in the life of a society. Just as my wife was responsible for deciding whether to undertake physical therapy, so it is desirable that somebody should be responsible for deciding to build up the social practices that are the analogues of my wife's muscles. For, in human interactions, we regularly see circumstances in which established social roles and conventions do not assign a responsibility at all or uniquely to one party. Because precedents may be vague or ambiguous, each party to the interaction may have some reason to believe that "responsibility does not lie with me." Such circumstances regularly produce the sprained ankles of social interaction.

A professor, for example, tells her students, "You are responsible for giving me your papers on Friday. I will collect them in class." The professor then falls ill on Thursday and does not come to her Friday class. Some students take her second pronouncement to mean that by coming to class with papers on Friday, they have fulfilled their obligations. But the professor takes her first pronouncement to imply that the students must get their papers to her office. Consequently, those who do not deliver their papers receive failing grades. Even in such a simple situation, it is unclear where responsibilities lie.

And consider how new technologies create new forms of harm to human beings. In the American Civil War, for instance, the increasing, but not great, accuracy of firearms resulted in a geometric increase in the number of wounded soldiers. Thus the leading cause of death in the Civil War was gangrene, resulting from untended wounds. Provision for tending wounds had not been an important function in previous wars. Whose responsibility was it, then, to see to the tending of so many wounds?[16] Other examples of harm are unrelated to war. Consider the industrialization of urban life in the past two centuries. Cancer certainly results largely from pollutant by-products of industrial manufacturing. Yet to this day people regularly do not know which new chemicals will prove toxic until a generation passes and the mortality statistics become clear.

These examples share a feature. Some social organization has set standards and delegations of responsibility that fail to account for a later development (the professor's illness, more accurate guns, atmospheric pollutants). Thus, previously delegated responsibilities could be (apparently!) fulfilled, while innovations gave rise to considerable harms. This feature is quite unhappy, since practices of accountability must be justified, if at all, in terms of their success in minimizing harm and promoting human flourishing. As my wife's stumbling was a critique of her habitual motions in walking, so cancer deaths become a critique of practices of pollution disposal. In general, new harms become critiques of older practices of accountability, and an argument for the evolution of new norms is implicit, just as my wife accepted the argument that she should undergo therapy. The emergence of unintentional harms argues for the need to take responsibility for the untoward consequences of practices, just as my wife's sprainings of her ankle argued for the need for her to strengthen her foot.

New practices, however, do not evolve simply out of the need to overcome harms. Consider, for example, the evolution of the role of the judge in the ancient Middle East.[17] For centuries, patriarchically organized tribes got along without judges for intrafamilial disputes where the authority of the father went undisputed. The interaction of families, however, led to disputes that no person had the recognized authority to resolve. In such circumstances, appointing adjudicators at least helps get disputes settled in a timely, orderly, and nonviolent manner; it may even facilitate fairness. This sounds like a straightforward evolutionary step.

The role of judge, however, clearly implies the need to compensate judges for performing a service that precludes producing their own food, and it became accepted in the ancient Middle East that disputants should pay judges. But whose responsibility was it to distinguish court costs from bribes? No one's, of course, in a strict and narrow sense. In this evolving situation, no considerations had been weighed, and no responsibility had been assigned. Yet surely the justifiability of a practice of adjudication involves making the distinction between court costs and bribes. For the practice aims at social benefits through attributions of responsibility, all of which is undermined if court costs go undistinguished from bribes. So, if we accept a narrow view of responsibility, we must conclude that a justified practice of judging will come to exist only if someone supererogates. But societies should not want the evolution of practices to rest on the good fortune that some *may choose* to supererogate.

The point of my section on collective goods (in Chapter 4) is that the risks implicit in this thinking argue for a stronger view of responsibility. The character of human interactions is bound to evolve, for both material and social reasons. As it evolves, ambiguities of responsibility will arise. Several manners cf motivation, ranging from desperation to selfishness to hostility to myopia, will then induce behaviors that result in inharmonious interactions. It thus seems desirable to create roles that promote the assignment of responsibility.

To summarize this point, I recur to Child's quotation of Lon Fuller, adding my own emphasis: "To embark on the enterprise of subjecting human conduct to the governance of rules involves of necessity a commitment to a view that man is, *or can become,* a responsible agent."[18] How could persons *become* responsible adjudicators without a distinction between court costs and bribes? Recall that prior to the distinction, the only extant definition of a "responsible" head of a family would have been one who protected and promoted the interests of the family. But that definition would strongly suggest that every head of a family, when giving money to a judge, should prudently attempt to convince the judge to rule in his favor. Thus everyone falls into a Prisoners' Dilemma in which court costs remain undistinguished from bribes.

Child accepts the similar argument that within the realm of international conflict and war, the usefulness of the concept of an aggressor diminishes because of the cloudiness that perspective often brings to its application. I draw the further conclusion that such practices as tolerate and support equivocation about this assignment of responsibility should be replaced. For if people agree, as Child and I do, that practices of responsibility are a social necessity, then the teleology I advocate seems but the smallest of steps: If we recognize that human society incorporates only imperfect—and sometimes fatally imperfect—practices of responsibility, then the desirability of responsibility involves the desirability of improving the extant practices of responsibility. Whoever wills the end wills the means thereto.

As a teleologist, then, I disagree with Child about the importance of incremental improvements of practices. Working out actual applications of a philosophical theory, he writes, "can be very difficult. But . . . the [Justified Violence] theory refers to some straightforward cases of aggression, in which equally clear rights of self-defense exist. For a philosophical defense of the view, we need only show that distinctions are sometimes clear and therefore that they can be applied in principle."[19]

I do not put a very high value on being able to show merely that in principle a view can be applied. For suppose that the Justified Violence View were clearly applicable in exactly one case. Suppose that in many other cases the view produced systematically ambiguous results, arising out of the problems surrounding intentions that I noted in Chapter 2. Suppose that in other instances the intuitionistic principles of the theory helped generate data sufficiently ambiguous to support propaganda machines on both sides of a conflict. On Child's account, the Justified Violence View could remain philosophically acceptable because Hitler was a clear aggressor, even if every other (unclear!) application of the view fed the fires of animosity and significantly increased the violence in the world!

Of course, I do not for a moment suppose that the Justified Violence View has only one clear application. But I believe a philosopher should endorse a stronger standard than that his theory has a clear application. If, of two theories of violence, A and B, the attempted application of theory A leads to significantly more violence than the attempted application of theory B, one ought to count that as an advantage of B over A. And if, over a moderate period of time, the attempted application of a third theory, C, leads to the same violence as B but leads to more of the positive contents of the concept of peace than does B, one ought to count that as an advantage of C over B.

Let us look at these practical standards for assessing theories in the light of the Soviet general's attempting to discern U.S. intentions. Commenting, Child says, "Neither the reams of factual information nor the conceptual apparatus . . . would have been available to the Soviet general. So surely this is a case where the Justified Violence View would not yield a definitive guide to action for him. And so much the worse for it. Yet I do not claim either universality or irrefragability for the Justified Violence View about the intentions of states."[20]

Two significant practical problems arise here. First, let us suppose that one were truly aggressive, but wanted to hide one's intentions. Clearly one should then choose to act so that one's (aggressive!) actions would be opaque to the Justified Violence View. Obviously, the facts that guerrilla soldiers do not wear uniforms and do not regularly fight fixed engagements on battlefields far removed from civilian settlements reflect the strength of this strategy. In other words, the prevalence of Justified Violence as a theory has bred violence the theory is unsuited to condemn—a very dangerous, yet predictable, strategic evolution.

Second, the Soviet general cannot accept the Justified Violence View simply because some of its applications are clear. He needs to act. For him, it is totally unhelpful to insist, as Child does, that his inability to apply the Justified Violence View is a mere contingency. The Russian general can take little comfort in the knowledge that in *principle* the intentions of the U.S. Navy could be known.

As a teleologist, then, I do not count a philosophical view acceptable insofar as it has some clear applications. Dangerous are the instances in which the regnant normative theory provides no clear direction or tolerates ambiguity and accordingly licenses adversaries to persist in hostilities. One makes significant moral progress if one can decrease the prevalence of such cases, either by supplementing or replacing the regnant theory.

Responsibility amid Adversaries

I turn now to what I regard as the center of Child's critique of my pacifist views. He urges that I do not adequately focus on the attack of an aggressor and that I do not view the aggressor's attack from the perspective of the victim. He finds me focused too exclusively on the preattack phase and on a policy perspective.

In part, I think it important to focus as he sees me focused. For in response to my focus, Child develops the Justified Violence View in important new ways. Speaking of contexts of policy formation, he urges the importance of considering the teleology of practices, going beyond what traditional advocates of Just War Theory have said. Very commendably, he says, "There is a place for considering 'the teleology of the practice,' namely, policy issues, and all of us as citizens, believing that violence is bad, should work hard on these issues."[21] If Just War theorists had traditionally taken this view seriously, then in addition to saying that going to war is justified only if one's war effort is defensive, and so forth, they should have said that going to war is unjustified unless, at earlier stages of what came to be a hostile relationship, a nation declaring war had consistently worked hard on defining tighter, mutually agreeable standards of responsibility. Accordingly, this major adjustment of Just War Theory is in principle of the first importance.[22]

Responsibility under Attack

But however important the policy emphasis may be during the pre-attack phase, Child is right to insist on an account of the attack phase.

Here he is concerned, in part, that I seem to place the burden of achieving an acceptable coordination of interests on the attacked, rather than the aggressor. Considering the situation in which an attack is imminent, Child asks, "Why ought the victim of an attack have this burden of new interest creation heaped on her, constraining her options for defense?"[23] Of course I have no argument that the attacked *deserves* this burden. Who *deserved* the burden of distinguishing bribes from court costs?

And who deserves the burden of devising the rechanneling of industrial pollutants so that cancer deaths can be controlled? Suppose that the answer to this question is ambiguous. Suppose that it is disputed, even to the extent that it is not ambiguous. Making these suppositions will leave untouched the undesirability of the cancer deaths. And consequently these suppositions cannot imply that no responsibility should be taken because of disputes about who should take it. Certainly Clara Barton did not deserve the burden of organizing nursing to tend the wounded in modern warfare, yet the world is better for the efforts she *cared* to undertake during the American Civil War. And with an altruistic motivation like a pacifist's, someone will *care* to address the moral problem of how to arrange for the responsibility so to be taken that the undesirable cancer deaths will be avoided, even if no one *deserves* to have this responsibility imposed.[24] The question of desert, then, is a bad question when it leads us away from caring to create improved social practices, practices that improve statuses for some but bring a net harm to none.[25]

The moral danger of this question is twofold. First, much violence is committed by parties that sincerely dispute who the aggressor is. In such instances, the view that the victim (read "our side") does not deserve to have the burden of practice improvement added to the burdens of self-defense is likely to lead to self-righteously insisting that the "aggressor" should make the first moves. These moves will need to include both nontrivial concessions and proofs of genuineness. Obviously, such moves are unlikely to come about if the parties sincerely dispute who the aggressor is.[26] And obviously they are unlikely to come about if "you" allow that "you" are the aggressor. So, in what cases are these initiations likely to be made? But surely it is undesirable for peace to wait for disputes in which either there is no perceived aggressor or the aggressor has a change of heart.

Second, suppose the burden can be taken. If, by taking the burden, the attacked creates a response that benefits at least one of the parties while harming none, then a better state of affairs has resulted from taking the burden.[27]

But can the attacked party take the burden? Of course, the answer is circumstance relative. And, as Child insists, the immediate circumstances of attack often severely constrain the attacked. But let us approach this issue slowly.

How an attack constrains an individual depends importantly on pre-attack preparations. In isolated situations, an attack constrains those whose defensive capacities allow them to ward it off much less than those whose defense is uncertain.[28] Employing developed capacities is typically not so constraining as attempting a defense without developed capacities.

But the question of constraints on the attacked is much different in circumstances where social support systems are available to the defendant. Obviously, if Mr. Green calls a bar and announces that he is coming to the bar to kill Mr. Blue, then Mr. Blue does not need any lengthy period to conclude that if the police are awaiting Mr. Green when he arrives, then the risk to his own life is minimized and the chances of apprehending Green (even nonviolently) are maximized. Because I accept Child's argument that some potentially violent uses of force deescalate violence, I can easily conclude that even if Mr. Blue feels threatened and has little time after Mr. Green announces his impending attack, still Mr. Blue can avail himself of the defensive, violence-deescalating capacities that society has readied in advance.[29] *It is immensely important that through deterrent and peace-building means society can steer events toward nonviolent interactions, through no worse than violence-deescalating means.*

Who Should Take the Party Perspective in the Attack Phase?

So am I allowing that in the attack phase it is appropriate to take the party perspective in defense of the attacked? Everything I have said notwithstanding, not entirely. Suppose the central values of a person's life are directly threatened; suppose it is appropriate (and possible) to defend the person (using no violence or using only controllable violence). Even then, almost no one needs to defend the threatened person. Had one person, witnessing the initial attack on Kitty Genovese, called the police, Ms. Genovese's life would have been saved, provided that (no more than) six police officers had warded off her attacker. But if no more than seven persons were needed to protect Ms. Genovese, it is undesirable to think, as Child does, that "society" has a duty to defend her. For the suggestion of this language, that persons should align themselves with the protection of Ms. Genovese, ignores the moral value of persons' aligning themselves with improving the safety of neighborhood streets. In a world of specialized labors it should not be too difficult to see that taking seven persons for the immediate protection of Ms. Genovese leaves twenty-some neighbors who need not interrupt their policy orientation.

Consistently with the rest of his views, Child affirms that the closer people see themselves to potential involvement in violence, the narrower the standard of responsibility they may justifiably take. But even if we allow this for persons directly involved in the violent interaction, this very allowance provides additional reason for concluding that others not directly involved need to broaden their standards of responsibility, in compensation for the narrowing of the standards of responsibility by others. How else are we to ensure that the narrowed perspectives of those closest to the violence do not undermine promoting the positive quality of peace?

Let me clarify this point by reiterating my previous arguments. Child argues that the responsibility persons should reasonably have accepted in contexts of policy formation is necessarily narrowed when those persons are subject to (imminent) attack. While most pacifists would resist this argument, I do not see how to make the resistance intellectually compelling:

1. When the issue is an attack on oneself, the fundamental question concerns the sort of integrity a human individual decides to pursue.

Nonpacifists and pacifists are likely to have different sentiments at this point. Some nonpacifists will reject the Socratic argument[30] that violence harms its perpetrator worse than its victim.

2. When the issue is an attack on others, what Gandhi alleged to be the "inevitably escalating cycle of violence" may not offset the moral compromise of those who are attacked but not defended.

Child argues cogently that not all cycles of violence are escalating. And I agree with him that using the Happening Theory to exculpate aggression morally or to justify acquiescence is a profound moral mistake. But from the conclusion that

3. *Persons under attack* have a narrower range of responsibility than do those persons at an earlier stage,

it does not follow that

4. The range of human responsibility in times of attack is narrower than at an earlier stage.

Even if the range of responsibility for the *persons attacked* is then narrower, a narrower range of responsibility *simplicater* would follow only if *everybody* were literally, individually, under attack. But there has never been a war in human history in which every human being has fought. Even in belligerent countries and even ignoring children, millions of men have been deemed too old or physically unfit for fighting, and millions more women have not been directly involved in battle. So the premise that those under attack have extremely limited duties to seek nonviolent options will leave unconstrained the wartime duties of millions.

I see a real problem in the analogy between attacks on individuals and attacks on nations. The analogy suggests that when a nation is attacked, the moral standards that apply to any individually attacked person are applicable to each citizen of a warring nation. But is it true that an attack on a nation is an attack on each of its citizens? It is true that defeat in war often leads to significant changes in the lives and lifestyles of individuals. But the idea that an individual is under attack carries a further meaning: that the individual must focus her attention and energies on the attack in order to repel it. True, the "war effort" potentially involves millions who are not soldiers. Yet, when a nation is under attack, for some individuals nothing is gained if their attentions and energies are focused on the attack. Indeed, large nations will include millions whose energies do not enhance the war effort.

Therefore, Child's premise that individuals under attack have only limited duties to attempt nonviolent responses has only limited application to war. The application is limited to individuals needed to repel the attack. It is a profound moral mistake to believe that whenever the repulsing of an attack requires the repulsers to adopt a party perspective, people, indeed whole nations, are relieved of responsibility for improving responsible social intercourse. The need for some to adopt a party perspective must not be misunderstood as an excuse for all to abandon a policy perspective.[31]

This, then, is the higher standard of responsibility I endorse: Since it would be desirable to avoid violence insofar as that can be done without (the violence of) capitulation, it is desirable for some persons to be committed to creating new interests that tend to be mutually beneficial. Good can come from this acceptance of responsibility, and no harm will result provided that the options created are no worse than as good for everybody as the status quo, while being superior to the status quo for at least some.[32]

An Example of Practice Improvement

Part of this commitment to reorganize practices is a commitment to minimizing the dangerous uses of presumptions. For example, a doctor is justified in *presuming* that a patient should be treated only when the doctor is ignorant of the patient's rational desire. A doctor may presume that an unconscious patient desires treatment because the patient's unconsciousness makes the doctor ignorant of the patient's willingness to consent to treatment. Accordingly, a doctor would be wrong to treat a conscious patient who clearly and knowingly refused consent. But if (1) the doctor is right to presume only when lacking the knowledge on which one more appropriately acts, then another condition is required before the doctor's presumption is justified: (2) Time must be of the essence, so that if action is not taken, very serious undesirable results will occur.

In a nonemergency situation, a doctor, instead of presuming, could simply wait for the patient to regain consciousness. In other words, without an almost inevitable jeopardy to basic values, a presumption would not be justified.

But now notice the implication to be drawn for practice improvement. From this premise:

> *Premise:* It is desirable for patients to be able to consent to any treatment they receive.

this conclusion will follow:

Conclusion: It is desirable to arrange Emergency Medical Services (EMS) so that the patients doctors receive into their care in emergency rooms are more frequently conscious or stable.

In other words, appropriate communication systems between EMS teams on the road and doctors in emergency rooms will allow doctors to supervise EMS teams. The teams can be instructed to perform services that not only minimize trauma to patients but also (and central to my point) create more situations in which doctors in emergency rooms need not presume because their patients are either stable or conscious. EMS practice is thus improved to the extent that, through it, the cases doctors handle less often require the making of presumptions that can interfere with significant values (in this instance, the patient's autonomy).

In Chapter 2, I noted the alienating character of the presumptions of the Justified Violence View. As doctors should, where possible, avoid making presumptions that jeopardize significant values, so we should also, where possible, avoid any alienation some presumptions may involve. The work of the pacifist, then, is like the work of the EMS team, in eliminating the need (and hence the justification) for dangerous presumptions.

Segmented Pacifism: An Alternative to Traditional Pacifisms

Segmented Teleological Pacifism as Empirical

In many ways, Child is correct that segmented pacifism is empirical. Any teleological pacifism—Gandhi's, King's, or mine—must consider how to move from a present state of violence toward the full-fledged peace indicated in Chapter 4. Any realistic path from a "present state of violence" must be empirically informed about that state. Accordingly, all of the following are empirical: the availability of goods relative to needs, the availability of goods relative to demand, the conventions for intra- and intersocial coordination, the interests relative to which parties will voluntarily move from conflicting to coordinating postures, the availability of persons to promote social evolution toward peace, the possibility of controlling violence nonviolently, and, to the extent that violence cannot be controlled nonviolently, the availability of genuinely violence-deescalating, violence-dominating strategies.

Thus the teleological success of a pacifist program depends on the circumstances of its employment. Indeed, moral philosophers, not grasping this dependence, have mistakenly questioned whether the roots of Gandhi's pacifism are moral. Contrarily, I argue that the specificity of Gandhi's tactics reflects his application of his pacifist principles to particular circumstances, rather than a lack of moral principles.

Gandhi devised his ideas for relations between intrasocial units of differing power. In order for pacifism to be viable in such circumstances, Gandhi needed to concentrate on the resources he had, the potential, nonresistant opposition of oppressed people to their oppression. On this point I have nothing substantial to add to what Gandhi so brilliantly defined. The important additions to Gandhi, for similar social environments, have come from King and Corazon Aquino.[33] Their tactics rely heavily on symbolic but substantial demonstrations of a public united in clear opposition to a perceived oppression. They rely on eliciting powerful public sympathies for those who resist a clear tyranny. Thus they rely both on the ability of a charismatic leader to unify the oppressed[34] and on the communication of the clear plight of the oppressed to people with the power to resist the tyranny effectively.[35] The workability of such a pacifist program is one of the monumental achievements of the twentieth century.

Yet its specificity means that it is not a pacifism suited to every social environment. A different pacifist program seems to me more suited to environments in which antagonists are each of significant power and in which the physical and social conditions of life lead the antagonists away from communication aimed at cooperative, constructive goals.[36]

What is not empirical is the commitment of the segmented pacifist to pursue a full-fledged peace without recourse to violence. For it is not empirical that, however favorably or unfavorably empirical matters may stand, it is desirable for some individuals to act in all feasible ways to make human environments more peaceful and to improve the empirical conditions that make peace feasible. Like any other pacifist, the segmented pacifist makes this commitment.

The Social Value of Disdaining Violence

But is such a pacifist commitment useful? This question is at least as old as Celsus's third-century exhortation to Origen that Christians should help the emperor "with all our power, and cooperate with him in what is right, and fight for him, and be fellow-soldiers if he presses for this, and fellow-generals with him."[37] To which Origen, the Christian apologist, replied,

> At appropriate time we render to the emperors divine help, if I may so say, by taking up even the whole armor of God. And this we do in obedience to the apostolic utterance which says: "I exhort you, therefore, first to make prayers, supplications, intercessions, and thanksgivings for all men, for emperors, and all that are in authority." Indeed, the more pious a man is, the more effective he is in helping the emperors—more so than the soldiers who go out into the lines and kill all the enemy troops that they can.[38]

Origen recognized that pacifists voluntarily accept the obligation of actively promoting the conditions of social intercourse under which persons would not incline toward violence. While others may feel they have done their duties by not harming anyone, by paying taxes to underwrite a police force, and, perhaps, by coming to the aid of a victim of violence, pacifists stand convinced that responses to violence that ultimately rely on (minimal, proportional, controllable) violence undermine the higher standard of responsibility of learning how to respond nonviolently but effectively to violence. Even if it is generally conceded that the pursuit of ideals goes beyond the call of duty, pacifists will accept the obligation of working to create the social structures that reduce society's reliance on violence.

If, then, the "pious" are to be more effective in helping the authorities, it would surely be because their piety consists in their ability to be motivated purely by a desire for social harmony, a desire that even the emperor's enemies can perceive to be in their own interests. Removing motivations toward violence and making nonviolent coordination mutually beneficial defend the innocent as surely as do guns and bullets. Individuals thus do a great good by creating the practices and institutions that make peace more real.

In accordance with this general line, I urged, in Chapter 4, that peacemaking roles are best created for pacifists, not for advocates of Justified Violence. But Child has not found this line persuasive. Referring to the questions raised by the conflicts in Northern Ireland and between the Israelis and the Palestinians, he has written to me: "That these questions are intractable for the MJV view is clearly true. My problem is that the assumption of pacifism seems not to help at all. The conflict-ing claims remain. I just don't see these questions as an issue between the MJV view and pacifism."[39]

But I do, since I believe that in some environments mediators com-mitted to pacifist principles will prove more effective than their un-committed counterparts. Against this view, Child has pointed out, quite reasonably, that procedures of mediation and arbitration work well within many societies and that their effectiveness does not turn on whether their practitioners are pacifists. This is true, but it ignores the advantages that established practices afford the intrasocial mediator.

Within the rule of law, it is explicitly beyond the authority of the me-diator to threaten violence in order to coerce agreement from the parties to the mediation. Indeed, the authority of the mediator is bounded by laws forbidding violent coercion. Instead of countenancing extralegal coercion, the rule of law ascribes to judges the powers to hold a person in contempt and to authorize the police to attach property. These prac-tices promote nonviolent conflict resolution by creating nonviolent forces (legal powers) and by dominating any (threats of) violence against those who wield these powers. Moreover, the desire of the mediator to work within that framework coerces the mediator to abide by the rules the framework provides: Within a rule of law, mediators would sub-stantially reduce their employability if they became known for (abusing their position by) gaining consent through threat of violence.

The international environment differs significantly. Consider, for ex-ample, the Israeli–Egyptian war of 1973, in which both the Soviet Union and the United States made overtures to mediate. The escalating military force such mediators would have been able to invoke and the lack of international conventions for restraining such force compro-mised their acceptability as mediators. Their power, unconstrained by established institutions, made them potential tyrants, especially given that their partisanship clouded whatever beneficence they might have had. Their rivalry made them ambivalently potential war escalators, rather than peacemakers. Accordingly, when the alliances of two bel-ligerents mean that each is in a position to resist mediation, then the only force that can be exercised in the situation is the force of the party who disdains the use of violence from the outset, one not aligned with violence but committed to the suasive powers implicit in new interest creation.

I thus answer Child's example of the successful intrasocietal, non-pacifist mediator as follows: When a mediator is not committed to nonviolence, it is a restraining social framework, such as we find within many societies' systems of law, which makes it possible to trust the mediator not to use violence to disadvantage one of the parties. When no external restraint system assures disputants that the mediator will refrain from violence, only a restraint system internal to the mediator—a firm commitment not to use violence, a commitment based on the mediator's own self-concept and sense of integrity—may be available to assure disputants of a would-be mediator's trustworthiness.

The Efficacy of the Segmented Pacifist

But perhaps the above argument is not yet fully convincing. For it focuses on the difficulties parties not inclined to pacifism will have in mediating. Can we move beyond Origen's metaphoric talk about the whole armor of God, to suggest the strengths pacifists bring to such difficulties? I think so.

The beginning of the answer to this question is implicit in the pacifist's positive concept of peace. The pacifist is committed to making the avoidance of violence compatible with building a much more encompassing peace. This intellectual commitment itself will make a small but real contribution to the pacifist's trustworthiness.

Second, the pacifist will enact that commitment in the form of the nonalienating presumptions I laid out in Chapter 2.[40] These presumptions, rather than cast suspicions and impose demands, offer prospective benefits to each of the conflicting parties. Of course these benefits give each party some reason for wanting to trust the pacifist, but more important is the fact that since adverse parties can also anticipate benefits, each party gains some assurance that the prospective benefits are attainable for all, since they are attractive to all.[41]

Third, a cluster of psychological, social, and historical considerations are available to supplement these theoretical reasons why the teleological pacifist can be more successful than his or her nonpacifist counterpart. Psychologically, the pacifist will exhibit a determination to pursue a positive peace. This determination will be winsome in its effect on adversaries, both because it exhibits an admirable steadfastness of character and because that steadfastness is aimed at the mutual advantage of the adversaries.

Socially, we may recall, the pacifist has lived in or studied environments in which mutually beneficial cooperation has been arrangeable without violence. Nobody denies that such environments exist, and as I have emphasized, pacifists will have cared to learn what they amount to, the attitudes on which they depend and the procedures that have produced them.

But the historical considerations are perhaps the most important.[42] The experience of arranging a mutually beneficial cooperation for conflicting parties will have given the pacifist useful perceptions, understandings, and dispositions others may not share. In considerable part following Gandhi, I note the following:

1. The pacifist will have cared to learn, from the perspectives of each adversary, the struggles adversaries to a conflict face.
2. The pacifist will be disposed to accept the adversaries' (nondominating) definitions of benefits and hazards.
3. The pacifist will use the reciprocity of his or her relationship to each of the adversaries as a basis for resisting adversarial definitions that rely on modes of domination. (For the pacifist can accept from one party only the like of which is also accepted from the other.)
4. The pacifist will have learned to recognize cues from a conflicting party as it moves toward a willingness to accept a particular compatibilist solution.
5. The pacifist will have learned to cultivate such cues into indications of a party's goodwill. For example, the pacifist will be disposed to consider expressing gratitude for the attitudes indicated by the cues (as a sometimes effective means to inducing parties to become committed to the attitudes).
6. The pacifist will be skilled at inducing each of the disputants to sense the similar cues from the other disputants.
7. Carefully avoiding the interpretation that a party's cues indicate its weakness, the pacifist will urge conflicting parties to build on those cues.
8. Throughout these efforts, pacifists will know how to use their own capital to facilitate agreement between disputants, for in some ways psychological capital expended earlier facilitates the later development of further capital.

In other words, the pacifist's experience will have taught strategies for building on cues—attitudinally, procedurally, and substantively—

so that conflicting parties are led to amicable, mutually acceptable outcomes. With a positive concept of peace as the unique motivation (as I urged in Chapter 4), we may imagine the pacifist (1) promoting the development of violence-defeating practices and institutions; (2) facilitating the coordination of human action to mutually advantageous ends; and (3) working to eliminate the incentives to violence that poverty and injustice are.

Aggressors and Pacifists

Do aggressive adversaries doom pacifist efforts? An antagonist with an aggressive nature the like of Hitler's can, according to Child, doom pacifist tactics from the outset. I disagree with this view, but I want to clarify the moderate way in which I disagree. I therefore begin by acknowledging that perhaps the most inventive new interest creation would not have stopped Hitler from pursuing the subjugation and annihilation of people. Similarly, I acknowledge that new interest creation may not succeed against every mugger who demands "your money or your life." Some persons will sometimes be incorrigibly bent on so subjugating others as to infringe their well-being. Thus, for example, although men can be raped, rape is clearly a crime predominantly committed by men against women, not for the pleasure of sexual experience but for the sake of sexual domination. Raped women are physically harmed not merely because they resist their rapists but because their rapists are intent on harming them. Even if I were to argue that in some cases therapy might eventually lead a man intent on rape to repentance, it would not follow that the woman or the therapist or anyone else could create an interest, at the moment of the impending rape, that would induce the incipient rapist to desist.

All these acknowledgments notwithstanding, my view is that persons do not have aggressive natures. The closest any modern geneticists come to the view that people have natures is that many genes prefigure (but underdetermine!) character traits. What primatologists tell us is that dissembling and alliance forming are central projects of social primates. The very attitudinal ambivalence that promotes intrasocial alliances and thus the dominance of some primates over their fellows similarly creates a niche for individuals (proto segmented pacifists) who are capable of discerning adversaries' ambivalence and who have developed the patience, attitudes, and skills to build these ambivalences into commitments to seek peaceful solutions to potentially violent conflicts.

For the peacemaking process I have sketched involves attending to the subtle nuances of many interactions. What SWAT teams have taught us is that, with proper attention to the right nuances, no greater force than the well-chosen word may be necessary to deter a violent person intent on violence. What I have suggested is that some environments will allow segmented pacifists much more than a well-chosen word.

Scarcity and Conflict

Part of my reason for qualifying my agreement with Child arises from noting the absence of scarcity from his definition of irreconcilable conflict. Such a definition hides the variety of reasons that may make a conflict irreconcilable. Suppose that, at bottom, the issue between the Israelis and the Palestinians were not unalterably a conflict about land to which each sees itself as having an inalienable claim.[43] The issue, for example, might be one of trust and reparations for past wrongs. If it were such an issue, it would not be an issue of essential scarcity. The meaning of "irreconcilable" would accordingly shift. Whenever resources become available through which the parties' interests can be simultaneously fulfilled, irreconcilable conflict can no longer mean that scarcity prevents the mutual satisfaction of desires. Irreconcilable conflict must then mean that at least one party lacks the will to be reconciled.

In a very important way, this is Child's point, for he is concerned that a Hitler or a rapist is intent on domination. Child is concerned that no new interest creation will satisfy the aggressor bent on subjugation. My concern is that the pacifist's insistence on diligently pursuing the policy role of interest creation will sometimes lead a conflictant away from (incipient or ambivalent) desires to dominate to desires that imply no hierarchical relationship over others. The typical ambivalence of human motives, which our evolutionary heritage as alliance builders has bestowed on us, means that interest creation often reconciles the conflicts Child calls irreconcilable. Indeed, while people also have a tendency to "dig in their heels" at certain points (and our evolutionary heritage has doubtless made such a passion profitable), counselors and mediators have the beginnings of an important body of knowledge concerning how to steer people away from the passion toward digging in their heels by taking advantage of some ambivalence toward reconciliative pathways.

Thus, as we consider "irreconcilable conflicts," the pacifist helps us to remember that we tend to view two very different sorts of conflicts as irreconcilable. One possibility is that the desires of at least one of the conflictants include desires to control the other. Then, given that the other's desires are incompatible with being so controlled, conflict, however ambivalently based, clearly exists. In that case, peacemaking means exploiting any discernible motivational ambivalence and using any real or creatable abundance as a lure for abandoning the desire to dominate.[44] The other possibility is that even though none of the conflictants' desires are desires to dominate others, a scarcity of goods or a conflation of ends with means prevents full satisfaction of all desires. If the conflict grows out of scarcity, then the pacifist will need to concentrate on enlisting cooperation and maintaining goodwill between the adversaries, while minimizing waste, creating new goods, or when goods cannot be expanded, devising good-faith compromises. Thus, means of creating new interests may either trade on our typical human motivational ambivalence to modify the desires underlying "irreconcilable" conflicts or bring new resources into existence.

Still, I must concede that Segmented Teleological Pacifism is not suitable for all circumstances. If action on a desire to dominate is imminent, the segmented pacifist *may* need force to dominate the portending violence. Whether nonviolent force will be available, when needed, is of course contingent. Similarly, we can imagine a world whose limited resources make extensive and extreme conflict irreconcilable. Under conditions of immense, unrelievable scarcity, the costs of continued deprivation might make the benefits of cooperation literally insignificant.

The applicability of Segmented Teleological Pacifism today depends significantly on the fact that in the past decade the means of feeding the entire human population of the world has been developed. It is of similar importance that the balance between human technology and human population should maintain that possibility. One can only applaud the recent efforts of many underdeveloped nations to control their populations, yet one shudders at other unabated birthrates. One can only commend such organizations as Habitat for Humanity, dedicated, as they are, to securing decent housing for the people of the world, yet one grimaces at the developed world's willy-nilly exhaustion of many resources. Were the technology not currently available to meet the basic needs of all people, one might argue that irreconcilable conflicts of rights are inevitable, and so values are bound to be trampled, no matter what happens. From this argument, one might conclude that recourse to violence is inevitable. And from inevitability, justifiability is a small enough step.

But at the macrocosmic level, the premises for this contrary argument are not available, and so the macrocosmic argument currently fails. It accordingly becomes desirable that the developed world's use of resources and the Third World's population retain or increase that possibility in the years ahead. It is extremely important that locally useful technology and food should become much more widely available throughout Africa, for the macroscopic irreconcilable conflict now threatening the world has its roots in the poverty that burdens so much of Africa today. Similarly, one must not underestimate the value of literacy in promoting autonomy.

Following this line, the focus of the argument concerning the viability of pacifist approaches to peacemaking comes to rest on microcosmic levels, on very real and intense conflicts between individuals and local groups. But if at the macrocosmic level no genuine scarcities make conflicts irreconcilable, and as long as the recognition of their undesirability prevents them from becoming irreconcilable, then the problem for the pacifist is to use the potential for constructive interactions to yield benefits that reduce and eliminate microcosmic conflicts and that induce individuals and leaders of smaller groups to stimulate interactions that yield new distributable benefits. For, clearly, when the means to feed and shelter the world are available, and when even the means to achieve worldwide literacy and provide a rudimentary education to all people are within the power of advanced societies to develop, the issue of peace in specific environments becomes largely an issue of distribution. The scarcities in our world today are at bottom local shortages in the midst of global capacities to create abundance. This is an immensely important fact, for, as President Aquino has argued to the communist guerrillas who opposed Marcos for seventeen years, surely even the costs of local guerrilla wars are worth bearing only if some political administration refuses to develop patterns of distribution that allow all people the opportunities to meet their own needs.[45]

And here we reencounter the tie between irreconcilable conflict based on scarcity and irreconcilable conflict based on a desire to dominate. When a pacifist addresses the aspects of a conflict plausibly based on scarcity, the face of the conflict is substantially changed. The most obvious change is in the extent to which the scarcity is alleviated. Less obvious, but clear, is the sympathetic response for realistic conflict resolution efforts that the pacifist's scarcity-alleviating action will build with the amenably intended. Still less obvious is the effect on the rhetorical case available to the conflictants; the claim that scarcity continues to drive the conflict becomes less plausible and, correlatively, the supposition that a desire to dominate motivates the conflict (if the conflictants are not reconciled) becomes clearer and, in many cases, more public. Yet, while this clarity tends to show reconciliation resisters in a bad light, the alleviation of scarcity and the appreciation of some newfound goodwill (on the part of the pacifist or on the part of one or more of the conflictants) will play on any motivational ambivalence the conflictants may feel, nudging them toward conciliatory paths.

In summary, then, I accept Child's view that some conflicts are in fact irreconcilable both because of unrelievable scarcities and because of willfulness. Yet, once a pacifist carefully notes these two sources of conflict, the pacifist will often be uniquely enabled to induce non-rights-violating resolutions of such "irreconcilable" conflicts.

Instituting Peacemaking among Nation-States

We may clearly imagine a nation-state that maintains a military through which it implements the defensive presumptions of rights theory. We noted, however, in Part I, that the contrariety between the presumptions of social protection and the presumptions of community building is not logical but at most practical. But since the ends of social protection and community building are desirable and are not essentially conflictual, it is crucially desirable to choose the harmonious means to these ends suggested by the positive concept of peace, rather than build means likely to be conflictual out of the alienating presumptions of the Justified Violence View.

The sort of social organization that facilitates nonconflict between social protection and community building is one in which different persons, in alternative social roles and practices, promote protection and community building. Having such persons so involved in one's own society, provided that they do not undermine each other, benefits the society. Therefore, having such persons so involved in each society, with the same proviso, is beneficial to all societies and to the community of societies.

Heads of state have traditionally had the ultimate responsibility for the protection of their societies; at this stage in human social evolution, they should also have the ultimate responsibility for the development of the community of societies. Consequently, peacemaking should be a task as close and as distant from the office of the head of state as is social protection. As Secretaries of Defense exist, so Secretaries of Peacemaking should exist, each with a function to perform independent of the functioning of the other. Because defense work is necessarily adversarial, Secretaries of Defense are not socially well situated for pursuing the social coordinations required to obviate any of a nation's defense needs.[46] With Secretaries of Peacemaking in place, Secretaries of Defense may continue to focus on defending their nations against the worst eventualities. They need not address how social evolution could obviate some of the needs for national defense. Instead, it will fall to Secretaries of Peacemaking to develop, among nations and their citizens, practices and institutions that lead to the development of harmonized and mutually advantaging interests.[47] Peacemakers may be assigned to discern (1) where coordination between adversaries can create new benefits for each; (2) where trading resources will produce comparable goods to adversaries; (3) what social problems can be profitably researched together; (4) what opportunities for broad scale cross-cultural contacts can reduce xenophobic suspicions and create new social realities; and (5) what publicly accessible social practices could be developed to alleviate sources of friction between adversarial societies. And Secretaries of Peacemaking from various nations may meet with one another to explore means by which peace, in its full meaning, can be further realized between and among their countries. Knowing the authority of Secretaries of Defense and the importance of not undermining their work, they will seek means to peace that leave undisturbed the military security of their nations. Working within parameters set by their heads of state, they will seek agreements that they can invite their heads of state to come together to ratify and implement.

In such a scheme, the responsibility of the head of state becomes to coordinate the work of the Secretaries of Defense and Peacemaking. If the presumptions of social defense and of community building are not contrary, it becomes the responsibility of the head of state to co-ordinate the work of the secretaries to achieve that compatibility. It is open to the head of state to take the view that the secretaries are undermining the effectiveness and the authority of the head of state whenever either of them proposes actions that tend to undermine the other. And each peacefully intended adversarial head of state can take this view without jeopardy because it will regularly be apparent to adversarial governments whether one's government is itself adopting this coordinative approach to its adversaries. Indeed, the use of a Secretary of Peacemaking gives heads of states genuinely interested in peacemaking a powerful advantage. Either one's adversaries will match one's secretary's initiatives or one's adversaries will be revealed not to be the friends of peace.[48]

Conclusion

Selective Convergence of Segmented Pacifism
and the Revised Justified Violence Theory

At the levels of violence between individuals and violence within society, then, the advocate of the Justified Violence View and the proponent of Segmented Teleological Pacifism must ultimately agree on the desirability both of disseminating the knowledge of defensive martial arts and of developing technologies that temporarily disable assailants without inflicting long-term harm. For the advocate of Justified Violence agrees that unnecessary violence is unjustified. (Indeed, one must be as perverse as a torturer to dissent from this view.) Thus, to the extent that it is feasible to make responsive violence unnecessary, the advocate of Justified Violence and the pacifist must agree that more violence has become unjustified.

Child and I also come to an important measure of agreement because of the ways our own views diverge from other Justified Violence and pacifist views. Child grasps the desirability of criticizing and reforming practices and institutions. Thus he incorporates into his final theory of Justified Violence much of the teleology I have advocated, even while it is obvious that the traditional theory, clearly expounded in Part I, takes no account of the potential evolution of practices and institutions. I, on the other hand, am a segmented pacifist. I defend the constructive peacemaking roles I believe members of a pacifist segment of adversarial populations are especially equipped to play, but I have accepted the positive value that deescalating forms of violence can have. I have commended the evolution of the rule of law that relies on the police officer's potential (and sometimes real) use of violence, but I argue that pacifists have advantages as mediators in present-day international contexts.

Summary and Prospect

In my introduction I ask whether one must define pacifism as the position that in *every* circumstance within *every* social setting, *every* individual is wrong and blameworthy if that individual uses *any* force against *any* other human being. In response, I offer the following:

1. I have argued that the problem is not about force but about violence. (Pacifism should not be defined in terms of nonresistance.)
2. I have defined violence in terms of the irreversible losses that make violence wrong, thereby avoiding the entanglements and self-deceptions that result from defining violence in terms of intention.
3. I have responded to the problem that violence may be necessary to prevent violence in a two-pronged way: *a.* I argued that escalating retaliatory violence is wrong. *b.* In response to Child's argument that potentially violent violence dominating is deescalating, I argued that extant social practices, including practices of violence domination, imply that human energies are available and could be utilized not merely to prevent hostilities but also to promote a fuller peace.
4. I then argued that in international contexts persons who promote peace are advantaged by having no club through which to threaten those who have the power to ignore those they do not trust.

I conclude the following:

5. The development of social practices and institutions that deescalate and minimize violence is desirable.
6. The creation of social circumstances (like those in our world today) that free some individuals to develop such practices and institutions is desirable.

7. Peace-loving nations ought to encourage an appropriate portion of their citizens to undertake work through which the improvement of human life may be possible.

Segmented Teleological Pacifism presupposes a society in which persons and groups can defend themselves against unprovoked violence (whether by potentially violent but controllable means or by unequivocally nonviolent means). The existence of these means, independent of the efforts of the segmented pacifist, creates a social space that, although not licitly occupied by free riders, is suitable both for developing nonviolent response patterns to conflict and for resolving, in mutually agreeable fashions, historical sources of conflict. The pursuit of these constructive goals in no way need undermine a society's established means of self-defense. Indeed, the direction in which the *aikido* metaphor points includes the construction of further, more assured means of nonviolent self-defense. But since the segmented pacifist's pursuit of the constructive goals of peace at least leaves defensive abilities intact, any constructive gain, in the availability of resources to needy people or the ability to negotiate conflict nonviolently, is a net gain.

My insistence that my view incorporates a higher standard of responsibility than Child's derives from my conviction that human beings should never acquiesce in circumstances in which nobody is responsible for the elimination of harm. When harm is not based in absolute scarcity, the teleological view of responsibility is that responsibility should be assigned for creating the social arrangements that divert antagonists into nonviolent alternatives. And when harm is based in scarcity, the teleological view of responsibility is that the harm should be allowed neither to escalate nor to persist.

I have now begun an argument for the construction of a pacific world. The martial arts make it possible for individuals to deflect violence from themselves. The introduction of publicly known laws, impartially administered, makes it possible for societies to minimize the violence of vengeance. Police use of stun guns has allowed communities to reduce the minimum necessary force required for law enforcement. Improved neighborhood lighting and community watch programs have reduced crime in many neighborhoods. The institution of a free press and, more dramatically, live pictures of television reportage police governments through public knowledge and thereby constrain the tyrant's options. With these precedents of violence reduction, the challenge facing adversaries and potential adversaries—indeed, facing all potential actors on the world stage—is to construct social practices and institutions that make international peace a stable reality.

Like other pacifisms, Segmented Teleological Pacifism retains an explication of ideals that will motivate some.[49] Focused, as it is, on the fundamental common goods of human life, Segmented Teleological Pacifism provides motivations and criteria for criticizing actions by reference to fundamental human goods. It thus replaces the ideological framing of criticism and the resultant objections of bias. Segmented Teleological Pacifism is unique in its commitment to practice evolution, which, as I argue in Chapter 8, it seeks to implement through a strategy of fail-safe incrementalism. Segmented Teleological Pacifism thus provides for the development of a practical, incrementalist program toward the realization of a peace that is more than the absence of war.[50] Through this program, as we see in Part IV, it creates new niches for the constructive evolution of social practices.

PART IV

THE WORK OF

PEACEMAKING

Introduction

The pacifism Scherer espouses in Parts II and III is neither a traditional universal pacifism nor a traditional personal pacifism. It responds to the objection against universal pacifism by acknowledging, or at least acquiescing to, the legitimacy of the defense of the innocent against imminent harm, even by violent means. It responds to the objection against personal pacifism with disdain for free riders. In rejoinder, it argues that a pacifist segment of a population has special dispositions and abilities for procuring and enhancing peace as a public good.

Accordingly, the Segmented Teleological Pacifism Scherer develops in no way contests the legitimate security needs of nations.[1] Segmented Teleological Pacifism per se implies no insuperable objection to such security systems of nations as protect the legitimate security needs of persons within the strictures of the Minimal Justified Violence View.[2]

Indeed, the segmented pacifist's rejection of the charge of free rider-hood employs a crucial premise: Providing for the legitimate security of citizens does not require the attention of every member of society. It is Scherer's claim that environments that meet citizens' legitimate security needs create opportunities for persons disposed to pacifism to provide valuable services that others would lack the will or the reputation to provide. Child agrees that this is so, absent the most extreme national emergencies (e.g., Britain facing Hitler in 1940).

Child argues that universal and personal pacifists do not see security interests as legitimate and see themselves as consciously sacrificing these illegitimate or imaginary interests. Child claims that this constitutes a moral mistake, but agrees that Scherer's version of pacifism does not make such a mistake. Scherer's segmented pacifism, unlike either a universal or personal pacifism, operates within a niche provided when legitimate human security needs have been served. Segmented Teleological Pacifism is thus a paradigm compromise in that it achieves the primary goals both sides seek without sacrificing too much of either position.

J.W.C.

D.S.

7

JAMES W. CHILD

On Avoiding War

When provision is made for meeting legitimate human security needs, the defender of the Justified Violence View and the segmented pacifist find common ground. They can agree on policy issues because they agree that peace is to be defined, at least in part, as the absence of war. The undesirability of the organized violence of war brings the defenders of the Justified Violence View and the segmented pacifist into agreement in three significant ways:

1. The moral obligation to secure persons from aggression requires, among other things, seeking improved international relations. At the same time, seeking such relations does not justify disregarding citizens' security.
2. Security Dilemmas, which the pursuit of security can create or magnify, are traps that potential antagonists should develop means to avoid.
3. The possibility of inadvertent war, which the pursuit of security can also create and magnify, ought to be minimized.

To some extent, I elaborate on each of these points in this chapter.

Properly Attending to Security

Much popular pacifist thought includes optimistic assumptions about human beings and their motives. Clearly, a universal pacifism would be much easier to defend from the premise pacifists sometimes casually use, that no persons are genuinely aggressive. A pacifist can all too easily lighten the burden of pacifist policy arguments by making some implicit, but nonetheless substantive, assumptions that err on the side of optimism, sometimes extreme optimism. This is one version of what I have earlier called empirical pacifism. Typically, these optimistic assumptions are both about the nature of possible adversaries and about the nature of adversarial relationships. All too often, they fly in the face of history.

Pacifists may be overly optimistic in their characterization of the nature of potential adversaries at two distinct levels. The first level is that of states[1] in the abstract. What sorts of states are possible on the international stage? What purposes do the governments of those states serve? What are the objectives, ambitions, and intentions of states and their governments? By assuming some very narrow and optimistic answers to these questions, pacifists may make the task of peacemaking seem far easier than it often is. The second level is in the assumptions a pacifist may make about the adversaries of a particular nation at a given time.[2]

Of Different Kinds of Adversaries

As we have seen, relatively equal adversaries will often be made anxious when the "security measures" of one potential adversary create perceived security problems for the other. This *is* our familiar Security Dilemma. It does not follow, however, that all cases of adversarial relationships are driven solely by Security Dilemmas and related spirals of misperception. Suppose at least one of two adversaries simply does not desire peace or desires it so much on its own terms as to require the nonexistence of its adversary or the violation of the basic rights (as I defined them in Part I) of the adversary's people, their conquest, their enslavement, or their deaths.

Are there any such cases? Have their really ever been genuinely aggressive states? Of course there have been. Standard historical treatments inform us that there have been many throughout history. The most familiar and least controversial example is, of course, Nazi Germany. Hitler waged war, not because he was anxious about the intentions or capabilities of his neighbors, but because he wanted conquest and an empire. His behavior toward Poland, the Soviet Union, and France did not result from the "anxiety" they caused him or from any fear of them.[3]

But Hitler is only the most notorious example. Japan's imperial ambitions in World War II were not much different. Did Japan's leaders have any reason to fear China, Korea, or Thailand? Or the Dutch (already conquered by Japan's ally, Hitler) in the East Indies? Or Britain, locked in a death struggle with Hitler? Yet Japan conquered part or all of these countries or their colonies.[4] These conflicts grew out of imperial Japanese ambitions, pure and simple. Japan did fear the United States, but only because it would frustrate imperial ambitions by stopping Japanese conquests, particularly in China.[5] In this case, the imperial ambitions came first; the fear of another great power followed. The ambitions were not the result of the fear, but the fear of the ambitions.[6]

Were Napoleon's conquests grounded in anxiety? Were the European powers' colonial wars, in the eighteenth and nineteenth centuries, driven by fear? Was Britain afraid of India, or France of Indo-China, or Imperial Russia of the Asian people whose lands it conquered? Nations arm, threaten each other, and go to war for diverse motives and reasons, some of them partly or wholly aggressive.

The Soviet Union: Still an Adversary?

Perhaps the most carefully analyzed and thoroughly chronicled adversarial relationship existed between the United States and the Soviet Union between 1945 and the recent gradual relaxation of tensions, which started about 1985. For forty years, that adversarial relationship loomed over all other issues of war and peace on the planet. And we must remember that even in this remarkable era of Mikhail Gorbachev and *glasnost,* the United States and the Soviet Union remain, in some important ways, adversaries. Each nation has approximately ten thousand strategic nuclear warheads aimed at the other. The Soviet Union has the largest armed force in the world.[7] The United States has the second largest.[8] Moreover, it remains true that both in types of weapons and in choice of strategic concept each military establishment is designed to *counter* the other. This is most graphically illustrated by one simple fact: The strategic missiles still point at one another. Though the adversarial nature of the relationship between the superpowers and their attendant alliances has attenuated greatly, with still promising possibilities for new forms of cooperation, these stark facts remain.

It is to be hoped that the degree to which we remain adversaries is more the result of institutional inertia than anyone's intentions. Still, massive nuclear arsenals on alert status constitute a reciprocal adversarial posture. Unwinding all this through bilateral and multilateral arms negotiations will take time, during which both caution and a prudent degree of readiness (of the nonprovocative sort) are very much in order.

But it is the adversarial relationship that existed throughout the cold war to which I want to devote discussion. For it represents a perfect test case of the issues discussed in this volume. Moreover, it gives us clues as to what we might expect or hope for or, and this is crucial, what we might *rationally fear* from the Soviet Union. That is, we pursue this seemingly moot topic of the Soviet–American adversarial relationship for two reasons. First, its well-documented and analyzed history constitutes a highly illustrative application of the Justified Violence View, with all the moral implications that entails. Second, there is at least some risk, discussed later in this chapter, that the adversarial nature of the relationship will be renewed. So the Justified Violence View could become a moral guide in a contingent future.

There is an open-minded, genuinely endearing attitude, typical of Western liberalism, that pacifist thought especially manifests. The Soviets, we are told by many observers, are just like we are. They have the same desires and aspirations; they fear the same things. For his own reasons, Scherer emphasizes human commonalities, and all of us would like, always and in all cases, to accept such a view of our adversaries.

Certainly, throughout the cold war the Soviet people were (and are) as good (in the sense of being worth as much) as Westerners. Believing in the universal equality of human beings, we must believe this. But normative claims about individuals tell us little about their moral status when organized as a polity. They offer no description or prediction as to their collective political and military behavior or their dispositions to behave, then or now. How do they see the world, themselves and us? In this sense, the history and tradition of Russia and the Soviet Union is profoundly different from ours. To believe otherwise, to expect them to respond to us as, say, the Canadians or the British might, is to misread history, culture, and political reality.

The history of any nation, the Soviet Union included, is crucially relevant to our assessment of its present tendencies and dispositions.[9] Lenin's self-confessed amoral tyranny[10] and Stalin's horrendous mass extermination campaigns[11] are as much a part of Soviet life and culture today as the administrations of, say, Woodrow Wilson and Franklin Roosevelt are part of what we have become. The repressions of Eastern European aspirations for democracy and self-determination lend perhaps the most obvious credence to this argument. Direct Soviet military repression occurred in East Germany in 1953, in Hungary in 1956, and in Czechoslovakia in 1968. Brutal Soviet threats kept hated communist regimes in Poland against civilian uprisings in 1956, 1970, and 1980. It is interesting that Gorbachev and other Soviet leaders have repudiated those repressions and to their credit chose the opposite strategy in dealing with Eastern European uprisings in 1989. Nonetheless, nations are not free of their recent pasts, of their inherited culture, or of their collective experience as a people. Indeed, the recent bitter recriminations over Gorbachev's, and especially Shevardnadze's, East European policy by members of the Soviet military and the Communist party are grim reminders of this. Nations are shaped by their pasts, which in turn mark clues to future behavior. To believe otherwise is to surrender to wish fulfillment.

The danger of the psychological processes of denial and wish fulfillment becomes more tempting especially now, when the Soviet Union is in the throes of an *apparently* basic reform and is led by a man more open and pacific, more familiar to us in his demeanor, more "Western," if you will. We consider this in the next section. If history is any guide, however, it is precisely now that a healthy dose of skepticism and caution is in order.

Gorbachev, Glasnost, *and Keeping*
Our Powder Dry

I believe we can say with reasonable assurance (as much as we ever can say in the life-and-death matters of world politics) the following: *If* Gorbachev succeeds in his programs of *glasnost* and *perestroika,* the world will be a much safer and more pacific place.[12] Consider the evolution of the Soviet Union under Gorbachev. Gorbachev urges massive

arms cuts by the superpowers and allows on-site inspection for verification; his predecessors built the most gigantic defense establishment
in history and continually resisted observation. He promises to cut defense spending; his predecessors adamantly refused. He admits that the
Soviet Union spends at least 20 percent of its GNP on defense (and
tells us it may be more, though he cannot be sure, because their ac-
counting is inadequate); his predecessors said it was less than 7 percent.
He promises to stop support for terrorist movements around the world
and appears to be doing so; his predecessors must have been supporting such movements, though they denied it. He admits that the great
phased array radar at Krasnoyarsk was an intentional violation of the
ABM treaty, and he disassembles it; his predecessors lied by denying its
true purpose while continuing its construction.

The undeniable moral progress of the Soviet Union in foreign affairs
under Gorbachev is astounding, even dizzying. Yet it also testifies to
the Soviet Union's moral retardation under its previous leaders. We
almost cannot overestimate the weight of Gorbachev's moral presence
as the leader of the Soviet Union, given the frighteningly aggressive
and amoral direction of Soviet policy in the postwar era before his
assumption of power.

Western skeptics about the Soviet Union, myself included, must not
be so narrow-minded as to refuse to see the awesome possibilities for
improvement. Societies do change for the better, sometimes from their
own internal, institutional dynamics, rather than by violent internal
revolution or conquest from outside. Contemporary Spain is an example. Twenty years ago, it was a classic dictatorship under General
Francisco Franco. Today, it is a parliamentary democracy with a free
press and free elections. That is a great deal of change, brought about by
peaceful internal reform in a short time. Certainly the largely peaceful
evolution (at this writing) toward democracy and free markets going
on in Poland, Hungary, and Czechoslovakia illustrates the enormous
potential for constructive change that Gorbachev's reforms seem to
presage for the Soviet Union. So we must not write off hope of change
in the Soviet Union merely because of fears or insecurities.

Will Gorbachev survive? And if he does, might political considerations force him to turn away from reform and toward renewed repression? Tremendous conservative forces in the Soviet Union are resisting
and will resist changes, especially liberal reforms.[13] These forces in-

clude the Red Army, the Communist party infrastructure, the planning bureaucracy, and, most ominous, the KGB, the self-proclaimed "sword of the party." Recently, the KGB has undertaken a massive public relations campaign, claiming to have changed its character. Moscovites attending a memorial service to its victims recently were not fooled. Their very strong feelings were that only the cosmetics were different. If they were not fooled, we should not be. The vast institutions that make up nations are not so quickly put into reverse direction.

All these deeply entrenched interest groups have much to lose in terms of power and privilege in the face of Gorbachev's reforms. Even worse, all these groups, and many average Russians (here we mean ethnic Russians) as well, possess a deep, almost visceral, fear of *anarchy*. Historically, anarchy has been feared when any disorder arises. This in turn leads to an obsession with order and a desire for strong leadership to provide it. Many observers of the Soviet Union and especially of ethnic Russian culture have held that this is the single most pronounced characteristic of Russian society and Russian history, as well as of Soviet life today.[14] Moreover, we are beginning to hear anxious rumblings from what the press has dubbed the (ethnic) "Russian right." Some of the more extreme of these people are ardent Russian nationalists, xenophobic, antidemocratic, and more than a little anti-Semitic. They openly express the fear of anarchy and propose repressive measures to cope with it.[15] Could we someday be facing a Russian Hitler?[16]

From 1917 to 1985, not one Marxist society successfully made the perilous journey from dictatorship to democracy. Now, Poland, Hungary, and Czechoslovakia appear to have done so. Still, we must hold our breath. Adam Michnik, a Polish historian and Solidarity leader, reminds us of the dangers of nationalism and xenophobia in the fledgling Eastern European "democracies," if we can call them that. Speaking of all of Eastern Europe he tells us: "One thing seems common to all these countries: dictatorship has been defeated and freedom has won, yet the victory of freedom has not yet meant the triumph of democracy. Democracy is something more than freedom. Democracy is freedom institutionalized, freedom submitted to the limits of the law, freedom functioning as an object of compromise between the major political forces on the scene."[17] Poland came close to democracy once before, in the early 1980s, only to regress, declaring martial law and crushing

Solidarity. Czechoslovakia began the journey in the Prague Spring of 1968, only to have Soviet tanks put an abrupt stop to it. It is true that Soviet armed force was responsible, directly or indirectly, for these reactions. It *appears* that armed force will not be a factor in the future. But Michnik reminds us that internal forces could do the same thing. Certainly in Tiananmen Square, China proved how very easy it is to fall from the path to genuine democracy.

So what are the chances for the Soviet Union, under Gorbachev or a liberal successor? What are the odds of a pacific planetary neighbor by the year 2000, where once we faced a monstrous Joseph Stalin and a Red Army five million men strong? Where even today we face ten thousand strategic nuclear warheads? The odds must be weighed in the light of two possibilities, each repressive, that might befall the Soviet Union. And these possibilities are, by my lights (and I say this regretfully), highly likely. Gorbachev might see the political handwriting on the wall and shift to a much more conservative and repressive line, as China's Deng has done.[18] Or, much more ominously, Gorbachev might be overturned by a highly conservative faction, which would not hesitate to inflict a bloody repression. The memory of Tiananmen Square persists. Either outcome could set the Soviet Union on a much more bellicose foreign policy. It is a tried-and-true technique of dictatorships to justify domestic repression by claiming foreign threats. Stalin was a master of the art, and Marxist ideology provides a ready-made worldview for such "threats."[19] So my pessimism persists even in the face of Gorbachev and his welcome reforms.

I hope I am wrong. And the reader may not agree with my pessimistic assessment of the odds against the permanence of a nonadversarial, pacific relationship between the United States and the Soviet Union. But anyone except a Pollyanna must admit that I *may* be right. That admission alone is all I need to make the policy I recommend rational: For the sake of our security, we should work with Gorbachev on arms control and on further integration of the Soviet Union and Eastern Europe into the larger world economy. We must do what we can to make Gorbachev or even more liberal successors succeed. We can aggressively promote a bilateral and multilateral arms reduction. This has the dual effect of reducing and relaxing still dangerous postures in our arms establishments while diverting scarce capital that the Soviets (and we) can put to much better use. Indeed, once we are convinced that

our expenditures cannot be turned to bellicose ends, and will be economically fruitful, the sort of Marshall Plan for the Soviet Union and
Eastern Europe suggested by Congressman Richard Gephardt might
well be in order. We may feel we cannot afford it. But considering the
cost of rearming for a second cold war and the huge benefits of an explo-
sion of free markets in so large a part of the world, perhaps we cannot
afford *not* to do this. Still, the caveat entered earlier must be honored.
The commitment to a pacific foreign policy for the Soviet Union would
have to be irrevocable. One key sign of this would be the displacement
of the Communist party from its still central role in Soviet political
life. Another would be the outright elimination of the KGB—a measure
called for by many Soviets liberals.

   We must do any or all of this with one very large caveat: We must
realize that whether Gorbachev or Soviet reformers generally succeed
or fail is essentially not in our hands. We can follow my recommenda-
tions (or Gephardt's) and help a bit at the margin, but the hard truth is
that such measures will not by themselves carry the day. The battles
for reform are primarily, even overwhelmingly, internal. So we must
be *prepared* for the failure of substantial reform, even as we ardently
hope for it. And we must accept our essential impotence in the matter.

   Even if I am wrong and the odds of the failure of Gorbachev's reforms
are low, the great stakes to be lost still require us to be prepared. We
must remember that the Soviet Union has not in a genuinely substantial way yet decreased its conventional military power or its nuclear
force, except for the destruction of the short- and medium-range missiles pursuant to its treaty obligations. In fact, one important feature
of the rejected Shatalim economic plan was a 20 percent cut in defense
spending. No doubt one reason for its rejection was resistance from the
armed services and their supporters. The Soviet Union still has larger
strategic nuclear forces and vastly larger conventional forces than we
have. The sheer size of the Soviet military is staggering, and too easily
forgotten in the West. The Soviet army remains *four times* as large as
ours. The Soviet military still has *four times* as many tanks, almost
six times the artillery, and over *twice* as many jet fighters and combat
support aircraft.[20] In short, they remain armed to the teeth.

   This vast force, in the hands of a militant and bellicose successor to
Gorbachev, would be extremely threatening. If, blinded by optimism,
we hastily disarm, in a foolish and gratuitous effort to show good faith

or in a shortsighted effort to save money, the results could be disastrous. For a still armed Soviet Union, led by a new aggressive leader (a Stalin, a Khrushchev, or even a Brezhnev), and facing a disarmed United States, could perpetrate blackmail so extortive as to compromise the basic rights of free people—perhaps profoundly, perhaps irrevocably.

Thus, we should encourage Gorbachev in any way we can that *does not weaken our security*. We must, as Oliver Cromwell cautioned his troops, "keep our powder dry." This means keeping our military prepared for the worst, while we hope and work for the best. We must let neither our fears of war nor our hopes for peace color our judgments as to what is real. We must practice neither wish fulfillment as to what is happening nor denial as to what could happen. We must disarm only as it is conclusively demonstrated that the Soviets have done so or are doing so, and we must be prepared to rearm rapidly and decisively (despite an inevitable Soviet propaganda barrage against it) should the Soviet leadership change for the worse. In terms of the lessons of this book, my policy affirms that we know our rights of self-defense and the defense of our alliance partners and that we continue both to assert them and to protect them with a *capacity* to defend ourselves. A capacity to defend ourselves and our alliance partners is a moral prerequisite that our government owes its people and that we, as voting citizens in a democracy, owe ourselves. How, then, while preparing for the worst yet remaining ready to exploit the best, can we deal most effectively with what must still be the primary desideratum: avoiding nuclear war?

Asking this question will give what follows a somewhat old-fashioned, cold-war sound. This is true and perhaps a bit artificial. But it is a logical consequence of our pessimistic working assumption about an at least possible reactionary shift in the Soviet Union. Moreover, it relates the best historical example of the Justified Violence theory in application. If it is not necessarily a guide to the future, it is a grand historical example.

Security Dilemmas

Nations tend to want peace "on their own terms," which means a peace with the "greatest possible security" for them. Such a peace may not be possible if each adversary seeks it. Moreover, though we live in a world in which peace in the abstract admired, many in the world have grievances, real or imagined, and many others fear violence. Those with grievances want peace only after the successful resolution of their grievances, and those who fear violence are convinced (often rationally and often irrationally, as I have argued) that they must prepare for the violence that may be necessary in their self-defense.

Even would-be aggressors will be concerned that the intended victims of their aggression may be or may become too strong to conquer or may be sufficiently alarmed to thwart a surprise attack. Suppose, for example, that I am unhappily correct in my pessimistic assessment of the prospects for enduring reform in the Soviet Union. Suppose that there were a conservative retrenchment against Gorbachev. Still, it would remain that the problems I am here introducing are *as much problems for the Soviet Union as for the United States.* Indeed, I believe they are *always* problems for nearly equal adversaries. Because of that near equality, each will have anxieties about what the other calls "the prerogatives of its security." In those prerogatives, each will see a need for self-protection. What does the Justified Violence View suggest about how international adversaries ought to respond to such problems?

The Security Dilemma captures the tendency of more weapons for one side to make the other side increase its arms, thus making the original arms less secure than before the arms increase. But the desire for security need not always provoke the same spiral from adversaries. Defensive weapons generally do not have the same effect as offensive weapons, and some offensive weapons have less effect than others.[21]

For example, intercontinental ballistic missiles (ICBMs), in recent years, have become accurate enough to knock out "hardened targets" such as other ICBM silos and command-and-control centers. (This capacity of modern missiles is called counterforce capability.) Unlike missiles on submerged submarines or airborne bombers, such land-based ICBMs are now vulnerable to counterforce first strikes. Thus, in any nuclear war, each side is tempted to attack those of the other side's nuclear weapons that they can knock out, namely, fixed-based ICBMs. Indeed, each side is tempted to start a war by striking the other side's missiles first, magnifying the Security Dilemma effect.[22]

This temptation to strike fixed ICBMs causes experts to call them *destabilizing.* In contrast, an invulnerable missile on a submarine, let us say, cannot constitute a temptation for either side to preempt, precisely because it cannot be attacked, preemptively or otherwise. Indeed, its security from first strike and threat as a second-strike weapon makes it profoundly *stabilizing.*

This gives us a hint to a way in which we can substantially lower the probability of nuclear war: by lowering the temptation of preemptive strikes. The most important way we can do this is by changing the composition of our arsenals, sometimes called *transarmament.*[23] This does not mean adding to the size of our arsenals; it means converting from reliance on a dangerously unstable to a more secure and therefore stable arsenal. This may appear to be a continuation of the arms race, and it will manifestly cost scarce tax dollars. But it will be making the world *safer.*

Transarmament and the Justified Violence View

Our notion of transarmament fits very well with the Justified Violence View. One of its key notions is not to do any more harm than is absolutely necessary to one's defense. Here, the shrinkage of the megatonage of the arsenals, the increasing of accuracies, and the restriction of attack to military (counterforce) targets all have the tendency to reduce what nuclear strategists euphemistically call "collateral damage"—more candidly, the unintended killing of civilians. This could be accomplished by dramatically reducing the lethal range of nuclear weapons as well as substituting conventional warheads for nuclear ones in some applications.[24] The replacement of nuclear warheads with conventional ones for some targets may seem visionary. But with the emergence of "ultrasmart" guidance systems, it is not. A way off in time, perhaps, but eventually realistic.

Moreover, insofar as transarmament means lowering the probability of nuclear war, it satisfies the Principle of Controllability. The Justified Violence View tells us we must do things that lower the probability of war before the fact. One such measure is transarmament to safer, more stable weapons, and it seems that our theory mandates it.

Moreover, transarmament makes us more secure without making the Soviets less secure. Indeed, it makes us more secure in part by making the Soviets more secure. It is a positive-sum game, making us both better off. Its only cost is the dollars and cents it takes to change the composition of the arsenal. If we genuinely want to lower the probability of nuclear war, the expenditure is worthwhile.

I conclude with two implications, the first immediate, the other practical but quite general. In these heady days of Gorbachev and *glasnost*, we may be tempted to forget such gritty problems and such tough-minded solutions, but let us not do so. For transarmament, as a stabilizing movement, can contribute to making the world more pacific. And if the promise of a completely pacific world disappoints, unstable defenses will again become promoters of war.

More generally, knowing what we do about Security Dilemmas and spirals of instability, we can see that the morality of any national defense is significantly (perhaps preponderantly) a matter of the stability of that defense. An unstable defense is the mark either of a covertly intended offense or of an irrational and negligently selected defense. For if the unstable defense is not intended offensively, then it provokes from its adversary an undesired spiral toward war. Thus the Justified Violence View carries with it the general implication that every nation has a duty to make its defense stable by avoiding the development and deployment of weapon systems whose value is compromised if they are not used offensively.

Notice that everything we say here is consonant with dramatic arms reductions, if such can be bilaterally negotiated. What is important is that the remaining nuclear arsenals be *stable*, regardless of their size. We can reach one surprising conclusion, too. *Stability is more important than size* as long as the arsenals are significant at all. How so? A nuclear arsenal one-tenth the size of either superpower's present arsenals could decimate either country. That we not have a nuclear war break out is the first priority. That it be fought with much smaller arsenals if it does break out, while important, is secondary.

Of course, there is the hope for the ultimate elimination of nuclear arsenals. Then the entire discussion is moot. But even today, such a prospect is visionary. It requires nearly complete trust and does not take into account the legitimate need to deter nuclear third powers. Reducing arsenals and making them more stable will prove much easier than eliminating them.

Avoiding Accidental and Inadvertent War

An "accidental nuclear war" is one that starts because of a computer malfunction or because a radar operator sees a flight of geese and believes it to be a missile attack or because a general goes mad and launches an attack that cannot be recalled (in the manner of General Jack D. Ripper in *Dr. Strangelove*). Accidental war has long been regarded as one of the most disturbing prospects of war in our time. It remains so today, for however good the present feeling between the superpowers, when their strategic arsenals are so large and pointed at each other, the threat remains. Whenever any power or, as today, two powers, keep nuclear forces in an alert posture, the possibility of such a war is real. But there are many things that we can do unilaterally to lower the possibility of accidental nuclear war.

For example, a program enhancing the security of the deterrent and pursuing transarmament can, by itself, lower the probability of accidental war. If a large portion of a strategic arsenal is vulnerable to a first strike, it must be kept on a high alert status. That means it must be ready to launch quickly, in immediate response to an attack. Of course, the quicker and more responsive you intend your counterattack to be, the greater the chance of launching by accident or mistake. In general, the more time an adversary has, the better, for the less likely is a mistake to be made or, having been made, to go uncorrected all the way to launching an attack. Security of the deterrent is what gives you time. Indeed, if the deterrent is completely secure—a submarine, for example—an adversary has as much time as it needs.[25]

There are other ways to lower the probability of accidental war. Most of the procedures for avoiding accident were put in place by 1970. Examples include the need for three independent missile officers to code and key the arming of a missile (a so-called permissive action link) on our Minutemen missiles or the "fail-safe points" our B-52s have, whereby, on reaching those points, they must automatically return home unless they receive a specific coded order from the president to proceed with the attack. These are good procedures. Nonetheless, they must continually be reviewed and updated. As we learn more about the management and control of complex systems in industry, government, and elsewhere, we must adapt those lessons to new measures to prevent accidental war. The Justified Violence View morally obliges us to spend the necessary tax money to manage the risk of accidental war and minimize it.

There is a profound difference between the incentive structure in arms reduction agreements and bilateral measures to prevent accidental or inadvertent war. When it comes to cutting levels of armament, it is in country A's interest that country B comply with the agreement, but that country A not comply (i.e., cheat). But in the mutual adoption of a measure against accidental war, it is in country A's interest that both it and country B adopt the measure. Even if country B cheats, country A is better off having complied and reduced its risk of starting an accidental or inadvertent war. Since this is equally true for country B, why would either cheat? Let us develop this point with respect to inadvertent war.

If a nation has a relatively stable arsenal and defense posture with which it faces a nearly equal adversary, neither surprise attack nor accident is the likeliest cause of its becoming involved in war. By far the greatest risk comes from a crisis situation between the adversaries escalating toward overt confrontation. In the nuclear age, there have been only three such crises, each involving the United States and the Soviet Union. Only one reached overt confrontation, although a second came too close for comfort. An examination of these crises can teach us much about avoiding inadvertent war.

The first was over Berlin.[26] For a period of several years (roughly 1958–1961), Nikita Khrushchev seemed obsessed with evicting the United States from West Berlin. By 1958, the exodus of East Germans into West Berlin, thence to West Germany and freedom, had grown so large that it became an embarrassment and then a severe economic problem for East Germany and its sponsor and protector, the Soviet Union. In 1989, under Gorbachev, the reaction to the same problem was to open the border and reform East Germany, ultimately letting it unify with West Germany. That was *not*, to put it mildly, Khrushchev's approach. Between 1958 and 1961, he explicitly and repeatedly threatened nuclear war. The American reaction was simply to stand firm and to do so without threats or inflammatory rhetoric. The crucial point is that, despite Khrushchev's bluster, neither side wanted war. As much as Khrushchev wanted the West out of Berlin and as much as he felt compelled to stop East German emigration, he preferred to avoid unlimited nuclear war with the United States. Certainly, the United States did not want war! Yet, war was a risk. Why? Precisely as Scherer asserts, and as we saw in Part III, because violence can get out of control; it can escalate. Neither side would have ordered a nuclear strike *ab initio* to get what it wanted. Nevertheless, shooting between East and West Berlin police could have escalated to shooting between U.S. and Soviet troops, which in turn could have escalated to a major conventional clash on the Central Front (East–West German border) between NATO and the Warsaw Pact. That would, with high probability, have led to unlimited nuclear war. For at each stage in the escalation, each party would have felt that it had to make this one more small step of escalation to win. In such circumstances, the eventual outcome is one neither party wants, and which each had hoped to avoid, but which they mutually bring about: *inadvertent war*. Indeed, inadvertent war is a terribly magnified possibility when the (threat of) violence on each side is continually inadequate to dominate the other's ability to escalate.

The driving force of the crisis was the unacceptability of the status quo. When the only possible change in the status quo—that is, Soviet eviction of the West from Berlin—is unacceptable to the other side, potential confrontation and escalation arise.

As we know, Khrushchev did find a solution to his (really, East Germany's) terrible emigration problem. He violated the four-power agreement and built a wall through Berlin, stopping the flow of refugees.[27] The Berlin Wall was a third option. From the standpoint of crisis management, we must say that the Wall was a strategically viable, if morally objectionable, solution. It brought the crisis well below the level of seriousness calling for a Western military response. It deescalated or dampened, rather than escalated. As morally offensive as the Berlin Wall was, it represents what Scherer calls "option creation," and to good effect. It arrested a spiraling escalation, which was threatening to get out of control. Certainly, the Wall was not a *good* solution to the crisis for either party, but if we consider the alternative, it was the least objectionable. In this is a lesson: Solutions that end crises threatening nuclear conflagration need only be tolerable to both sides. They often will not be preferred and are seldom cost free. In that sense, they are often zero- or negative-sum games.

The most overt and graphic confrontation in postwar history is so familiar as to need no description. It was, of course, Cuba in October 1962. For our purposes, however, it had all the characteristics of the Berlin crisis, including the terrible danger of inadvertent war.

Each of these crises occurred before the development of counterforce weapons, that is, during the era of mutual assured destruction. The crises were dampened because each side knew that if it launched an all-out nuclear attack, it could only destroy its opponent's cities, and the other side would not be stopped from retaliating. But consider what would have happened if the same events occurred in an era of counterforce with the reciprocal fear of preemption discussed earlier.[28] In general, imagine the following circumstances:

1. Neither side wants nuclear war.
2. Each side has the capability of preemptively destroying many of the other's missiles, thus substantially limiting damage to its homeland. But, to achieve this, each must strike first.
3. A confrontation looms. It appears that a series of reciprocal moves of escalation will, more or less inevitably, occur with no obvious or easy stopping point short of unlimited nuclear war.
4. In virtue of (2) and (3), each side is fairly sure that the other is considering a preemptive strike.
5. Each side knows that it can limit damage only if it strikes more quickly than the other.

The fearful mechanism of inadvertent war is now obvious. How do we disarm such a mutually constructed and reciprocally operated doomsday machine?

The problem of inadvertent war is best dealt with by a set of unilateral measures and, if possible, by a set of bilateral measures adopted in concert and cooperation with one's adversary. But one does not require mutual willingness to adopt the unilateral ones.

We may analyze the purely unilateral measures in the light of the story of the third nuclear crisis in American–Soviet relations.[29] In 1973, during the High Holy Days of the Jewish year, on Yom Kippur, the Egyptian and Syrian armies attacked Israel in a lightning surprise assault. In the first few days of the struggle, it appeared that Israel might lose. The Egyptian army succeeded in crossing the Suez Canal and hurling the Israelis back into the Sinai Desert. Finally, the Israelis regrouped and, with enormous courage and tactical brilliance, mounted a successful counterattack, driving the Egyptian forces back against the canal, crossing it at one point, and surrounding and trapping one entire Egyptian army (the Third).

At this point, it looked as if Israel might take Cairo and conquer the whole country. Soviet Premier Leonid Brezhnev decided that he could not tolerate the complete collapse of his then client, Egypt. So he sent an urgent message to President Richard Nixon telling him that if he (Nixon) could not stop the Israelis' advance, the Soviet Union would put in paratroops, in direct protection of the Egyptian Third Army. Brezhnev immediately put his most elite paratroop divisions on alert and began transporting them to Egypt. Thus, Soviet troops and Israelis (our closest allies outside NATO) would soon have been killing one another. At the same time, a large number of ships, carrying some sort of nuclear devices, left Soviet Black Sea ports, headed for Egypt. We never knew exactly what they carried, but we must surmise them to have been tactical nuclear weapons.

Again, we see a Soviet leader directly creating a confrontation to prevent an eventuality considered unacceptable. Surely, Brezhnev did not want general nuclear war. He did not even want a direct confrontation with the United States. He had a very limited ambition: to save Egypt from Israeli conquest. Yet he risked inadvertent war to achieve this ambition.

In any event, lest the reader think I am merely using the Soviet policy as a whipping post, consider that the next move in the crisis belonged to the United States, and it was a dangerously mistaken one. President Nixon informed the Soviet Union that such a move of their troops was unacceptable, and he *put all our strategic nuclear forces on alert.* The message was obvious. We were using threats of nuclear force for coercion. Threats, after all, can be quite real without being explicit.[30]

Such threats raise a moral question. If the risk of escalation to unlimited war is so great that it would be immoral to use nuclear weapons, is it immoral to threaten their use? What would the Justified Violence View tell us about the morality of using nuclear threats during a confrontation? The most obvious moral principle that is a candidate for application to this question is the rule of proportionality. Is the gain achieved by the threat (the prevention of the installation of Soviet troops, in the example) worth the cost paid, the risk of all-out nuclear war? We have seen the large (and, unfortunately, still growing) premium on a first strike that vulnerable counterforce weapons create. So great is this premium that some analysts have concluded that once both powers reach maximum alert status, nuclear war is almost inevitable.[31] Even threatening nuclear war in a confrontation poses more than a near-zero risk of bringing it about.

Moreover, we must apply the Principle of Controllability. It disallows means that, because we cannot control them, might get out of hand and create massively disproportionate harm. But inadvertent war is precisely the result of an escalation that no one party is in a position to control. Thus, all in all, one must conclude that Henry Kissinger made a mistakenly risky and, accordingly, immoral move here. Precisely because nuclear coercion involves nonnegligible risks of nuclear war, the principles of proportionality and controllability make immoral the use of nuclear threats to obtain policy objectives short of preventing an adversary's use of nuclear weapons.

Does this mean that we are impotent to protect our legitimate interests in the world? Certainly not! We have rights to our security. What it means is that we must prepare moral means suitable for that protection.[32] The Principle of Controllability tells us exactly what was the appropriate U.S. response. What would have been the least risky means of stopping the Soviet move? The answer is obvious: adequate conventional forces. In this case, that meant a powerful rapid-deployment force conjoined with naval and aerial domination of the eastern Mediterranean. Such conventional force would have been at least as effective as nuclear threats and much, much safer.

Another lesson is implicit in the 1973 example. Neither superpower can make commitments to defend interests that are undefendable with conventional forces. For to do so implies a willingness to use nuclear threats to defend those commitments, and nuclear threats imply to the party threatened a willingness to use nuclear strikes.

The general implication of the moral requirement of controllability is simple: Nuclear powers must have the moral courage to decide and stick to the consequence of their decisions. Either the defense of a strategically important area is worth the cost (in tax dollars) of a controllable defense or it is not. If not, nuclear powers have a moral obligation not to try to protect it on the cheap by nuclear threats, which, in a crisis, might play a major role in the path toward inadvertent nuclear war.

The best unilateral path for any power to lower the probability of inadvertent war is for it to tailor its foreign commitments to its ability to carry them out, using conventional forces that do not trigger inadvertent escalations. Nuclear powers should keep the threat of nuclear retaliation for only one purpose: deterrence of nuclear attack against oneself or one's allies. If superpowers were restrained in this fashion, nuclear war would recede substantially into improbability, since inadvertent nuclear war, growing out of a confrontation, is by far the greatest danger to the peace and safety of the world. Knowing what we do about the Justified Violence View, we can see that we are not only morally entitled but morally obliged to follow this course.

It has probably occurred to the reader that I have made some highly convenient but also highly controversial assumptions in our discussion so far. I seem to presuppose that moral defense or deterrence using nuclear weapons is possible, albeit it must be suitably limited and controllable. It must not be used where conventional force would work, and it can be used or threatened only to prevent *nuclear attack*. Still, I tacitly assume that nuclear weapons have a morally permissible place in a nation's armory and strategy. Needless to say, many people disagree with this. Many who are not otherwise pacifists are what I call "nuclear pacifists," that is, they believe that no use (or sometimes even no threatened use) of nuclear weapons can ever be morally permissible.

I have not argued against nuclear pacifism here and, conveniently, have held that nuclear weapons are justifiable in the same way, in principle, that other weapons are. Needless to say, this is highly controversial. But it is also far too large an issue to consider at length here. I refer the reader to my book *Nuclear War: The Moral Dimension*, which argues this thesis at length.[33]

Armed Conflict in a Post–Cold-War World

Obviously, in what I have said about the probable continuance of the cold war, I have risked being written off as a congenital pessimist. Let us then make an assumption, one often nowadays taken as implicitly true. Let us assume that the cold war is over. What does this tell us about the future of armed conflict, of purposive international violence? I am afraid that such a scenario only amplifies my pessimism.

If the cold war is ending, it is doing so, at least in part, because at least one party is losing the capacity to participate. I have held that the Soviet Union remains a military superpower. It does and will remain so for some time. Nevertheless, its profound economic weakness and political instability presage an age of only one superpower. And what of that superpower? Our own economic power is on the wane. Indeed, at this writing the economy of the United States seems to be weakening at an accelerating pace, and a near-universal consensus exists that we must cut defense spending dramatically. So we are well on our way to a multipolar world where many powers have at least regional capacity to do great harm.

It is shocking that nations like Iraq, Syria, North Korea, Vietnam, Israel, and South Africa have large and highly destructive military and paramilitary establishments capable of wreaking havoc in wide areas of the globe. This only exacerbates the general fact, long held by conflict analysts, that multipolar systems of power are inherently less stable and more prone to conflict than the bipolar system now presumed to be waning. The comparison of Europe immediately before August 1914 and Europe from 1945 to 1985 makes the point most clearly.

As I write this, Iraq has invaded Kuwait and stands confronting a U.S.-led multilateral force on the Saudi Arabian border. Though many things can be said to have "caused" Iraq to do what it did, the eclipse of Soviet power must count heavily as one. Numerous pundits have loudly acclaimed that such a confrontation between a Soviet client and the United States occurring several years ago would have risked nuclear war. It is, we are told, due to the reorientation of Soviet foreign and military policy that we have avoided a Cuba-style superpower confrontation over Kuwait. This may be true, but what is more likely is that several years ago the Soviet Union would not have permitted a client state to commit so blatant an aggression, *precisely because it would have brought about a superpower confrontation.* That is, the superpowers in a bipolar world had huge incentives (their very survival) not to permit many sorts of very dangerous violence.

The new instability in a post–cold-war world has been observed and commented on, however. Typically, it takes an ethnocentric and even implicitly racist tone. The Third World, we are told, in areas like the Persian Gulf, will be the locus of this new instability. Yet I believe Europe promises to be one of the biggest powder kegs of all.[34] Hungarians and Romanians fight pitched battles with thousands of casualties in the streets of Timisoara (in western Romania). Yugoslavia threatens to fly apart through ethnic strife. Bulgarians turn on their indigenous Turkish population. Without the Red Army, chaos threatens in Eastern Europe. And as German nationalism stirs, NATO is fading into irrelevance. American troops in Germany are rapidly becoming a thing of the past.

Nuclear proliferation threatens to arm many of these contending parties with nuclear weapons, which means various intraregional clashes could go nuclear. As long as Saddam Hussein remains in power, no one would be very surprised at a nuclear war between Israel and Iraq, or one between India and Pakistan. Less often considered, but by no means impossible, might be a nuclear war between Germany and Poland or between Hungary and Romania, or a nuclear civil war in a fragmenting Soviet Union.

Indeed, all these problems are made worse, as problems of violence and conflict typically are, by a host of possible Security Dilemmas. We have become so accustomed to seeing the like of Security Dilemmas and Prisoners' Dilemmas in a bipolar world that we forget how many more such dilemmas and how many fewer accompanying stabilizing effects exist in a multipolar world. Indeed, one of the best applications of the theory of the Security Dilemma in print is Michael Mandelbaum's "Israel, 1948–1979: Hard Choices of the Security Dilemma."[35] Here a series of Security Dilemmas emerges in a zone of regional strife and, principally, with conventional weapons.

All of this sounds so bad and the world so dangerous and unstable that pacifism becomes tempting. If only all these contending parties would stop fighting, threatening, and preparing to fight. And as we saw with pacifism generally, if it would truly become universal, all would be well. But it will not, and not one contending party dares trust its opponents.

So, again, the best we can do is to fall back on our moral right to defend ourselves. But we have learned a great deal, for we now know the severe moral limits that justify the defense. We cannot go beyond them. Moreover, we must remember that our moral responsibility requires that our means of defense be controllable and that our strategies must be nonmyopic. That is, we must proceed with an awareness of the various dilemmas that face us and do our best to avoid their worst effects.

Summary

The Justified Violence View justifies a program of national defense. But no one should conclude from the Justified Violence View that one strong national defense is as good as another. One strong defense may reassure one's adversary of one's nonaggressive intentions, while another defense goads one's adversary to develop more costly and less stable counters. A national defense can and should be evaluated both morally and strategically. My argument in this chapter is that both evaluations lead to identical conclusions on three fronts.

1. A nation-state best and most morally attends its own security by weapon systems and strategic doctrines that minimize aggressive threats to one's adversary without compromising one's security.
2. Alone and in concert with an adversary, a nation-state can take steps of transarmament that make adversaries mutually more secure by reducing the escalatory consequences of any use of violence without giving either adversary an advantage over the other.
3. A nation-state needs a variety of fail-safe devices and a variety of defensive response capacities if it is to minimize the possibilities of accidental and inadvertent war. These are best designed in concert with adversaries, and the logic of these measures provides mutual incentives to such action.

Especially in a time of international accord, these opportunities must be grasped.

Thus, at this very practical policy level, we see more fully the extent of the commitment to peace built into the Justified Violence View. For the view directs us not only to minimize the responsive violence we must use in defense. Instead, when we are not imminently threatened, it directs us toward defensive strategies that avoid motivating one's adversary toward violence or even undue preparation for violence and creates incentives toward safer relations. Thus the enactment of these policies shows the peaceful intentions and goodwill of the advocate of the Justified Violence View. Now more than ever, the teleological pacifist and the advocate of the Justified Violence View mesh. Indeed, both are crucial to real progress.

Toward an Enriched Peace

An Initial Model of Peacemaking

The thrust of Child's argument is that by making one's defense more secure, by avoiding heightening spirals of violence, and by minimizing the risks of accidental and inadvertent war, it is possible to reduce the overall likelihood of war. All these emphases, Child stresses, are compatible with a justified defense of citizens' rights. With these war-avoidance strategies, I am in substantial agreement.

Therefore, the thesis I pursue is a complementary one. I urge a parallel variety of strategies aimed beyond the avoidance of war at the development of peace positively defined. My motivations for this emphasis are, however, not only the obvious one of the value of a positive peace but also that the repercussions of the Security Dilemma may derail Child's well-intentioned suggestions. For nations, even nations in pursuit of peace, desire something more than peace, namely, peace on their own terms, in contrast to the terms of their enemy. And, as George Kennan has noted,[1] the function of any nation's military advisers is to bring their nation to view peace in terms of its own security. As Child's discussion of the Security Dilemma makes clear, such security will regularly include either foreseen or inadvertent or (at the least) perceived insecurity for the potential enemy.

The "enemy" therefore may demur from a peace so defined. However much the enemy may prefer peace to the continuation of a tense, traumatic, and expensive status quo, still the enemy may prefer continued hostility to a peace designed to its adversary's security specifications. If each adversary resists a peace on the terms of its adversary, continued adversarial relations, with their inevitable tensions, suspicions, misunderstandings, and displacements of war to lesser powers, become the best obtainable option.

In such circumstances, morality demands our insistence that the best available option is inadequate. For when existing options are unsatisfactory, it is morally unsatisfactory to choose what we call the lesser of evils. A morality rooted firmly in common human values requires us to *create* the superior option whose prior existence cannot be assured. And if the specialized role of the military adviser can promote national security, then segmented pacifists can improve our available paths toward peace.[2]

On Creating Options

During the hottest days of summer, electricity may be in short supply in some areas of the United States. The shortage is most likely to occur in the heat of the day, in late afternoon when industrial, commercial, and residential use are all high. Since, without the newest technologies, electricity cannot efficiently be stored, less efficient equipment for the creation of electricity has been traditionally used to meet the peak demand. But the use of less efficient equipment means more waste of material resources, a higher average cost of energy production, and the possibility that the production system will be overburdened, causing a blackout or brownout.

Nobody wants these results. Yet such results occur because nobody has the option of avoiding them. On the one hand, residential users are individually insignificant. They are (and feel) as powerless as individual citizens feel in foreign affairs. On the other hand, most industrial and commercial users each see a unilateral disadvantage in individually curtailing electrical use during prime time. Their need to avoid a competitive disadvantage is as important to them as is the need of heads of state to avoid jeopardizing the security of their nations.

Of the states facing this problem, Florida was one of the first to create another option. Instead of settling for the status quo, with parties individually deciding whether to curtail late-afternoon electric use, the Florida Public Services Commission decided to charge customers more money for the use of the less efficiently produced electricity! Through its action, the commission created the options of (1) curtailing use; (2) buying cheaper electricity; or (3) paying for more expensive electricity. Earlier, only the options of curtailing or consuming had existed. The happy fact is that customers, faced with the redefined options, shifted their demand to nonpeak hours significantly enough that the production of electricity became more efficient (thereby avoiding the overburdening of the system) and the bills of customers declined despite the new, albeit one-time, cost of a second meter.

The problem of achieving peace in certain environments bears an analogy to this energy problem. The environments are ones in which reasonably stable, though adversarial, relations exist.[3] Given this stability, the analogy I draw between the problem of curtailing electric use and the problem of achieving peace is no more and no less than this: Each problem involves four possibilities:

1. A peace designed to maximize our security relative to our adversary's security. (Unrestricted energy use by me, while all of you practice conservation.)
2. A peace designed without predominant attention to any one nation's security. (Conservation practiced so widely that efficient electricity remains available on demand.)
3. Continued adversarial relations. (Unrestricted electric consumption by all alike.)
4. A peace designed to maximize your security relative to ours. (Conservation practiced by me, while all of you do nothing to curtail your electric use.)

In each problem, when each party pursues its individual best interest—(1) or (3) being preferred to (2) or (4), respectively—the result is that everybody winds up with (3), when everybody would prefer (2) to (3).

Thus, I wish to address two different problems. Problem A asks: If everybody prefers (2) to (3), how is it possible to restructure the interchange between the parties seeking peace? Problem B asks: Even if one party is sufficiently aggressive that, because of its pursuit of (1), it is willing to forsake (2) and acquiesce, if necessary, in (3), how can adversarial interactions be so structured that when each party acts as that party thinks appropriate to its own circumstances, the result is the peace everybody should prefer, (2), rather than (1) or (3)? My strategy is to begin with the easier case, problem A, but to intersperse extensions of my argument to the harder case, problem B.

The Problem of Contingent Assumptions

The electricity example also illustrates that creating options may involve risks. Brownouts, for example, might continue even after the installations of the second meter. To the extent that (1) option creation is forced to rely on assumptions, (2) the assumptions themselves involve contingencies, and (3) those contingencies lie beyond the control of the option creators, option creation may become a risky business enjoying only sporadic success. Since national security tends to make humans risk adverse, option creation, if risky, may become an ignored strategy. If option creation, then, is to be a successful peacemaking strategy, peacemaking models need to be built on *sparse* assumptions *within* human control. Thus I begin my discussion of option creation with a historical model that makes few assumptions, with the ultimate goal of constructing a model that virtually eliminates even these few.

Graduated Reciprocation in Tension Reduction

In any long-standing adversarial relationship, as Child has observed, each side will have developed defensive postures that provide no continuing security to one's side but that disturb one's adversary. Such postures can serve an important peacemaking purpose because the fact that the original purpose has been mooted implies that while the adversary will appreciate the termination of an annoyance, the risk in abandoning the mooted need is zero. Thus, either side may take the lead in a process of graduated reciprocation in tension reduction (GRIT).[4]

The general principle involved is that what creates a gain for one adversary need not create a cost for the other. This principle applies to positive, as well as negative, elements of peace. Thus I observe that the elimination of outmoded defenses is not the only means by which to create a gain for one adversary.

Consider an example from international business. Honda, the Japanese auto maker, has been shipping auto parts in crates to an assembly plant in the United States (Marysville, Ohio). From Honda's viewpoint, the crates, having protected the auto parts en route, become a liability. But farmers near Marysville grow grain, which is exported to Japan. The price for which the grain sells in Japan depends on how bruised it is on arrival in Japan, and shipping the grain in the auto-part crates substantially reduces bruising. Thus, when Honda gives the used crates to area farmers, Honda avoids paying for their disposal, while the farmers enhance the quality of the product they deliver.

From each side of the adversarial relationship, the argument is the same: When an action improves the lot of the adversary and sweetens the adversarial relationship for both at no cost, that action is a bargain. Emergency medical aid and cultural and academic exchanges all illustrate the point. And when such exchanges are reciprocal, each adversary gains major benefits at no more than minor cost.[5]

The Reciprocation of Initiatives

Indeed, the only thing that could be better than a tradeoff of something worthless for a less resentful relationship would be the reciprocation of the same![6] After all, the reciprocation of initiatives indirectly facilitates the continuation of initiatives. For reciprocation not only lifts burdens from the original initiator but also serves as a token of gratitude for the original initiation. It is better than a mere diplomatic expression of appreciation, no matter how sincere, because the reciprocation provides an actual benefit to the initiator.

And the reciprocation need not always be related to the same issue as the original initiative. For example, when one adversary finds the need for some defensive posture mooted, the opponent may not be equally secure with respect to that same posture. Fortunately, the process of reciprocation need not require the noninitiating nation to march to the tune of the initiator. But what reciprocation must, by definition, require is that the noninitiator create some benefits for its adversary.

Reciprocation also encourages the originator to look the harder to undertake further initiatives. This encouragement comes from two directions: Taking further initiatives tends to promote a process that, from a self-interested viewpoint, is beneficial. Not taking further initiatives manifests a suspicious apparent unwillingness to continue a mutually beneficial process.

Reciprocal acts may also expand the creatable options. Consider again the example of the auto-part crates. Once the farmers use them to send grain to Japan, the question arises whether the crates are clean and strong enough for sending auto parts back to the United States, thus saving the cost of a new crate. And each reciprocation carries with it some suggestion that a measure of cooperation is recognized as mutually beneficial, even when no formal agreement has been reached. And thus a peace-building program may develop concretely the feedback loops I suggested in Part II between the conjuncts of peace.

The Expansion of Reciprocated Initiatives

The strength of GRIT lies in its recognition that the course of events continually generates a variety of initiatives that a nation and its citizens may take at little or no cost, and sometimes even with some benefit to itself, yet with a clear, substantial benefit for the adversary. Such actions stimulate reciprocation, for each adversary can see that the series of reciprocations is mutually beneficial while each of the early actions is no worse than cost and risk free, and the act of non-reciprocation will carry the considerable cost of manifesting apparent ill will. Those who are rationally self-interested, as national leaders are charged to be, will have the best of reasons to accept GRIT.

When the sequence has produced repeated benefits for each side, the continuation of the sequence can itself become the rational goal of each party. Consider any social organization whatever, a marriage or a business. There are always issues about which the spouses or partners might conflict. Yet violence is not inevitable. The parties often choose to avoid areas of disagreement, not because they are blind to the conflicts, and not because nothing is at stake. Instead, they choose to avoid the conflict because they realize that a major part of what is at stake when one party will not ignore an area of conflict is the positive value of the relationship independent of the conflict. Thus the continuation of the sequence implies not only the eventual accumulation of many benefits and the reduction of many costs but also the possibility (initially little more than a bare possibility) of beginning to transform the adversarial relationship.

It can therefore become rational, once there is a repeated reciprocation of initiatives, for either party to initiate actions that involve risks, provided that the harm risked is *reversible* and *contained*. It will be obvious from the outset—indeed, it can be publicly noticed—that if harms are suffered because advantage is taken when risks are incurred, some curtailment of the reciprocated overtures must result. When reciprocations are creating substantial benefits for each, curtailment will be mutually undesirable. Thus, if the risk-taking initiator calculates carefully, it can be obvious to everybody that the gain the adversary might have from taking immediate advantage of the risks being run will be less than the gains available from continuing the cooperation already achieved, especially as projected into a future of expanded tension reduction.

Assumptions and Limitations of GRIT

The strategy of gradual reciprocal initiatives of tension reduction has three potential problems, each of which seems to have played some role in American–Soviet relationships between 1968 and 1985. The first problem arises because the initiatives of any one party are taken without the consent of the other. True, they do not harm the other, but they do pose a problem for the other. If the continuation of the series is to be assured, the other must find a close reciprocal with which to respond. Although the reciprocation need not be identical, a close reciprocal is of practical importance because of the differences of perspective, history, and modus operandi that is inevitable between adversaries. Security advisers will tend to exploit these differences to argue for the minimal value of the reciprocation.[7] Although closer reciprocals are not guaranteed to overcome this obstacle, improving the isomorphism of the reciprocation reduces the plausibility of these detracting arguments.

Close reciprocals, however, are not always easy to spot or create. And while one deviation threatens the continuation of the series less as the deviation is smaller, the series is longer, and the deviator takes other compensatory initiatives, still the hard-liners in each camp will continually find some perspectival ammunition with which to minimize the benefits derived from the adversary's initiatives, even while emphasizing the risks and the liabilities implicit in one's own initiatives. More distant reciprocals intensify this tendency. And for these perspectival differences there is no full cure, although I later suggest how communication, multiple initiatives, and microcosmic actions can substantially minimize this difficulty.

The second problem arises partly because GRIT will almost inevitably not define the totality of the relationship between two adversaries. Some long-standing problems, apparently resistant to GRIT treatment, may continue to fester. Third parties may feed the adversity between the nations. A strategy of GRIT may thus fall victim to a change in leadership or to an extended crisis that disrupts leaders from their tension-reduction initiatives.[8] Since GRIT is fragile, I must suggest how to make tension-reduction initiatives more resilient.

The third historical problem with a policy of GRIT arises directly from the way in which the history of any adversarial relationship colors any gradual initiatives for tension reduction. In the mid 1970s, for example, influential people in the Soviet Union saw the United States as attempting to bully it through superior military force. When the Soviet Union responded with an arms buildup, influential people in the United States saw the Soviet Union as attempting to gain military superiority over the United States. When these influential people convinced a wide constituency within the United States of the aggressive military aims of the Soviet Union, the United States began a new arms buildup of its own. And when the rough parity of military strength between 1983 and 1985 came to include Soviet superiority in certain categories and Soviet plans for advancements in arenas of American superiority, the argument became current in the United States that any Soviet offer was made from momentary Soviet strength in order to perpetuate temporary American weakness. Thus does an adversarial history tend to increase both the likelihood and the plausibility of discounting the "initiatives" of one's adversary. Accordingly, more comprehensive peacemaking programs need to involve the capacity for creating a new postadversarial history.

A More Comprehensive Model of Practical Segmented Pacifism

A program of GRIT may encounter any of the following difficulties: (1) The resolution of some problems requires the cooperation of more than two parties; (2) some problems are so interconnected that they must be resolved interconnectedly; (3) the resolution of some problems requires substantial risks; and (4) adversaries may be unwilling to jettison perspectival or ideological descriptions of some problems. What can be done about such problems?

Let me suggest a package of tactics that well-intended adversaries will want to adopt, each initially for its own well-being and ultimately for the well-being of humankind. Less tractable problems facing such adversaries can often be avoided or postponed. And even if they are beyond solution in their original form, they may nevertheless become resolvable after intervening events modify their "intractability." Such a shift is often the result of the evolution of microcosmic social environments where scores of thousands of individuals initiate relationships in which old problems find no continuing place.

Peacemaking and Gandhi's Strategy

Certainly Gandhi used such environments to considerable advantage. Part of his genius (and King's, following him) was to appreciate the value of working among one's antagonists. One of the complications of international struggles is that such social environments are not central to the lives of the adversaries. An extra creativity is therefore required to transpose the tactics of Gandhi or King to international relationships. But Gandhi's writings offer clues about how to undertake this work.[9]

The first step in Gandhi's program is a shared understanding of the problem. A "problem" in the requisite sense is that one or more of the values fundamental to human life is unrealized or jeopardized, in whole or in part, for some people. The fact that the values of human nutrition, safety, health, education, opportunity, and integrity are usually uncontroversial facilitates defining problems in such terms. However many sources of disagreement adversaries may have between them, a good problem definition will stand independent of such sources of disagreement as who or what is responsible for the problem and who (besides the people who have the problem) will benefit from a certain solution to it. Accordingly, disagreement about problem definition arises either from conflating the activity of problem definition with some more controversial question or from ill will and disagreeableness. If conflation is the cause of the problems, then the peace-seeking dispositions of the pacifist in conjunction with careful analytic skills carry with them the prospect of eventual, mutually acceptable problem definition, at least for many issues.

But suppose ill will, hostility, or aggressive intent lies at the basis of the disagreement. Even here, the pacifist can make considerable headway if rather evenly matched adversaries have rather stable military defenses. If, in other words, the military balance of power does not favor the "aggressor" sufficiently to make the aggressor ready to war against the other, then the pacifist's dispositions will create a dilemma for the aggressor. For if the pacifist's obviously nonselfishly motivated actions are rejected, the aggressor will create a public appearance of his nonpeaceful intentions. This appearance will provide military strategists in the opposite camp with stronger arguments for building a more resolute defense apparatus, thereby making the aggressive intention more difficult to fulfill. But if the pacifist's initiatives are not rejected, then the would-be aggressor takes one small step, and moves the nation one step, toward a peace not desired.

Gandhi's second step toward mutual understanding is the clarifications of essential, long-range interests shared by the potential adversaries. Human health and safety, human education, and the improvement of the economic lot of people are very important to this discussion. Not only do the long-term interests of human beings necessarily rest directly on these fundamental values, but additionally improvement in each of them tends to reduce the attraction of violence. Fortunately, human health, safety, and literacy tend not to be highly ideological issues. Importantly, it is in the self-interest of potential adversaries to keep them nonideological.[10] For to the extent that these issues remain nonideological, adversarial thinkers will find it easier to modify their traditional approaches, both to adapt to new circumstances and to resolve continuing problems.

Consider, for example, the opportunity created by the international problem of alcoholism, a problem that crosses the ideological borders of the world. There is no distinctively adversarial definition of alcoholism, and there is no distinctively adversarial conception of goals for the rehabilitation of alcoholics; ideology does not determine what the problem of alcoholism is. Yet individuals suffer from alcoholism, and societies suffer from the violence and the irresponsibility of their unrehabilitated alcoholics. And this suffering sufficiently grounds the conclusion that effective approaches to the problem of alcoholism are desirable. Thus the characteristics of the problem of alcoholism make it apt for joint research projects and cooperative preventative and rehabilitative programs.

Nor is alcoholism an extraordinary problem. One has but to consider the problems of air and water pollution to see how they reflect a structure similar to that of alcoholism. The problems can be defined at a technical, nonideological level, and adversarial societies throughout the world have much to gain, both for individual victims of the problem and because of the social costs of the problem. It was thus fortunate that even during cold-war years, the United States and the Soviet Union initiated scientific exchanges to research pollution problems.

These coordinations illustrate Gandhi's third step, the tentative formulation of a limited goal for cooperative action. The adversaries need a practical, short-range goal to which each can contribute without substantial risk. The goal should be as isolated as possible from the controversies between them. Projects with multiple linkages are inevitably susceptible of alternative interpretations, favoring one party or the other, and thus geometrically increasing the difficulty of reaching an agreement.

Gandhi's salt march and Martin Luther King, Jr.'s bus boycott tell us that the ideal response to such snares will incorporate symbols of the loss of the basic goods of human life: She starves; he is tortured; they "simply disappeared." The essential goods of human life, in other words, are negated. Such messages, so basic and concrete, carry symbolic power: The rightness of responding to human victims is not confined to one malnourished man or one woman who will not sit in the back of the bus. Such violence will not be justifiable, whatever one's history or initial presumption.

Clear symbols easily move human beings to the conviction that if being human stands for anything, it must stand for not acquiescing when the basic needs of human life are deprived from the downtrodden. In the visual world television has created, every downtrodden group has the power, in conjunction with a media team, to manifest their plight to decent people who will sense the portrayal symbolically. And when repressive governments keep such images off their television screens, they thereby create the underground communication systems that broadcast their repression and cast them in the pose of opponents of positive peace.

Following the tentative formulation of a short-term cooperative goal, Gandhi's fourth step is face-to-face discussions between the persons under whose authority any agreement must be authorized. The tentative formulation of even a short-term goal is sure to need careful refinement, and the difficulties of negotiating intelligently are at least minimized by the increased information made available to both sides in face-to-face meetings. Negotiators and intermediaries not only create the potential for misinterpretation of authorities but also distance the authority from the proceedings, thus tending to make negotiation positions more rigid and to convey the distinct impression that the adversary finds the discussion unimportant.

These Gandhian tactics offer considerable promise for conciliation. They tend to uncover and to create real possibilities not only for reducing the attraction of violence but also for preparing for a real peace. They also underline the value of working among one's adversaries. The value of this work lies in part in being able to display one's goodwill to one's adversaries. Verification problems can be minimized within microenvironments. Moreover, working with the needy enables parties to display their goodwill to distant audiences who will appropriately sympathize with those who coordinate their actions to benefit the downtrodden. But the value of working among one's adversaries transcends these self-interested goals. For only the routines of normal daily life provide one with a real-life definition of the humanity of one's adversaries. One cannot know what problems mean to one's adversaries (when they struggle, how they struggle, and why they struggle) until one sees that struggle. The humility that I argued to be part of the pacifist's motivation has been a humility reinforced in the minds of pacifist leaders who could see not only the obvious inhumane lot of their people but who had the strength of character to elarn the humanness of their oppressors. Without compromising one's love for one's people, the pacifist leader who lives among antagonists learns to care for the humanity of the oppressor, a care that made Gandhi advocate conceiving every struggle as a positive struggle in favor of human beings and basic human values, rather than a struggle against antagonists. Here is a powerful interpretation of the paradoxical maxim not to struggle against those who struggle against one: struggle instead with them toward a better human future.[11]

The Gandhian Program in the International Context

The application of a Gandhian program to an international environment, however, raises a number of issues that deserve direct discussion. For special problems arise about information because of a lack of microstructures and because of the multifaceted character of peacemaking. I turn, then, to these special problems.[12]

Information

When two countries do not trust each other, each may incline to minimize the flow of information about itself to the other. For reasons of national security, even a nation that regards its openness as a virtue will substantially restrict the flow of information to a potential adversary. In some instances a policy of minimal information flow may be supplemented by the flow of deliberate misinformation. Moreover, it is always within the power of national leaders to color the information about a relatively unknown "enemy" either by selective presentation of data or by the presentation of data through the filter of the habits of thinking prevalent in one country but uncommon in another. Consider the response of the press in the United States to the tragedy of Chernobyl. Articles through which Americans learned that the Soviets "refused" to "admit" the "enormity" of the "catastrophe" overwhelmed discussion of technical and medical problems.[13] While no one should deny the importance of good information for resolving problems and for preventing their recurrence, no one could deny the ideological casting of issues in the American press: Both the choice of topics of discussion and the connotations of terms chosen for pursuing the discussion showed an unmistakably ideological casting of issues.

A people's limited knowledge of foreigners facilitates such casting, which in turn perpetuates xenophobic biases. But potential adversaries need not be convinced of the value of positive peace in order to want to respond to the problems that xenophobia inevitably produces. Instead, they need only be willing to explore its reduction. Both modern media systems and exchange visits of professionals provide members of the adversarial societies with opportunities to reach beyond their culturally honed sensibilities, beyond an initial reconfirmation of the "queerness" of the other, to an underlying recognition both of the common humanity of adversarial people (the shared concerns for food, community, shelter, education, medicine, and the arts) and of the particular, acculturalized sense of being human through which another people, however peculiarly, impart meaning and order to the routines of human life.

Developing Microcosmic Structures

The goal for communication between nations can be marked by the standard of communication that often obtains in small towns. In a small town one often hears from a friend what a "terrible thing" is happening in some organization of which the speaker has no direct experience. The hearer of the report, however, may know and trust people in that organization. Yes, they might make mistakes; yes, they might be focused on their own sticky problems. But surely, the hearer thinks, surely such "terrible things" cannot be happening. Within small communities, problems are often resolved at this point, or tensions at least reduced, because the hearer of the report calls friends in the organization. Inquiries are made: What has been going on? Is there any foundation for the spreading rumor of "terrible things"? With a constructive response to such feedback, an organization can avoid much needless grief. The development of such microcosmic structures is immensely important in response to the problems that arise for GRIT because of changing leadership and intervening difficulties. These variables are the *inevitable* discontinuities of international relationships. If such discontinuities are not to disrupt international relationships, the relationships need to rest on a vast microcosm of structures that hold the international relationships stable through inevitable periods of macrocosmic disruption.

The best communication, in other words, is not limited to mass media. Not only are mass media too macrocosmic and impersonal; they also fail to provide the interactive feedback that is the strength of small-town communication. Thus the increase of microcosmic communication would improve both the stability of relationships and the lot of those who communicate.

Microcosmic relationships also ease the responsibilities of heads of states charged with the security of their nations. The development of a multitude of international microcosmic relationships means the creation of vast networks of persons who come to have interests in nondisrupted friendships and interdependent prosperity. The more numerous and strong those interests, the more it is contrary to the interests of heads of state to threaten those interests by maintaining adversarial stances. The leader who seeks peace gains new means of achieving peace, while the leader who sought conquest is coerced from his goal by emerging interests of his own people.

Abstractly, this is a point about the interplay between the security-maximizing presumptions of the Justified Violence View and the positive peace-maximizing presumptions of Segmented Teleological Pacifism. In adversarial relations, either side can propose allowing the development of a vast microcosm of relationships that do not impinge on the security of the other. If the two adversaries are genuinely seeking peace, they will be able to discover together several ways of developing non-security-impinging microcosmic relations. Thus, in order to avoid clearly manifesting more hostile designs, even the aggressive adversary is coerced to allow the development of such a microcosm of relationships. But as the microcosm expands and the relationships become more central to the lives of the participants, the aggregate of the microcosms moves to stabilize itself. This movement toward stability inevitably includes a movement toward dampening the thrust of the alienating, security-focused presumptions.

Consider France and Italy, enemies in World War II, but joining a united Europe in 1992. Because they have, during the intervening years, built up a multitude of common interests, France and Italy do not contemplate war against each other today. It is not merely that, as the world happens to be today, much of what advantages one also advantages the other. Instead, and more important, the intervening interactions of France and Italy and of French and Italian people have *created* the interests that now bind the nations in alliance as they were once knotted in hostilities. Patterns of postwar economic development argue that microcosmic interactions can become the means of providing a mutually beneficial access to opportunities for mutual advantage.

Just as Child has argued that transarmament makes military security more stable, so I argue that microcosmic relationships make any obtained benefits of positive peace more stable. Some problems need not be resolved by agreements between nation-states. Leaders often cannot take particular initiatives toward peace because of the lack of development of interests in which the adversaries could potentially cooperate. What the initiative of citizens can do is to create the common interests on which leaders can build. Leaders need only avoid forbidding citizens from exploring and implementing what benefits each and harms none.[14]

When ideological concerns are set aside, the problems of negotiation become the standard problems when two parties foresee that there do exist conditions of coordination better for each than reaching no agreement. The standard problems are that (1) since more than one mutually suitable arrangement is possible, the negotiators need, perhaps through their negotiating process, to create a salience[15] that makes one of those

suitable arrangements mutually attractive; and (2) the process of negotiating must remain simple enough not to generate significant costs of
its own for either party.

But the convergence of these two problems is that since both parties
have more to gain from agreeing than from failing to agree, it behooves
each party to take a negotiating posture of trying to propose a model
that creates an appropriate salience.[16] Although, rather than agree to
the other's proposal, the other adversary may counterpose a different
salience, still the genuine attempts of parties to incorporate elements
attractive to the other into the proposals they make will not only convey goodwill but minimize negotiating costs by focusing the efforts of
the negotiating team on collecting the best of various proposals into
one package.

And here we grasp a central conclusion of social philosophy:

> *Conclusion:* In negotiation structured by Gandhian precepts,
> "best" comes to mean, in substantial part, not
> adversarial advantage, but the coordinated,
> mutually advantageous, stable, and self-enhancing
> convergence of interest.

In summary, then, the pacifism of Gandhi rests on working in the
midst of one's adversaries. Thus the application of Gandhi's program
to international relations requires the development of microcosmic
social environments where the power of Gandhi's approach can manifest itself. Peacefully intended adversaries, however, will be able to
allow citizens disposed to pacifism to create such environments. Aggressively intended adversaries will find themselves coerced by the
combination of the strength of the adversary's military and the undesirability of manifesting one's aggressiveness. In either event, citizens
disposed to pacifism will have the opportunity to cultivate the stability
that positively peaceful environments tend to develop.

Tough Times, Troubleshooters, and the
Suspectedly Aggressive Adversary

The long-range goal of a planned program of coordination for adversaries is the development of a myriad of mutually beneficial relationships. Yet, for all the benefits a planned program of coordination may
have, all relationships encounter tough times. Moreover, differences

in presumption and history are certain to imply that the toughness of those times will be perceived as largely the adversary's responsibility.[17] Hence the realization of a brighter future requires special structures for navigating tough times. If a defensive reorientation is not to become the sole order of those anticipatable tough times, the work of peacemakers must incorporate the work of troubleshooting.

Organizations that function well appoint troubleshooters in anticipation of tough times. The goal of the troubleshooter is to obtain or maintain a stable environment for presumably nonaggressive coordinations. Accordingly, the office of troubleshooter should be established when the value of continued (and possibly expanded) cooperation is undisputed: The benefits of cooperation need to be clear and the costs low. The troubleshooter's job thus becomes that of maintaining or improving a desirable state of affairs.

Thus, the mind set of a troubleshooter is aimed away from questioning the legitimacy of the functions of interacting organizations. The troubleshooter presumes that, with proper precautions, the functions are legitimate and coordinatable. It therefore becomes the business of troubleshooters to *prevent the introduction of incompatible means* in the pursuit of legitimate functions. Troubleshooters must thus have the experience to spot emerging difficulties and the know-how to solve problems[18] before they become disruptions and thus threats to the mutual value of cooperation. Moreover, troubleshooters must have appropriate discretionary authority inasmuch as effective troubleshooting often demands timely action.

But who could adversaries agree to appoint as troubleshooters? To the extent that adversaries do not trust one another, they probably will not approve appointing a troubleshooter from the adversary's camp. Moreover, untrusting adversaries will fear that "neutral" troubleshooters may prove self-interested and unreliable. The alternative, then, is to team pairs of troubleshooters, one from each of two adversarial nations, to work together. How could such teams work? Since troubleshooters are appointed when it is evident that the adversaries are experiencing new benefits from their increased cooperation, preventing the disruption of benefits will be the troubleshooters' primary responsibility. For when adversaries are experiencing new benefits, it has become in their interest to secure and enhance those benefits.

Thus troubleshooters from adversarial nations will agree to follow clear, predefined procedures, understood by both and arranged in advance. They will agree on this point because each will see that not to agree, even to demur in part, would signal to the other that the one aimed not at successful cooperation but at adversarial advantage. Obviously such a signal would force the second party into the defensive mode of protecting one's government, rather than the coordinative role of troubleshooting. Thus, since the goals both sides seek are mutually advantageous, both troubleshooters will agree because neither will want to undermine the potential of cooperation. Moreover, they will reach an agreement in which each has the assurance that their communication with each other will be full and open. For, again, to demur from such an agreement will signal to the one the bad faith of the other "troubleshooter," again undermining any attempt to act in bad faith.[19]

The Desire for More than Peace

Earlier, in discussing the desire of adversaries for peace, I noted that peace is hard to come by because the adversaries each want something more than peace. But if we pay attention to the course of the argument thus far developed, we reach the conclusion that the adversaries can have much more than a negative peace.

Some problems, however, are less corrigible. For all our creative ability, both technologically and culturally, conflict will remain. Yet these less happy cases will not make violence inevitable if the perception emerges that the already created convergence of benefits and a further potential convergence outweigh the remaining conflict. It is an indisputable fact that through the coordination of human efforts, social organization has the power both to create economies of scale and to allow human beings to reach thresholds beyond which cooperation becomes mutually advantageous. Thus the avoidance of international violence does not require the utopian panacea that conflict should cease. A strong assurance of the avoidance of violence can rest simply on a mutual recognition that the economies of scale and all the other advantages of cooperation outweigh, and promise to continue to outweigh, any status some nation might obtain only through the costs of destroyed cooperation.

Since this point is so central, I pause to reinforce it. There will certainly be those who, with good reason, will want to qualify the importance of the goals defined here by reference to political liberty or economic justice. A social order seriously compromising these fundamental social virtues would be sufficiently undesirable as to make many ready, on occasion, to challenge even the fundamental goals I have enunciated. I do not wish to object to such a plausible position: It is very hard to argue against freedom or justice. But if the position is not to be challenged, then how important are the goals I have enunciated? Might it not be reasonable to compromise them, at least somewhat, for the sake of these fundamental social virtues?

It could be reasonable to compromise those values I have enunciated only if they were in inextricable opposition to the fundamental social virtues. For only their opposition could make it necessary to choose between them. (And if the opposition were contingent, it would be wise to reengineer the contingencies!) Yet the positive concept of peace implies that the fruits of peace include the basic social virtues. But if the basic social virtues flow from peace, they are surely not inconsistent with it. Indeed, the fundamental economic lessons of the past twenty years would seem to be that production improves when people stand to gain from the improvement, provided that the people have the educational background and the capital resources to shape their own lives.

But if the basic social virtues are the fruit of peace rightly pursued, then we must surely follow Immanuel Kant in saying, "Whoever wills the end, wills the means thereto." If it can be agreed that no great good need be seriously compromised in willing those means, then it is hard to see how agents could seriously disagree about moving toward the construction of a pacific world.

Conclusions

Adversaries, in pursuit of peace, should want to be in a world where the nutrition and the health of people is improved, where both alcoholism and air pollution are more tractable. They should want to be in a world that increasingly supports people's health. They should want to be in a world where the resources required for human sustenance are available to all and where literacy improves the economic lot of people. They should want the spread of prosperity and literacy to be wide enough[20] that the stabilization of the world's human population comes above our perceptual horizon. They should want to be parts of societies taking active steps to stabilize family life through the reduction of unhappy marriages with the divorces those marriages engender.

And they should want to be in a world in which people live under the kinds of government that suit them.

They should realize, therefore, the advantages of living in a world where cooperative strategies that improve the achievability of these goals are employed even by potential adversaries who see each other as military threats. They should want to live in a world in which former adversaries are increasingly less interested in attacking each other because each is increasingly advantaged as each increasingly benefits the other. They should want to live in a world in which the cautious new allies begin to look toward the time when they so enjoy their camaraderie in the course of their regularized round of cooperative activities that they come to appreciate and respect what they learn of those with whom they cooperate.

From what position would the enunciated goals be objectionable? In a world of stable deterrents, no adversary can afford to object. But as each adversary assents, the world of their interaction evolves away from the sources of their conflict toward mutual advantages grown out of their consensual cooperation. And as adversaries are pushed toward this stability, so are they increasingly drawn by its desirability. For the goals are desirable for reasons based on everyone's situation as a human being, independent of whatever ideological convictions any may have. Indeed, these goals are not merely unobjectionable; they are so valuable and so fundamental that only a considerable conflict between their achievement and the achievement of other fundamental human goals could seriously call their rational pursuit into question. Accordingly, the more peacemaking and troubleshooting efforts magnify the value of peace, the greater can become the reasonable assurance that the nations of the world will be unmotivated by warfare. For the goal of peacemaking is to provide such benefits for all, through coordination, that the continuation (not to mention the continued enhancement) of the status quo is a far more reasonable option than its destruction through warfare.

The Structure of the More Comprehensive
Model of Applied Segmented Pacifism

So far in this chapter, I have dotted my pages with examples of the option-creating peacemaking strategies I advocate but which traditional Just War Theory has never urged. I have emphasized examples to exhibit the practical character of my proposal. Now I want to show the structure of my argument. For someone might suspect that I am proposing no more than a hodgepodge of tactics that may or may not work. I, contrarily, believe that I am proposing a systematic plan for regularly making the quest for a positive peace an alternative preferable to war.

It is a powerful strategy to ask adversaries to define their goals non-ideologically. Restricting their answers is pragmatically required for mutually agreeable progress. (Otherwise, divergent histories and pre-sumptions will undermine the constructive agenda.) Restricting their goals is morally justified by the fundamental character of the common human goods. Such restriction is hard for an adversary to balk. On the one hand, balking is a public notice of bad will. On the other hand, the balanced, mutual benefits of not balking make balking perverse among somewhat militarily evenly matched adversaries. Thus the restriction is hard to appear to oppose and hard to want to oppose.

At the same time, answers to the question will include many goals that can be approached through what are called Pareto optima. The idea is that some actions benefit some without harming any. Whenever one nation so acts as to benefit another without harming itself, it indirectly induces the other nation to a reciprocal action as a means toward inducing further initiatives on the part of the originating nation. Because exchanges of Pareto-optimal initiatives are mutually benefi-cial, the continuation of such exchanges is rational for each party. Such exchanges will be rational as long as the benefits to each party remain explicit and obvious.[21]

In order for the benefits to be explicit it will be advisable to allow the adversaries to present their views directly, regularly, and widely to the people of the other nation. In order for the benefits to be obvious it will be necessary to begin by defining benefits in terms of local issues with few linkages. And if such local issues are not above the adver-sary's initial threshold of recognition, it is mutually advantageous for the adversaries to seek out such issues and find ways of pursuing them cooperatively.

Once such a series of exchanges has been initiated, a series of bene-fits will (by hypothesis) be experienced mutually. Thus, an impetus to the continuation of such a series will exist. Similarly, since the series is geared to provide ongoing mutual benefits, it will be rational to prevent the series from terminating. Because a series of reciprocations between heads of states is fragile, it will inevitably terminate unless it is undergirded, both symbolically and substantially, by a vast microcosm of interests.

The continuation of a properly undergirded series of national reciprocations will be threatened only if one of the conditions that made the series feasible is violated: Either the communication lines break down or the complexity of issues makes relative advantages and risks nonobvious. If either condition were to occur, suspicions might arise that could both end the series of exchanges and give rise to a feeling within the adversarial camps that new (and costly) protections might be prudent in the light of the adversary's suspicious behavior.

The continuation of the series, however, is mutually advantageous, and the extent to which resources can safely be transferred from defensive protection toward production of goods for human needs will be but one instance of a pattern of exchange from which everybody benefits. Thus, inasmuch as the causes of series breakdown can be known and isolated, it becomes mutually advantageous to create social and technical structures that prevent series breakdown by making any unilateral deviation from cooperation self-revealing. For self-revealing deviation is self-defeating deviation. Thus the key to the continuation of the series of exchanges beyond its early no-cost, no-risk steps is to make the costs and risks of later exchanges acceptable by making any deviation from the series self-revealing, so the costs and risks become either negligible or fail-safe.

Thus each will know that the willingness of each to perpetuate the mutually beneficial exchanges depends on the adoption of a stance of goodwill toward the other. That is, when parties agree to make deviation self-revealing, they agree that whatever suspicions they may have borne and whatever security they may have reserved, the arrangements they make to ensure that their actions are transparent so simplify the relationships between them as to assure them that their suspicions are either mooted or at least focused on the arrangements that guarantee the self-revealing character of deviations from an ongoing series of mutually beneficial and, in the long run, perhaps, mutually disarming exchanges.

One of the best ways to approach agreements in which deviation is self-revealing is to seek microcosmic agreements: (1) In many small networks the appearance of deviation registers early, and in general the potential for deviation is more self-policing and self-correcting; (2) because the agreement is microcosmic, the risks of its failure are containable and bearable; (3) better modeling information can result from a specific cooperation because information is more clearly definable and collectable; (4) a network of intersocial microcosmic agreements is much more stable than macrocosmic agreements alone can ever be.

In conclusion, then, when the continuation of the series requires actions that involve substantial costs or risks for the initiator, the series can continue on a rational basis only if deviation from the series becomes self-revealing or the risks are self-limiting. Therefore, the advantage of the continuation of the series translates itself into the advantage of creating the technology and the social structures through which these results occur.

When deviation is so structured as to be self-revealing, the created structure makes deviation self-defeating: Structuring deviation to be self-revealing makes nondeviation the only rational move. Thus Kant's dream of perpetual peace comes into view. Peace can become perpetual when the radical honesty enforced on parties for whom dissembling is self-defeating guarantees that only paths of continued cooperation remain open. Peace is then realized as the stability of coordinated, mutually beneficial interactions among all who interact.

Beyond the Limits of Rationalism

Yet, for all its benefits, the peace I have envisioned still seems to me inadequate. Alternative choices may be irrational and self-defeating, but that proves only that they should not be made and that it is contrary to each party's interest for them to be made. It does not prove that they *will not* be made: (1) Such erroneous choices may arise from quite innocent misinformation or from inadvertent or unperceived linkages; (2) even if no erroneous choice is made, the execution of orders given by heads of state may create appearances or real harms that were neither intended nor foreseen in the original order; (3) actions following from permissions given by heads of state may create appearances or real harms unforeseen when the permissions were granted. The argument so far has merely been that it would be rational to begin a series of exchanges, such that if that series were properly organized, its perpetual continuation would also be rational. From that argument, one cannot conclude that the series will perpetuate itself.

Thus stronger conditions must be met in order for peace surely to perpetuate itself. What is required is a kind of "inner strength" of the peacemaking process. But what does the metaphor of "inner strength" mean? I believe we can adequately define inner strength by viewing a theoretically mutually beneficial series of exchanges as a system and then using two concepts drawn from systems theory in our definition. By the *inertia* of a system, I mean the tendency of a system to continue as it has functioned despite the introduction of a new and potential disruptive element into the system. When human beings run across a grassy lawn with heavy shoes, the shoes tend to disrupt the growth of the lawn. But a well-established lawn can withstand a degree of trampling. Even when blades of grass bend and break, a grass plant need not die. The inertia of the grass plants is their tendency to continue to grow despite being trampled.

Besides inertia, however, the lawn also has *resilience*. Enough trampling will actually kill some grass plants. Neighboring plants, however, will tend to spread, filling in the hole left by the dead plant. Resilience, then, is the tendency of a system to restore itself to its original functioning state after its functioning has been disrupted. For human beings to ensure the perpetuation of peace, then, requires that mutually beneficial series of exchanges incorporate inertia and resilience.

Perhaps most important, the inertia of the system will depend on how transparently each party can demonstrate the value of continuing the cooperation. A history of exchanges will of course help. But beyond history, leaders can demonstrate the value of continued cooperation in their responses to inadvertent loss. They will often be able to minimize, to compensate, to work fastidiously to prevent recurrence, to modify a dangerous continuation of the series, and to make heartfelt symbolic gestures. The employment of segmented pacifist peacemakers will make it easier for heads of state to take such actions without appearing weak. And the motivations I attributed to peacemakers will translate as the perceived genuineness of their efforts. Indeed, even the states will appear genuine in their concern for one another. After all, they have allowed or created the structure within which the peacemakers operate.

Peacemakers will incline to take the West African perspective that failures of the coordination are "our" problem, a joint problem about the continued viability of mutually beneficial exchanges, rather than "your" problem about "your" unfortunate loss. Indeed, it will be their function to induce heads of state to create the viability of their perspective. For, as happy spouses know, to the extent that the interests of two parties begin to merge, it becomes artificial and queer to think anymore about the interest of the one and the interest of the other. When it is genuinely true that when you are unhappy, I am unhappy, then it will be true that your loss is my loss, and your problem ours.

The individuals in a relationship will either have or lack inertia to continue in that relationship. Resilience, in contrast, does not lie solely within individuals. True, the disposition of an individual may be resilient. Even in the wake of discouraging events, some individuals will have the resilience to begin a new day with a fresh look at how the goals they still hold dear can yet be rescued from the failures of earlier efforts. I will have more to say, connecting such individual resilience to traditional conceptions of pacifism, in the next section. For now, however, I turn to the resilience of a social system.

Even as the resilience of a lawn to cover bare spots left by the death of individual plants is independent of its inertia, so the perpetuation of peace need not depend solely on rational processes even in conjunction with the inertia of the parties to continue the relationship. What systemic resilience means is that within a system lies a power to compensate for the failure of components of the system.

Thus, in a society, systemic resilience is the ability of some individuals to step into roles others have played. Human societies, of course, cannot hope to match the resilience of a grassy field in which any neighboring grass plant, through seeding or spreading, can replace any dead grass plant. Clearly, however, it is only self-interest for nations to create a very large number of relatively autonomous interacting agents, each involved in a series of mutually beneficial exchanges. As long as states do not prevent their citizens from developing self-interested interchanges with citizens of foreign nations, a myriad series of mutually beneficial exchanges will result. Each of those series, then, provides the interacting nations with some capacity to restore any exchanges undone by the contingencies of human life. The decentralization of exchanges between adversarial nations, because of the resilience it builds for maintaining whatever improvements in relations leaders may seek and permit, is itself a powerful step from suspicious misgiving toward the perpetuation of newly originated peaceable coordinations. For many small-scale exchanges are much more resilient than a few large, centralized ones.

In every successful relationship, issues remain. Among the remaining issues, some will seem amenable to treatment, others not. A relationship is richly peaceful when the mutual perception exists that it is better (for the sake of all the relationship yields and for the sake of all it means) to temporize with the issues that do not seem amenable to treatment than to force the issues and jeopardize the relationship. A relationship remains richly peaceful when the mutual effort exists to build on existent ties to improve interactive flourishing and transform the structure of less tractable situations.

Is Peace the Art of Buying One Another Off?

Is this proposal of mine really pacifist? Is it not a betrayal of the ideals of Gandhi and King? My honest answer to such questions must be yes and no. These great leaders improved their societies not only by disdaining violence but by building the foundations of a self-perpetuating peace. Thus has pacifism become a strong, if underappreciated, social force in our century.

I have tried to explicate the large extent to which the pacifist's argument has its foundation in rational self-interest. For it can become self-interested to develop an inertia to maintain the path from self-interest to better relations; it can be self-interested to assure the resilience of mutually beneficial exchanges. I have tried to show that a better, pacifist, and reconciliatory future is available, even though differences of perspective, history, and ideology can lead from frustration with adversaries to bullets directed at antagonists. I find it very hard to escape the conclusion that although everyone theoretically agrees that the paths of peaceful resolution of differences should be exhausted before hostilities are begun, in fact antagonists regularly read "peaceful" negatively to mean "nonhostile," rather than positively to mean "constructive of a reconciliatory and cooperative future."

Just-war theorists, fortified with the alienating presumptions of rights theory, have not stood against this movement. Estranged antagonists quickly exhaust nonhostile means of resolving their differences, whereas, if I understand the pacifist tradition, it maintains correctly that constructive means of conflict resolution are cultivated by the very process of genuinely seeking a cooperative conflict resolution. I believe I have remained true to the tradition in making explicit that the tactics of these people have a hard-headed basis.

Pacifism and Love

The view I have developed, however, diverges from those of so many great pacifists, at least because I ignore the important role of love in their work. I hasten now to correct that omission. It can hardly escape notice that real pacifists have regularly been motivated by extraordinarily strong feelings of love for their fellow human beings. These feelings contrast with the alienations against which Chekhov, Ibsen, and Wilder have warned us.[22] To the extent that one has been reinforced in dividing the world between "us," whose ways are at least decent and well intended, and "them," whose ways are no better than puzzling and untrustworthy, one will feel the duty to self-protection. The actual disposition to construct a reconciliatory, coordinative peace has historically rested on a willingness to act out of love. I have cast my argument in such a hard-headed way because I believe that the contrary dispositions toward self-protection are so prevalent. Love can appear soft, whereas pacifism will be acceptable to the strong only if pacifism is itself strong.

Yet if the love of which Tolstoy spoke was long suffering, surely it was not blind. Indeed, far from denying the importance of love, I want now to emphasize another role love plays in pacifist views. Consider the Confucian image of the Golden Age or the Christian view of the Kingdom of Heaven.[23] These are views of an ideal human community. Yet it will not be too difficult for most human beings to recognize that they have from time to time enjoyed relationships of camaraderie with a select few others that could model the kind of human community so widely idealized in human writings. One reason Gandhi advocated living among one's adversaries was surely that the eyes of love or, less romantically, the self-reflective eyes of human dignity and self-perpetuating prosperity, can then see the common human struggles besetting one's adversary. When a winter blizzard comes to the midwestern United States, we are all snowbound together, the neighbors check on one anothers' needs and rally to clear the street for emergency needs, the common vulnerabilities of human life coming into clear view. It is good to be reminded of the ever-so-human nature of such desires and fears.

Another reason Gandhi advocated living among one's adversaries was to combat the intellectualistic suspicion that a person may not respond with genuine concern for one's well-being when one has acted with genuine concern for that person. But Gandhi sensed that if one genuinely sought a common good, one's adversary would in the course of time see one's motivations on the face of one's actions: Love is disarming, and the sight of such love can powerfully affect the suspicious. Here is the motivational foundation of the special ability of the segmented teleological pacifist to pursue peace. Moreover, when love makes one feel good about both oneself and what one is doing (or trying to do) for others, love perpetuates itself as one's motivation independent of feedback concerning the immediate affect it has on another.

Love is a powerful motivator, and the pursuit of a community of love is a stirring goal. In love, then, we find a resilience of the segmented pacifist. But, for the pacifist, peace is not merely a goal; it is an experienced, if embryonic, reality. Recall the words of Tolstoy. Writing ever so elegantly, surely Tolstoy was aware of the energy and the peace one claims when the power to affirm replaces in one's life the will to destroy, when the courage to love replaces the need to defend. Is this not the experiential reality to which Jesus referred when he said, "The Kingdom of God is within you"? One cannot expect the mere commitment to the noble principles of Just War Theory (nor even an intellectual assent to pacifism) to motivate persons to seek beneficial options for their adversaries, to learn the struggles one's adversaries face, and to help both sides benefit.

I have tried to emphasize the importance of resilience in the pacifist world whose construction I urge. In fact, I have understated its power. In Part III, I set aside the usual pacifist argument that there is always a superior social alternative to participation in war. For I believe that a successful pacifist argument can build on, rather than challenge, the role of the military adviser. I also believe that those who have been deeply hurt and those who viscerally fear being out of control may find such a premise unpersuasive. They will ask the pacifist to admit that a successful response to violence sometimes requires violence. But will these admissions not undermine the pacifist's continued use of the premise that a superior option always exists? At that early stage in my argument I could only accept the incompatibility of the premise with the admissions.

But now the importance and power of resilience has become a part of my pacifist view. The larger the number of people enlisted together in communities, the larger will be the number of people whose inter-actions will fortify them to set aside personal hurts for a nobler human cause, the cause of the common human needs, with which they have come to identify. As this larger number of people organizes itself, the resilience of the pacific community increases. This resilience means that, in the light of a setback to the cause of human community, the will exists to develop a larger variety of measures designed to minimize the harm, to compensate for the harm, to create alternative communal structures, and to devise further safeguards against the destruction of community.

Socrates claimed that it is a greater evil to cause pain than to suffer it.[24] The claim I make is that to the extent that people come to identify with the communities of which their pacifist activities may make them a part, they will come to identify themselves in such a way that they can do better than merely agree with Socrates: They can agree without being forced to acquiesce in continual suffering. They can agree and find their resilience, their imagination, and their resources sufficient to create a new road to a pacific community. The presence of such a moral will is the final safeguard of a positive peace. Its emergence is the triumph of the pacifist spirit.

The Challenge of Pacifism

The effectiveness of any pursuit of a positive peace must have its origi-nal appeal to adversaries. One cannot expect to persuade one's adver-saries that they ought to be motivated by idealism or love. From the point of view of either antagonist, such motivations would be impru-dent and potentially disastrous. What antagonists must see, in order for them to be moved, is either the sufficient power to move them out of their antagonistic stances or the sufficient fail-safe benefit available to them by modifying their stance. Gandhi, King, and Aquino have all developed the first of these alternatives. They have each used resources nobody thought could be mobilized, with the result that their adver-saries retreated, rather than sustain (what their adversaries regarded as) substantial losses. In contrast, I have developed the second: I have proposed the self-interested pursuit of low-cost benefits on the parts of the adversaries, with the result that the pursuit of these benefits transforms the character of the previously adversarial relationship. On the assumption that the appeal of distributed benefits can move people, I have devised a pacifist program for the construction of a stable, prosperous, and peaceful world community.

The pacifist need have no illusions about the arduous task of reversing the animosities of generations. But the pacifist can sense that human community is possible, that fail-safe cooperation can turn to a grudging admission of the problems of the adversary, that a grudging admission can turn to a small gesture of common human kindness, and that some such gestures will be reciprocated in ways even our own narrow socializations will allow us to see. Then an awareness of reciprocated actions, especially reciprocations not fully required by the bare bones of the interaction, can become a sense of the community of our efforts and a sense of what we are making of our future. And our sense of our common future can become a genuine concern both for the well-being of the others in our community, without whom our future community is jeopardized, and a genuine concern for the well-being of others not yet integrated into our community, without whom the joy of our community is incomplete, even as the future of our community is jeopardized.

This chapter poses a challenge because I have begun, I believe, by proposing nothing but the following of self-interest. Only as the following of certain interests leads self-interestedly to the transformation of interests does my package develop. Never does the transformation lead to an argument that it is desirable or necessary to ignore or to compromise the self-protection of people. Never does the transformation lead to any argument that it might become desirable or necessary to compromise, in the case of even a single person, the common, basic values of human life. And so I close with this challenge: If it is possible to obtain, or even grossly to approximate, the positive peace I have described, and if this peace is possible without any violation of the common, basic values of human life, exactly what might be the argument to denigrate the social efforts toward this peace?

Concluding Social Scientific Postscript

In 1985, when I conceived writing my portion of this book, the prospects of anything like Segmented Teleological Pacifism seemed, to many rational observers, quite limited. But since then, an amazing momentum has developed that encourages reading my views not as visionary optimism but as theoretical explanation of events. Events in China notwithstanding, 1989 and 1990 were widely viewed as years of great moral and political progress.

I do not entirely share the optimism of this reading, for several reasons: (1) Democratic reforms, though welcome, carry difficult baggage with them; (2) cultural reforms, though needed, are not easily accomplished; and (3) economic reforms, though vital and passionately desired, require broadly based dispositions, practices, and institutions. Let me explain each point further.

Democracy is not an efficient form of government. Autocracy is more efficient. The great benefit of constitutional democracy is that, among systems for maintaining social order, it is less disposed to great harm because of the checks on abuses that grow out of its openness and divisions of power. This disposition greatly benefits prosperous jurisdictions, but not the desperate. The desperate will be disposed to seek quick improvement, which democracy with its intentional divisions of power is ill suited to provide.

The hunter–gatherer and agricultural organizations of society that dominate our human past have been passed by. They are ill suited to the quality of technology and the quantity of people of our time. The newer organizations of human society grew out of the European Renaissance, where the state was little more than a confederation of lords, and the church and the feudal organization of life came to be supplemented by guilds of artisans, merchants, seafarers, and bankers. Yet even in that favorable evolutionary environment, Adam Smith's *Wealth of Nations* was not published until over four hundred years after the church had recognized that such borrowing of funds at interest as facilitates commercial enterprize does not constitute usury. Modern Western democracy evolved only as, and to a large extent after, the simple organization of feudal life receded.

To glimpse the practices and institutions Western economic life involves, consider a mundane question: How much debt is it reasonable for a productive unit (a family or a nation) to undertake? Standard answers to this question require a calculation: (1) The rate of interest and the swiftness of repayment must be measured against the projected increase in the rate of productivity. But (2) the projected rate of productivity must itself be defined in terms of the strength of the market for the product. Of course (1) requires practices of contracting and institutions for the protection of contracting, and (2) requires not only knowing how to project worker acceptance of a new technology of production but, indeed, the very existence of markets, along with ways of estimating their strength.

In the light of such considerations, here only indicated, one can hardly be sanguine as one looks east of Western Europe. It is hard to escape the conclusions that World War II ended only in 1989, that an international Marshall Plan need not and cannot await the total dismantling of entrenched adversarial relations, and that a monetarily based plan is going to require the substantial supplement of human resources. Citizens of advanced nations will need to become teachers and models of alternative social organizations.

I say these things for the simplest and most basic of reasons. People are not inclined to be patient when plans for economic or political reform leave them starving. People will sacrifice themselves for the clear benefit of their children, but they will not willingly sacrifice themselves for the sake of political causes divorced from life's central passions and projects. The social evolution that created the modern West will not be repeated at the pace at which it originally occurred—either it will be catalyzed through agency within economically developed nations or a different evolution, perhaps less morally happy, will occur.

Child claims that Gorbachev's problems are largely internal, with the implication that they are problems the people east of a united Western Europe must resolve for themselves. But let us look a bit more closely. The Balkan states have not resigned themselves to solving their problems independently. Instead, one witnesses scientific, technological, and commercial alliances with Sweden, Finland, and Norway. Hungary and Czechoslovakia seek similar alliances with Austria, Germany, and Switzerland. Gorbachev's problems differ from those of leaders in these nations partly because of the geographic, ethnic, and religious differences the Soviet Union encompasses and partly because of the geographic remove of the Soviet Union from the West, but they are problems susceptible of interdependent resolution.

In most developmentally minded countries, the power of ethnic nationalism is, to a significant extent, the attraction any historically nurtured identity has for people whose objective circumstances give them little else on which to build. Their identities, their lives, their projects are in want of motivational foundation, and the power of the attraction is fueled by the desperation of their circumstances. Certainly leaders whose power grows from that desperation will (continue to) be very credible in the eyes of their followers when they brand the West in general and the United States in particular as their enemies.

My argument, then, is that if we accept Child's view of Gorbachev's problems as mainly internal (and hence beyond our reach), we accept the view that the projected and desired hopes for political and economic reform so prevalent in 1990 are likely to be quashed: (1) Without broadscale aid, proffered and accepted, the reforms are likely to come slowly and unsteadily; (2) desperate people will not willingly tolerate slowness plus unsteadiness. Consequently, less friendly and less democratic governments may easily arise, either because a people's revolution creates them or because a people's revolution is defeated.

When Florida realized that it was composed of individuals, commercial enterprises, and industrial enterprises, none of them in a position to avoid continued inefficient uses of energy, the state wisely decided that rational players should not want to continue playing negative-sum games. When the structure of a game demands that rational players play it in a negative-sum way, it is wise to remember that the only demand on the players is that if they play the game, they play it in a negative-sum way.

There is no abstract demand that they play the game. Child urges that the circumstances of a person literally under the gun may constitute a demand on that person to play the game. The argument of the segmented pacifist, however, is that the circumstances of the person literally under the gun are not universal. When the structure of a game is negative sum and the dire circumstances of some parties demand their participation, morality places a significant, perhaps an enormous, demand on parties who do not share those circumstances. Far better than allowing oneself to be sucked into the consequences of the continuation of the game is the altruistic impulse[25] to catalyze the transformation of the game's structure.

The positive concept of peace therefore implies the wisdom of rejecting the conventional concept of the internal political and economic reforms of a nation-state as outside the province of another nation-state and its citizens. Prosperous nation-states, whose stability in considerable part depends on the prosperity and freedom of its citizens, should want to encourage the broadest range of secure, fail-safe, and damage-controlled initiatives with the reform minded. In turn, reform-minded governments, whose stability in considerable part depends on the willingness of its people to endure continued hardship, should want to provide the broadest range of assurances to those interested in significant initiatives. Securities can be improved; fail-safe packages can be rendered more feasible and damages less likely and less extensive. These possibilities portend positive-sum exchanges.

Windows of opportunity are not always long lived. Actions must be not only forthright and immediate but also substantive and self-reinforcing. The avoidance of nuclear war, as great a goal as that, must not overshadow the pursuit of positive peace. The need of our time is for hundreds of millions of people whose circumstances are not dire to invent the evolution of many series of positive-sum games, scientific, technological, economic, educational, and cultural, each based on the assets available to the agents. Without such evolution, the bud of peace is likely to fade, not flower. Yet, with such evolution come not only diminished threats of war but building blocks of a true and substantial *shalom.*

JAMES W. CHILD

Afterword

The inconceivable has happened. Unless appearances deceive, the events of August 19 through September 6, 1991, have changed the world forever. The cold war, it would appear, is over, completely and irrevocably. But the reason for its ending is even more startling. It is over because one of the parties no longer exists, at least not in a recognizable form. At this writing, the Communist party of the Soviet Union has been dissolved, as has the Union itself as the strong, centralized government we had grown to know—to be replaced, it is supposed, with a loose confederation of republics along the lines of the European Community.

All of these monumental developments can easily transfix our critical faculties. Yet a degree of skepticism and prudence is in order. We must remember that there remain approximately twelve million Communist party members in the Soviet Union, a million or so of whom were professional party functionaries, presumably now to be unemployed. To them, we must add three-quarters of a million professional military officers and non-coms as well as three-quarters of a million KGB officers. Some, although by no means all, of these people must be embittered and deeply alienated by the rapid movement toward a multi-party, democratic confederation and free markets.

This group might still form what the Soviet liberals now fearfully call a "party of revenge." Indeed, Victor Alksnis, the archconservative "Dark Colonel," who led a like-minded bloc in the Supreme Soviet, has said that the botched coup of August 19–21 was only a "tactical defeat." The battle, he claims, is not over. Likewise, all the nationalist and xenophobic forces referred to in the text remain, waiting for the liberals to fail, waiting perhaps for a cold and hungry winter.

Still, no one can deny that the developments of these historic weeks are profoundly positive, full of promise for a happier, more peaceful world. Can we make sense of them given the two paths toward peace set out in this book? Yes we can. By practicing firm war avoidance under a right of collective self-defense, the West, especially NATO, contained what almost all, including Russian liberals, now agree was a potentially aggressive dictatorship. In the years from 1945 to 1985, the West maintained a stable, strategic balance, avoiding both nuclear war and acquiescence to Soviet military threats. In deterring aggression the path I advocate in the text was a necessary condition to peace.

Many of the measures Scherer advocates played as crucial a role, as well. The institutions of peace, including international organizations, arms control, trade and cultural ties, and a general willingness to engage in peaceful intercourse built a foundation of trust, especially during the Gorbachev years of 1985–1991. The West showed the Soviet people as well as their leaders a peaceful face. Because of this, the vast majority of them came to feel safe without the protection of a giant military machine and the discipline of a militant Communist party and KGB. Moreover, during the momentous weeks of August 1991, the ability of the Soviet people to communicate with the West and through it with each other was central in the failure of the coup. People understanding each other was, as Scherer claims, crucial. This was truly a people-to-people revolution, sometimes mediated by governments, often not.

Where do we go from here? The Soviet peoples face the daunting task of building not only a new political system but a new civil society. How might their future course be charted along the two paths toward peace delineated in this book?

Foremost among the tasks of the Soviet peoples is the establishing of the rule of law. There must be effective, *legitimate* sovereign power in order to provide for security and social stability. Yet it must operate within the confines of the rule of law. The temptation to punish Communists merely for their political beliefs must be avoided. Any punishment to be meted out to genuine criminals of the past regime must come within the framework of the due process of law. In all of this, the responsible use of force attended by violence is only acceptable when necessary and rigorously circumscribed by the rules of the justified violence view. Remember, unnecessary use of violence is *ipso facto* illegitimate, inviting escalating responses, and ultimately social chaos.

The rule of law, however, only establishes legitimate political authority, and Soviet society also lacks a freely evolved social order. The Soviet Union was a totalitarian social order in the technical sense of that term. In other words, the party and the state infused every aspect of social life. The political sphere replaced the civil society, namely, the economic, the social, and the cultural spheres. As Scherer discusses, a free civil society grows spontaneously, out of people-to-people contacts and resulting practices of reciprocal coordination. Indeed, the free markets the Soviets so badly need are good examples of such spontaneous structures.

Part of the necessary foundation of free markets are codes of laws governing property, contracts, corporations, and the more specialized institutions of a commercial society. In the West these foundations themselves evolved out of people-to-people contacts, over a period of centuries. The new free confederated republics, however, will lack the luxury of that slow evolution. As the United States, in its infancy, adopted most of the framework of the English common law of commerce, so the new republics must, for the time being, weave huge chunks of existent frameworks into the legal fabric of their society. A comprehensive, relatively stable, confederation-wide commercial code, undergirding markets, is a key necessary condition for attracting foreign capital and making effective use of it. Without foreign capital, the confederated republics, especially without the Baltics, will undergo sufficient human suffering to fuel discontent and civil discord. A revolution and some form of tyranny could easily follow.

In the long run, of course, the commercial code of the confederated republics must evolve in response to the spontaneous decisions of many people-to-people contacts within the republics and between their people and the people of other societies. These contacts can and should develop into commercial, technical, cultural, academic, and personal ties. For people outside the republics to initiate and to strengthen such ties will help the Soviet peoples build a new civil society. Moreover, these activities will help to ensure that the republics are peaceful. Civil wars, inter-republic wars, and wider wars are all discouraged when it is plain that they jeopardize the benefits of a productive economic union and social system. The more alike the foundations of our commercial societies become, without sacrificing our cultural and historical plurality, the less likely we are to have conflict.

Beyond this, the West must be willing to mount a substantial aid effort. Short-term humanitarian aid will doubtless be needed this winter and, perhaps, for several winters to come. The cost of our refusal might well mean the return of tyranny. Moreover, the slower Western governments are to act, the greater will be the amounts of aid required. Long-term investment capital to build a new economic infrastructure, dedicated to pursuits of peace, not the implements of war, is essential to save what was the Soviet Union from counterrevolution, xenophobic nationalism, indeed even nuclear civil war or nuclear terrorism. Just what form this capital infusion will take is yet to be worked out. No doubt, much of it will and should flow from private investors to private entrepreneurs. Some of it, however, will doubtless have to be mediated in some way by Western governments, if for no other reason than to provide insurance against political instability. Such long-term aid must, of course, be contingent on a shrinking military budget and continuing democratic and free market reform. But that the Western governments should provide this capital, or at least facilitate its provision by those private parties who are willing to provide it, cannot be doubted. It is a matter not only of charitable motives but also of the interests we in the West have in common with the interests of the Soviet peoples. Exploiting common interests to the benefit of both parties is a central tenant in both paths toward peace. The dividends such capital aid will pay to our world and the world of our children are incalculable.

Humankind stands at the beginning of a bold new adventure. It is fraught with terrifying dangers of inter-ethnic bloodletting and nuclear instability. But it also offers peace, prosperity, and human happiness realized on a scale undreamed of a short decade ago. As we begin this venture, we must not forget, however, the lessons learned along the two paths toward peace.

NOTES

Chapter 1: A Defense of Justified Violence

1. This point neglects the terribly difficult problem of defense by deterrence and punishment as deterrence. Since punishment is not our subject, we likewise avoid discussing punishment as a form of deterrence. There is one caveat: Only punishment as *specific deterrence* could ever be considered under a right of resistance to attack. That is, if you have a history of violently attacking people, punishing you (violently or otherwise) could deter your future attacks and be seen as defending your potential future victims. Suffice it to say that this is a deep issue and is sufficiently removed from our topic to allow us to avoid it. Note, however, specific deterrence is not the same thing as the preemption of a violent attack using violence. Preemption will prove most relevant to our concerns.

2. In describing the assault of the Greek hero Diomedes on the Trojans, Homer says, "As for Diomedes, he raged so widely across the plain, it was hard to tell whether he fought more on the Achaean or the Trojan side. Like the swelling flood of a thawing river, no dikes could hold him. For as no walls of fruitful vineyards can embank the torrent of its fresh, spring flow, but in a moment does its rain-swollen fury burst through, laying waste the hard fought gains of noble men, so Diomedes, displaying that same ungovernable violence, stormed the dense battalions of the enemy, driving them back, though they were many. But, confused before him, they dared not withstand his onslaught." Homer, *Iliad* 5:85–94, as translated by Donald Scherer from the 1931 Oxford University Press edition of the text prepared by Thomas William Allan.

3. Concerning Samson, the biblical writer tells us that "when he came to Lehi, the Philistines came shouting to meet him; and the Spirit of the Lord came mightily upon him, and the ropes which were on his arms became as flax that has caught fire, and his bonds melted off his hands. And he found a fresh jawbone of an ass, and put out his hand and seized it, and with it he slew a thousand men. And Samson said, 'With the jawbone of an ass, / heaps upon heaps, / with the jawbone of an ass / have I slain a thousand men.' " Judges 15:14–16. And of Joshua and Israel, it is said that when "Joshua and all Israel saw that the ambush had taken the city [of Ai], and that the smoke of the [burning] city went up, then they turned back and smote the men of Ai. And the others came forth from the city against them;

so they were in the midst of Israel, some on this side and some on that side; and Israel smote them, until there was left none that survived or escaped." Joshua 8:21, 22.

4. In addition to several passages that more directly echo those quoted above, we find the following endorsement of virtues based on norms of violence: "Wiglaf spoke in sorrow of soul, / With bitter reproach rebuking his comrades: / 'I remember the time, as we drank in the mead-hall, / When we swore to our lord who bestowed these rings / That we would repay for the war-gear and armor, / The hard swords and helmets, if need like this / Should ever befall him. He chose us out / From all the host for this high adventure / Deemed us worthy of glorious deeds, / Gave me these treasures, regarded us all / As high-hearted bearers of helmet and spear—Though our lord himself, the shield of his people, / Thought single-handed to finish this feat, / Since of mortal men his measure was most / Of feats of daring and deeds of fame. / Now is the day that our lord has need / Of the strength and courage of stalwart men. / Let us haste to succor his sore distress / In the horrible heat and the merciless flame. / God knows I had rather the fire should enfold / My body and limbs with my gold-friend and lord. / Shameful it seems that we carry our shields / Back to our homes ere we harry the foe / And ward the life of the Weder king." *Beowulf and the Finnesburg Fragment*, trans. John R. Clark Hall (London: Allen and Unwin, 1950), ll. 2631–2654. We have occasion to discuss oaths of vengeance and the emotions that support them later.

5. They may tell us something about human beings and their innate tendencies. Indeed, that these emotional appeals so often work and that we are so fond of telling such stories offers at least prima facie evidence that we do, as a species, tend to violence in the way many thinkers (Freud and Lorenz among the more prominent) claim.

6. See their essays in Jerome A. Shaffer, ed., *Violence* (New York: McKay, 1971); and Robert L. Holmes, *On War and Morality* (Princeton: Princeton University Press, 1989), chap. 1.

7. This point oversimplifies two issues. First, it reinforces my admittedly controversial claim that violence must be intentional, which entails that there can be no violence that is the result of negligence or unavoidable accident. Second, it ignores a distinction often made between violence as purposive and nonpurposive violence done knowingly. An act done for some other purpose may have violent consequences that were known to follow but were not the purpose of the act. Such are often called *double effects*. Here I mean to include under the intentional condition foreknown effects, even if they are not the purpose of the act. Thus, if we blast an enemy bridge (not by itself violence against persons) and in the process knowingly kill

some people crossing the bridge, that act constitutes violence by double effect and is for my purposes an act of violence. Given these provisos, my oversimplication in the text is benign.

8. Thus our definition excludes the kind of case to which Newton Garver refers in his article "What Violence Is," *The Nation*, June 24, 1968, 817–822, reprinted in A. K. Bierman and J. Gould, *Philosophy for a New Generation*, 4th ed. (New York: Macmillan, 1981), p. 218. He quotes the following from the *New York Times*:

> Phoenix, Ariz., Feb. 6 (AP) Marie Ault killed herself, policemen said today, rather than make her dog Beauty pay for her night with a married man.
>
> The police quoted the parents, Mr. and Mrs. Joseph Ault, as giving this account:
>
> Linda failed to return home from a dance in Tempe Friday night. On Saturday she admitted she had spent the night with an Air Force lieutenant. The Aults decided on a punishment that would "wake Linda up." They ordered her to shoot the dog she had owned about two years.
>
> On Sunday, the Aults and Linda took the dog into the desert near their home. They had the girl dig a shallow grave. Then Mrs. Ault grasped the dog between her hands, and Mr. Ault gave his daughter a .22-caliber pistol and told her to shoot the dog.
>
> Instead, the girl put the pistol to her right temple and shot herself. The police said there were no charges that could be filed against the parents except possibly cruelty to animals.

As morally outrageous as this story is, and as *wrong* as what the parents did was, on our definition (or I believe on any correct definition) this is not violence. Indeed, it serves to warn us of a mistake that Garver may have fallen into, one we all often commit. We find something such as racial discrimination or verbal sexual harassment so morally outrageous that we label it violence. This is a metaphorical usage, and we court confusion, perhaps even moral mistake, if we conflate it with literal usage. As Reinhold Neibuhr pointed out, there are other kinds of *evil* than violence. Sometimes violence is not even the worst evil.

9. "Violent institutions" are also discussed in Garver, "What Violence Is."
10. Holmes, *On War and Morality*, chap. 1.
11. Thomas Nagel, "The Limits of Objectivity," *The Tanner Lectures on Human Values*, vol. 1 (Cambridge: Cambridge University Press, 1980), pp. 109–110. For further elaboration of this same point, see Nagel's *The View from Nowhere* (Oxford: Oxford University Press, 1986), pp. 156–162.
12. It may be that this right is not absolute and can be overcome in some very

unusual cases. That is, we want to leave the door open for paternalism, wherein we can overcome a person's will and force a painful medical procedure on the person for his or her own good. Failing that, at least, we may want to justify the same for purposes of the general welfare, to stop an outbreak of a highly infectious disease, perhaps. Nonetheless, the right not to be put involuntarily in pain is a *very strong* presumptive right.

The notion of rights more generally are presumed throughout and will constantly cause trouble between Scherer and me. We have both tried not to turn this work into a debate on liberal rights theory. Suffice it to say here that I make the traditional assumptions of liberalism that people have a variety of very basic and very strong (if not absolute) rights. The list will emerge throughout this discussion.

It is obvious that I cannot plumb the foundational issues of basic rights, their meaning and justification, in a work such as this. It is equally obvious that both their nature and existence is problematic. For me, in this work their existence must occupy the role of a *working hypothesis*.

13. Garver, "What Violence Is."

14. See William Prosser, *The Law of Torts* (St. Paul, Minn.: West, 1964), pp. 32–36.

15. See Wayne R. LaFave and Austin W. Scott, Jr., *Handbook on Criminal Laws* (St. Paul, Minn.: West, 1974), pp. 604–605; and *Model Penal Code* 211.1(1)(c).

16. See *Model Penal Code* 213.0(2) and 213.1(1) or *Ohio Revised Code* 2907.01 (A).

17. Generally, torture would be aggravated battery (or in the language of some codes, "aggravated assault"). See, for example, *New York Penal Law*, 120.10. It is still occasionally considered mayhem. See LaFave and Scott, *Handbook on Criminal Laws*, pp. 614–615.

18. Can violence ever be consensual or voluntary? Yes, it certainly can. One good example is boxing. However we feel about boxing, I believe that most would agree that since two boxers in a ring have both consented, have both been compensated, and have both trained, and since they are more or less evenly matched and their activity is governed by rules, enforced by an omnipresent referee, the boxers are not dehumanized in the way a rape or torture victim is. (This is *not* to say there is nothing dehumanizing about boxing. I believe there are several such things.)

19. Here I am clearly relying on the moral philosophy of Immanuel Kant, as set out primarily in *The Fundamental Principles of a Metaphysics of Morals*, trans. Lewis White Beck (Indianapolis: Bobbs-Merrill, 1954). It was Kant's view that the heart of any moral philosophy must be in the recognition that human beings are, to use his language, "ends in themselves not means

only." That is, their value is ultimate, not instrumental; they are not to be *used* as things are used.

20. We do not take up the very difficult question of conscription in this work.

21. 80 *Corpus Juris Secundum* 1317. See also, Baron de Montesquieu, *The Spirit of the Laws*, trans. Thomas Nugent (New York: Scribner's, 1949), bk. XV, pp. 235–237. John Locke, *Second Treatise of Government* (New York: Cambridge University Press, 1960), secs. 17, 22, 23, 135, 137; and Jean Jacques Rosseau, "The Social Contract," in *The Social Contract and Discourses*, trans. G. D. H. Cole (New York: Dutton, 1950), bk. I, chap. IV, pp. 7–12. See also "A Discourse on the Origin of Inequality," in ibid.

22. Just what the right to life consists in is not clear. Is it a right to continued life? Is it a right to invade others' rights, even to take their life to protect your own? See Judith Jarvis Thomson, "Self-Defense and Rights," in *Rights, Restitution and Risk* (Cambridge: Harvard University Press, 1986), chap. 3, for a deep discussion of these issues.

Perhaps the right to life is only the right not to have your life wrongfully taken, but of course that only forces the issue back to the question of "wrongful taking." But whatever this right consists in and however it is analyzed, most agree we have it, and Western law presupposes it.

23. Charles Fried, *Right and Wrong* (Cambridge: Cambridge University Press, 1978), pp. 44–45.

24. In the language of modern action theory, these acts are intentional "under the description" of rights-violating activity.

25. Perhaps the most famous recent statement of the contrast between a theory of value and a theory of the right is John Rawls, *A Theory of Justice* (Cambridge: Harvard University Press, 1971), pp. 446–452. But I learned more about these issues in conversations with L. W. Sumner than from any written material.

26. Jan Narveson, "Pacifism: A Philosophic Analysis," *Ethics* 75 (1965): 259–271.

27. Deriving a right to self-defense and a defense of innocent others out of the clash of rights of the attacker, the victim, and the defender can be seen as an in-house argument among rights theorists, and since Scherer has little sympathy for rights theories and rights language generally, our exchange avoids this thicket.

28. There are several excellent discussions of the right of self-defense. See Thomson, *Rights, Restitution and Risk*, chap. 4. In what follows I rely on Philip Montague, "Self Defense and Choosing between Lives," *Philosophical Studies* 40 (1981), and a critique of this paper contained in David Wasserman, "Justifying Self Defense," *Philosophy and Public Affairs* 16, no. 4 (Fall 1987). Also, I am indebted to "Justifying Self Defense," an un-

published paper by Jefferson McMahon and to conversations with him on the subject.

29. My definitions of violence and aggression greatly simplify my task. For the most serious problems in self-defense come from the possibility of "innocent aggressors," whose behavior is not wrongful. Within this large literature, the reader might see Eric Mack, "Three Ways to Kill Innocent Bystanders," *Social Philosophy and Policy* 3, no. 1 (Autumn 1985): 1–26. For us, a violent attack is ipso facto intentional and, if not itself defensive, a wrong committed by the attacker.

30. Cf. Thomson, *Rights, Restitution and Risks*.

31. Fried, *Right and Wrong*.

32. The analysis that follows tracks very closely with that set out in James W. Child, *Nuclear War: The Moral Dimension* (New Brunswick, N.J.: Transaction Books, 1986), pp. 27–28.

33. This construction of a national right of self-defense is due entirely to Locke. See *Second Treatise on Government*, chaps. 2 and 8. A good secondary source is Richard H. Cox, *Locke on War and Peace* (Washington, D.C.: University Press of America), esp. chaps. 3 and 4.

34. See D. H. Baker, *An Introduction to English Legal History*, 2nd ed. (London: Butterworth, 1979), chap. 24; or S. F. C. Milsom, *Historical Foundations of the Common Law* (London: Butterworth, 1969), pp. 352–374.

35. Authoritative discussions can be found in James Turner Johnson, *Just War and the Restraint of War* (Princeton: Princeton University Press, 1981); and Michael Walzer, *Just and Unjust Wars* (New York: Basic Books, 1977). Shorter treatments include Child, *Nuclear War*, chap. 2; and James E. Dougherty, *The Bishops and Nuclear Weapons* (Hamden, Conn.: Archon Books, 1984), chap. 2.

36. A further discussion of this very problematic provision of the Justified Violence View must be deferred until later.

37. This definition is taken largely whole from Kenneth Boulding, *Conflict and Defense* (New York: Harper, 1962), p. 5.

38. See Wasserman, "Justifying Self Defense," p. 371ff.

39. This perspective was pointed out to me by Scherer.

40. This may be an example of an "agent sacrificing permission." Cf. Michael Slote, *Common Sense Morality and Consequentialism* (London: Routledge and Kegan Paul, 1985), chaps. 1 and 2.

Chapter 2: A Critique of Justified Violence

1. Child's philosophical reflections, as his endnotes document, are themselves built on the writings of many other prominent philosophers who have contributed to the Western liberal tradition.

2. See p. 33 in Child's Chapter 1.

3. The Balantas and the Djolas, the so-called primitive tribes Walter Rodney discusses in *A History of the Upper Guinea Coast, 1545–1800* (Oxford: Clarendon Press, 1970), are the nonstate, egalitarian tribes to which I refer.

Child takes no position on the question of punishment. Nor do I discuss West African conceptions of justice in order to relate punishment either to pacifism or to the Minimal Justified Violence View. Instead, I am attempting to elicit what might be a better goal than the defense of human rights, what sort of action might protect the values that the construct of rights is designed to protect without the unhappiness that has accompanied safeguarding those values by action based on the assertion of rights. For an advocate of Minimal Justified Violence, the justifying motivation for action is the violence done against a victim of aggression. The following discussion is pertinent because it explores this question: "What alternative motivation might ground the justification of a different action?"

4. What I mean by social practices contrasts with Alasdair MacIntyre's views in his *After Virtue* (Notre Dame, Ind.: University of Notre Dame Press, 1981):

> A practice involves standards of excellence and obedience to rules as well as the achievement of goods. To enter into a practice is to accept the authority of those standards and the inadequacy of my own performance as judged by them. It is to subject my own attitudes, choices, preferences and taste to standards which currently and partially define the practice. Practices of course, as I have just noticed, have a history: games, sciences and arts all have histories. Thus the standards are not themselves immune from criticism, but none the less we cannot be initiated into a practice without accepting the authority of the best standards realized so far. (p. 177)

In this passage, MacIntyre makes many claims. He immediately involves the normative ideas of standards of excellence, obedience to rules, and the achievement of goods. A dialectic between them is suggested, but remains unexplicated. In these general ways, my view coincides with MacIntyre's.

In contrast to MacIntyre, who shuns the biological basis of Aristotle's views, I note the biological root of the concept of a social practice in the fact that human beings are social animals. Evolutionary theorists tell us that human community is valuable because human interdependence facilitates meeting the needs of adult humans. Human beings are thus interdependent in their needs for food, protection, nurture, and affection. The things that are fundamentally good for a human being are accordingly things good for all human beings. And to the extent that interdependence has facilitated the achievement of these goods, these goods are also social. Human society, then, rests on biological commonalities, namely, the large extent to which the fundamental human goods are both goods for all persons and goods obtained through interdependence.

The justification of any evolution of social practices cannot rest on what is peculiarly of value only for some, since the justification must appeal to a basis on which people can be expected to agree. Accordingly, the justification of the evolution of social practices must finally appeal to goods in common. (MacIntyre emphasizes the function that teleology plays in Aristotle and in Christian thought, but he never affirms the pivotal role of goods in common. When, however, the issue is one of the criticism of a practice, goods in common provide the only available, that is, "in common," basis on which human beings can hope to agree.)

The initial list of these goods is derived from the social animals we have been for perhaps two million years. (One might speculate that the emotions of social animals have evolved to facilitate the success of the animals in surviving, reproducing, and insuring the survival of dependent young, given ambivalent alliance formations in social environments.) Additions to that list of goods in common arise when generally beneficial social practices create additional common goods, among which one might well number the virtues and the values arising from reflective self-understanding.

One feature of a practice is that it may operate in conjunction with other practices so as to achieve goods, define standards of excellence, and generate rules of conduct that would not be derivable were the practices not operating simultaneously. Accordingly, my talk of practices will often fudge whether I am referring to a single practice or some cooperative set of practices.

5. Can there be psychological violence without physical violence? I think so. Almost every human being has affectional ties. As Child's reference to Garver indicates, some of those ties are strong enough that one would prefer harming oneself to disrupting those ties. Sometimes others know those ties exist. This knowledge can be used to compromise the person with such ties. A system of law may find it difficult to respond to such cases. After all, the affectional ties of individuals differ, and these ties will be difficult to prove within the standards of proof courts feel constrained to employ. But this difficulty of proving within a judicial practice should not blind us to so pernicious a reality as a demonic torturer may employ.

6. The importance of this point is suggested by a study conducted by the psychologist Philip Zimbardo in 1987. He divided student volunteers into two groups: prisoners and prison guards. Each group was asked to play its appropriate role relative to the other. An environment was provided that closely approximated an authentic prison. The "prisoners" and the "guards" were observed for ten days. Within days, the "prison guards" began treating the "prisoners" in humiliating fashions, the "prisoners" came to feel de-

meaned, and the "prison guards" began to feel justified in their "necessarily harsh" treatment of the "prisoners." Toward the end of the ten days, the prison guards were becoming increasingly sadistic and the prisoners were responding in an obedient and timid manner.

7. Bryce Lyon, *A Constitutional and Legal History of Medieval England* (New York: Norton, 1980), pp. 83–86, gives an interesting account not only of the practice of revenge in England in the centuries immediately following the departure of the Romans but also of the complex evolution toward a practice of providing compensation to the kindred of whoever suffered violence.

8. Obviously, what I argue here concerning acts of revenge has its analogue in war, as Gandhi urged. When nations A and B wage war against each other, we can easily imagine that whatever violence B can muster will lead A only to undertake more violent aggression. This syndrome of new aggressive violence and new retaliatory violence may repeat itself indefinitely, however trivial the original source of conflict. This is one aspect of the escalatory cycle of violence Gandhi believed to be part of its very nature.

9. Historians now commonly view the French insistence on the return of Alsace-Lorraine in this light.

10. The view sketched is only a part of Gandhi's theory of *satyagraha*, literally, "insistence on truth." Having here expounded Gandhi's view as it implicitly criticizes Child's, I postpone until Part II a further exposition of the constructive portion of Gandhi's view.

11. That rights can be violated only by human action will seem to some a definitional truth. But it remains that the goods that rights are designed to protect are often compromised or negated by natural or social conditions not intended to bring about harm but that could be controlled so as to prevent harm. Here I merely foreshadow the difficulty explored later concerning the inclusion of "intention" in one's definition of violence.

12. In *The Cherry Orchard*, Anton Chekhov presents the alienation of Mme. Ranevskaya at the loss of the cherry orchard, in chilling contrast to the oblivious Anya and Trofimov, especially in the final scene where Mme. Ranevskaya takes her poignant leave of the orchard, while the gay voices of Anya and Trofimov are heard offstage, followed finally by the sounds of the strokes of an ax against a tree far away in the orchard.

13. In *A Doll's House*, Henrik Ibsen concentrates on the alienation between Nora and her husband, Torvard, who in the final scene says to the departing Nora, "Let me help you if you are in want." At which point the following dialogue ensues:

> *Nora:* No, I can receive nothing from a stranger.
> *Torvard:* Nora—can I never be anything more than a stranger to you?

> *Nora:* Ah, Torvard, the most wonderful thing of all would have to happen.
> *Torvard:* Tell me what that would be!
> *Nora:* Both you and I would have to be so changed that—. Oh, Torvard, I don't believe any longer in wonderful things happening.

From *The Works of Henrik Ibsen* (New York: Blue Ribbon Books, 1928), p. 215.

14. In *Our Town*, after Emily's funeral, Emily senses that she can return to her previous life, and against the advice of the others in the cemetery, she returns to relive her twelfth birthday. But having returned, she finds the moments of life and the relations to others so precious that she realizes how mundane they are for the living. Finally, Wilder has her retreat to the cemetery, saying, "I can't. I can't go on. It goes so fast. We don't have time to look at one another." Thornton Wilder, *Our Town* (New York: Harper & Row, 1938), p. 100.

15. It is Roberto Unger, in his book *Knowledge and Politics* (New York: Free Press, 1975), who has made plainest to me how the allegedly subjective and individual character of all human desire is at the heart of the modern mentality and the center of the modern political organizations that replace the ancient Greek philosophical view that what is good for human beings can be derived from what is essential to human nature. Since I do not believe in essences, it is not my intention to resurrect ancient philosophical views. Instead, my argument is that a careful examination of human experience makes it evident that the desires for life, self-development, prosperity, and justice are neither arbitrary nor merely subjective. Their roots are in both the common human sentiments and the universal conditions of human life.

16. Very significantly, no nation must submit itself to the jurisdiction of the World Court.

17. Many will be ready to ask whether I mean my views generally enough to include, say, Hitler's march into Poland in 1939. My reply here is that the argument I have just given is part of a dialectic. If my general argument is faulty, the question is how the case of Poland in 1939 shows its fault. I leave this to Child.

18. The superior alternative for intrasocial conflict is defined in the discussion of *aikido* and stun guns and somewhat modified in Part III; the superior alternative for intersocial conflict is defined in Part IV, partly by what Child says about making military arsenals safer and partly by my peace-building proposals.

19. I recur to this topic to discharge the difficulty of interpreting the evidence in the section on violence and in Part III.

20. I detail my views of how the value of life and the value of human life relate in "A Disentropic Ethic," *The Monist*, January 1988.

21. Both meanings of "partial" are appropriate to this sentence.

22. The reader is reminded that even in a society with an established legal system, much of life is so conducted as not to fall within the compass of the system.

23. To see how far-reaching are the reversibility of presumptions about intentions and perspectival histories based on facts derived from contrary understandings of the status quo ante, notice how those premises drive the following litany of adversarial babble: "I didn't really want X; I only said I did as a negotiating posture." "If I had said what I really wanted, the extent of my true weakness might have become apparent." "I said I intended to get X because I did not see any other means of securing my true goal, Y." "I realized we could achieve what we both wanted through means Y, but I never thought you would be willing (or able) to cooperate on that." "When I said I wanted X, I never thought it would harm you." "Your insistence on Z seemed to pose threat T to me." "Even though we both wanted Y, it was obvious neither of us would take the first step toward bringing Y about, and it wasn't obvious how to take our steps in unison." "I interpreted what you did as breaking the bargain we actually made, while you interpreted what you did as pursuing the goals we shared in making that bargain." "I agreed to plan Z, which provided adequate security when the threat we faced was limited to technology W, but I do not agree that Z is adequate to the threat posed by new technology U." "When I got what I wanted, I didn't want what I got."

24. For a full discussion of the complexities arising out of attitudes toward others who have attitudes toward us, see David Lewis, *Convention* (Cambridge: Harvard University Press, 1969), chap. 1.

25. Seymour M. Hersh, *The Target Is Destroyed* (New York: Random House, 1986), pp. 17–18.

26. I do not need to overstate my point. I admit that two or more individuals can share a single intention, provided sufficient convergence in their beliefs and desires. My argument is simply that in an organization as large as the government of a contemporary state, such convergence will seldom exist, the occasions on which it may exist will in no way be especially easy to spot, and, in particular, the intentions can in no simple way be read off the behaviors of military vehicles.

27. Moreover, defining violence in terms of the use of great force seems mistaken. One does violence against a person as much by slow-acting, but secretly injected, lethal poisons as by exploding a grenade in the person's face. Of course, many actions are violent in their effect only because they are violent in their manner. If they were done less swiftly or with lesser force, they might be warded off. If they were done in a less violent manner, nonviolent responses to them would more easily and more often be

effective. Yet what is bad about violence is totally divorceable from any forcefulness of manner. And we have yet to inquire whether nonviolent force must be ineffective against swift and forceful attempts to commit violence. Might not the capacity for effective nonviolent response be relative not simply to the swiftness and forcefulness of the initiative but also to the training, technology, and alertness of any respondent? Surely the issue of what violence is should be kept separate from the issue of what response to violence may be justified, at least until the possibility of nonviolent response is considered. I shall do this, while quite reasonably reminding myself that some violence occurs swiftly and with great force.

28. We may restate those difficulties as follows:

> *a.* Adversarial presumptions play a dangerous role in the defining of intentions within evidentially underdetermined contexts.
>
> *b.* Histories are infected by this danger because the courses of action that become histories are the enactments of commitments based on presumptions about adversarial intentions.
>
> *c.* The divergent actions and statements typical of authorities within nation-states often make the concept of the intention of a nation incoherent.
>
> *d.* When adversaries attempt to keep their intentions concealed from each other, the difficulties of *a* through *c* are immensely compounded.

29. Yes, I do think these difficulties apply even in the case of Hitler's Germany. But understand how specifically I make my point. I am speaking only about intentions. In my mind, German intentions have little or no relevance to a moral judgment about the activities of the Third Reich. Accordingly, the moral judgment of those activities seems to me sufficiently clear, even though I have little epistemic confidence in assertions about national intentions.

30. The logical point is that the facts sufficiently underdetermine these ways of talking that they are regularly compatible with whatever course of action leaders choose to follow. (Not that leaders do not sometimes lie or otherwise misrepresent the facts to their people; they do.) My point is that misrepresentation need not be much—and on occasion may not be any—of what they do. The underdetermination of languages of the right in conjunction with the power of leaders to create such realities as suit their purposes will often suffice for a leader's adversarial purposes quite independent of straight-out lying.

31. The record of the use of rights talk within societies is somewhat better. The rule of law, when properly administered, can lead to a social order in which the violence typical of revenge practices can be curbed. One must not there-

fore be contemptuous in criticizing the use of rights talk within societies. The argument I have made, however, is that the alienation of individuals from the community of human concerns is a significant price, a price one might hope not to need to pay were the appropriate social practices and institutions to develop.

32. Jean Hampton's recent work on explaining the origin of the state emphasizes the roles of coordination games in the evolution of social structures. See Jean Hampton, *Hobbes and the Social Contract Tradition* (Cambridge: Cambridge University Press, 1987).

33. Indeed many developments in world events since I began this manuscript in 1985 offer confirmation of my view. But I note that I began this manuscript in 1985 to caution the reader against interpreting me as assuming the inevitability of the history of the late 1980s; my arguments do not assume anything like the history of Soviet politics in the late 1980s.

Introduction to Part II

1. We mean here *sincere* threats, that is, ones that the threatener is prepared to carry out. It is not clear that a pacifist would have to reject bluffing uses of threats of violence.

2. Robert L. Holmes, "Violence and Non-Violence," in *Violence*, ed. Jerome A. Shaffer (New York: McKay, 1971), p. 113.

3. Jonathan Glover, *Causing Death and Saving Lives* (London: Pelican, 1977), p. 256.

4. *Tolstoy's Letters*, vol. 2, *1880–1910*, trans. and ed. R. F. Christian (New York: Scribner's, 1978), p. 707. The reader should note that although the cited passage from Tolstoy focuses on not killing, Tolstoy himself actually advocated the more radical view of nonresistance.

5. This is close to Child's theory, developed in Part I. It is also close to Reinhold Niebuhr's view, discussed later.

Chapter 3: Problems with Traditional Forms of Pacifism

1. Quoted in Joan V. Bondurant, *Conquest of Violence: The Gandhian Philosophy of Conflict* (Princeton: Princeton University Press, 1958), p. 24. For a further elaboration of this key notion, see pp. 23–26 and 111–113. See also William Borman, *Gandhi and Non-Violence* (Albany, N.Y.: SUNY Press, 1986), chap. 1.

2. "Not reducable" here can mean at least two things and we want to construe it most broadly to include *both*.

    a. An ultimate value is not *commensurable* with other values such that units of that value can be translated or reduced without remainder to units of some other value, as quarts to pints.

    b. There exists no other value that "trumps" or lexically dominates it. Lexically, *u* dominates *v* just where any amount of *u*, however small, is better than any amount of *v*, however large.

Note that an ultimate value typically will both trump all other values and reduce them to it, but not conversely. My colleague Tom Attig raised this issue.

3. See Bondurant, *Conquest of Violence*, esp. chaps. 2 and 4; Borman, *Gandhi and Non-Violence*, esp. pt. I; and Bhikhu Parekh, *Gandhi's Political Philosophy* (Notre Dame, Ind: University of Notre Dame Press, 1989), chaps. 3 and 4.

4. Reinhold Niebuhr, *Christianity and Power Politics* (New York: Scribner's, 1940), esp. pp. 8–18.

5. Mary Midgley, *Wickedness: A Philosophical Essay* (London: Routledge and Kegan Paul, 1984), p. 2.

6. This last is an empirical, ultimately psychological, claim, that stands in need of confirmation, although it is often asserted as a first principle. Indeed, if the historian Crain Brinton was correct, it is most often when a people discover hope and rising expectations that they become violent, in what he called a "revolution of rising expectations." So the most exploited and repressed may not be the first to have recourse to violence.

7. Ibid., p. 26.

8. I do not want to attribute particular cogency to my anecdotal impressions of the nature of human beings. This, after all, is an empirical question and a matter for social science. I offer them only as an *example* of a relatively optimistic view of human nature that, nonetheless, will not support pacifism.

9. Thomas Schelling, *Micromotives and Macrobehavior* (New York: Norton, 1978), chap. 3.

10. It probably is smaller, since I believe the very large majority of humans has a deep aversion to killing others of our species.

11. This Prisoners' Dilemma is just a modified version of the more well known one that applies to disarmament between the superpowers.

12. Coercion is a terribly complicated concept, which has spawned a huge philosophic literature. For good coverage of the problem and extensive references, see Alan Wertheimer, *Coercion* (Princeton: Princeton University

Press, 1987). We need not get too deeply involved in these issues, however. Our intuitive notion of coercion will serve us well here.

13. The notion of force is itself very complicated. See Jerome A. Shaffer, ed. *Violence* (New York: McKay, 1971). For our purposes, however, we can work with our intuitive conception of force.

14. James Buchanan, "The Gauthier Enterprise," *Social Philosophy and Policy* 5, no. 2 (Spring 1988).

15. It might strike you that such a chaotic society would soon run through its stock of cars and that there would be no way to renew the stock. Who would "buy a car"? If this wholesale thievery were generalized to all items of private property, would the practice of buying anything not immediately consumable ever make sense? However degenerate and collectively irrational a society like this would be, it could become stable in its anarchy for all of its citizens would be in an n-person assurance game. Thus it would be irrational for any one person to try to reestablish the institution of private property, for whatever they tried to buy or own would be stolen. This is true even though everybody would be better off with secure private property.

16. Schelling, *Micromotives and Macrobehavior*, pp. 83–133, esp. pp. 94–99.

17. Jan Narveson, "Pacifism: A Philosophical Analysis," *Ethics* 75 (1965): 254–277.

18. I presented this argument in James W. Child, "The Immorality of Pacifism," paper read for the Icelandic Philosophical Society, Reykjavik, Iceland, March 6, 1988.

19. John Rawls, *A Theory of Justice* (Cambridge: Harvard University Press, 1971), p. 388.

20. Wesley Newcomb Hohfeld, *Fundamental Legal Conceptions* (New Haven: Yale University Press, 1919), p. 65.

21. Immunities as rights are discussed in ibid.; Samuel Stoljar, *An Analysis of Rights* (New York: St. Martin's Press, 1984), pp. 61–62, 70; Carl Wellman, *A Theory of Rights* (Totowa, N.J.: Rowman and Allanheld, 1985), pp. 75–80.

22. A good discussion of the relation of rights to "ought" statements and a good argument in favor of their independence occurs in Judith Jarvis Thomson, *Rights, Restitution and Risk* (Cambridge: Harvard University Press, 1986), pp. 12–14 and 118–119.

Chapter 4: Creating a New Pacifism

1. Felix Gilbert, *Machiavelli and Guicciardini* (Princeton: Princeton University Press, 1965), p. 165ff.

2. Throughout my exposition of Confucius, I follow the scholarship of Arthur

Waley. See *The Analects of Confucius*, trans. and ed. Arthur Waley (New York: Random House, 1938).

3. Many biblical scholars note that the concept of *shalom* (especially as developed in the deuteronomic tradition) has the features I here attribute to Chinese sources.

4. As a key to understanding the evolution of practices, this is an example of how problems evolve out of the ways in which previously defined problems come to be met.

5. Here I respond to Child's "related argument" presented on p. 73ff. in Chapter 3.

6. The poet Delmore Schwartz explicates for us the character of these despicable tendencies. Asking what the finished murderer must know, he writes,

> You cannot sit on bayonets,
> Nor can you eat among the dead.
> When all are killed, you are alone.
> A vacuum come where hate has fed.
> Murder's fruit is silent stone,
> The gun increases poverty.
> With what do these examples shine?
> The soldier turned to girls and wine.
> Love is the tact of every good,
> The only warmth, the only peace.

Delmore Schwartz, "For the One Who Would Take Man's Life in His Hands," in *Summer Knowledge: Selected Poems* (New York: Doubleday, 1959), p. 54.

7. The ambivalence implicit in feeling pleased that the murderer shall die and in feeling repulsed that one feels pleased is an instance of the attitudinal flexibility I introduced in (6) on p. 92.

8. I do not say (and have not argued) that any person of any integrity will share this perception. I have thus not argued that any person who lacks this perception lacks integrity. Accordingly, when police officers endanger their own lives rather than fire into a crowd of innocent persons, they display an admirable integrity. Surely when police officers shield the innocent with their own bodies, the admirability of their action is not compromised simply by their returning an assailant's fire. The account I am giving shows only what may motivate the pacifist and what rationale the pacifist may feel. I am not arguing that the pacifist is justified, much less that everyone with other motivations and rationales is unjustified. Even if a pacifist's use of violence would violate the pacifist's not irrational and not immoral sensitivities, it does not follow that anyone who lacks those sensitivities is irrational and immoral.

9. In this regard, the experience I recall is Jean Valjean's, as written by Victor Hugo in *Les Miserables*. When Jean is apprehended after taking the silver candlesticks from the priest's home, the priest pronounces them to be a gift to Jean.

10. And such creations will not be like the rights-based responses I criticized in Chapter 2 for intensifying conflict. For these responses will aim, instead, at community building and community restoration, goals less divisive and more integrative.

11. My view is, thus, in fundamental accord with the view of Robert Frank, *Passions within Reason* (New York: Norton, 1988), that in a society genetically different predispositions of different individuals may be reinforced in a variety of social niches existing in equilibrium with each other. I am greatly indebted to Professor Frank's exposition of these ideas.

12. I am not so convinced as Child, however, that they do not "wear signs." We know, for instance, that 80 percent of all violence is committed by males. We know that 80 percent of all violence is committed by persons aged 15 to 29. We know that violent behavior is significantly correlated with intelligence, with having been abused as a child, and with success in school. We know that violence is infrequent in well-lit public places. To this day, our knowledge does not allow us to read violent criminality unambiguously off our correlations, but many (albeit equivocal) signs of violent criminality are clearly distinguishable these days. Nor would I be one to think that we have reached the pinnacle of such knowledge. Again, in accord with Professor Frank's application of evolutionary theory to human society, we should expect that the ability of persons to spot difficult-to-hide indications of antisocial intent would confer some advantage.

13. See p. 80 in Child's Chapter 3.

14. I owe many of my thoughts about the wisdom of defining force broadly to Aldous Huxley, *An Encyclopedia of Pacifism* (New York: Garland, 1972), esp. pp. 51–52.

15. "By the time of the Feudal States, 770–448 B.C., kung fu was already widely established and held in some measure of esteem," according to Christopher Keane and Herman Petras, *Handbook of the Martial Arts and Self-Defense* (New York: Barnes and Noble, 1975), p. 1.

16. Emil Farkas and John Corcoran describe *aikido* as an "unarmed method of self-defense founded in Tokyo in 1942 by Morihei Uyeshiba, and based on the principle of harmony and nonresistance to one's opponent." *The Overlook Martial Arts Dictionary* (New York: Overlook Press, 1983), p. 4.

17. "More than thirty different sects of aikido exist today. . . . Minoru Kirai's korindo aikido . . . is strictly self-defensive." Ibid., p. 5.

18. An account of a small *aikido*-trained woman defeating a male master of another martial art is to be found in John Stevens, *Aikido: The Way of*

Harmony (Boulder, Colo., and London: Shambhala, 1984), p. 15.

19. How tragically ironic it is, then, that cities in the United States, with their routinely armed police forces, have murder rates astronomical in comparison to cities in Great Britain where even today the police are not routinely armed.

20. "Thirty-seven Who Saw Murder Didn't Call the Police," *New York Times*, March 27, 1964, p. 1.

21. It is certainly relevant to note that increased street lighting regularly leads to decreased crime.

22. The two products known under the popular names of stun guns are the Taser and the Nova XR 5000. "Both . . . work by putting just enough electricity into the body to interfere with the normal electrical circuit of the nerves and muscles. This interference causes instantaneous involuntary muscle spasms." The Taser has an effective range of fourteen feet, while the Nova requires that the instrument be held against the person to be subdued. This information comes from "Stun Guns—How Dangerous?" *Popular Science* 227 (October 1985): 92–93. The title is misleading because the article reports no long-term side effects and concludes that "the electric subduers have a clean bill of health."

23. The moral defender of Minimal Justified Violence, however, gains no real advantage in arguing that the effectiveness of a nonviolent defense is relative to the form of aggression. Although this is true, it is a truth about "effective defense," having nothing specifically to say about nonviolent defenses. The effectiveness of violent defenses, just like that of nonviolent defenses, is relative to the form of the offensive violence to which they respond.

24. Jan Narveson, "Pacifism: A Philosophic Analysis," *Ethics* 75 (1965): 257–291.

25. Ibid.

26. Note that my response to Narveson is based on my rejection of pacifism as a ban on all resistance to violence. Instead, my response relies on my exposition of the varieties of nonviolent force.

27. John T. Noonan, Jr., provides a clear discussion of ancient norms concerning the widow and the orphan in his *Bribes* (New York: Macmillan, 1984), p. 5ff.

28. Exodus 23:9 and, similarly, 22:21.

29. Pacifists are often imagined as persons removed from the scene of violent conflict. Historically, this image is false. Pacifists on the battlefield have attended the wounded and dying, activities of positive moral and social value, yet work statistically more life-threatening than combat.

30. The distinction between personal and universal pacifism thus becomes crucial because of threshold effects.

31. These words derive, with only somewhat altered meaning from Origen, who says: "At appropriate time we render to the emperors divine help, if I may so say, by taking up even the whole armor of God. And this we do in obedience to the apostolic utterance which says: 'I exhort you, therefore, first to make prayers, supplications, intercessions, and thanksgivings for all men, for emperors, and all that are in authority.' Indeed, the more pious a man is, the more effective he is in helping the emperors—more so than the soldiers who go out into the lines and kill all the enemy troops that they can." *Contra Celsus*, trans. Henry Chadwick (New York: Cambridge University Press, 1953), p. 509.

32. Alfred Kahn was, I believe, the first to suggest the practice.

33. It is only too obvious that one can resolve conflicts based on a scarcity one has the power to alleviate.

Chapter 5: On Justifying Violence

1. We shall ignore the interesting borderline cases of whether negligent behavior can be violent. I am inclined to think not, but the issue is not of immediate moment. But see the discussion of escalation and the responsible use of violence.

2. Lawrence H. Davis, *The Philosophy of Action* (Englewood Cliffs, N.J.: Prentice-Hall, 1979), pp. 4–5.

3. Here I rely on Donald Davidson's notion of action that is a doing, intentional under some description. See his *Essays on Actions and Events* (Oxford: Clarendon Press, 1980), pp. 57–61, 109–110, 193–195, and passim.

4. Lon Fuller, *The Morality of Law* (New Haven: Yale University Press, 1964), p. 106 and passim.

5. Ibid., p. 162.

6. Notice that our mugger uses the threat of violence. But once we assume that the mugger *is* prepared to use violence, we know that the threat is, in the relevant sense, sincere. Then, from the viewpoint of our example, it seems to make little difference whether our mugger *threatens* violence or actually *uses* it.

7. It is no accident, in violations of the criminal law, that the state assumes the role of the prosecution, that is, a *party* in the case. The police are the agents of the state *as a party* to the unfolding conflict, although they are also empowered under some conditions to prevent it before it unfolds.

8. See p. 44 in Scherer's Chapter 2.

9. There are numerous excellent discussions of Munich. Perhaps the most thorough is Telford Taylor, *Munich: The Price of Peace* (New York: Doubleday, 1970). Another good account, which provides a broader perspective, is

Donald Cameron Watt, *How War Came: 1938–1939* (New York: Pantheon, 1989), esp. chaps. 2–5.

10. See Ronald Dworkin, *Taking Rights Seriously* (Cambridge: Harvard University Press, 1977), chaps. 2, 3, and esp. 4, on applying rules in easy and hard cases.

11. There may, of course, be justifying or excusing circumstances that surround the attack, but absent those, fault lies with the initiator (who will usually also meet our definitional test of an "aggressor").

12. The notion of "attempted crimes" in particular and the area of "inchoate crimes" in general, including conspiracy and solicitation along with attempt, have given legal scholars considerable problems. Nevertheless, the law in its homely way has evolved a workable, if not elegant, conceptual framework with which to deal with them. See, generally Wayne R. LaFave and Austin Scott, *Criminal Law* (St. Paul, Minn.: West, 1972), pp. 414–495.

13. There is a vast literature on the subject, but a few works stand out. For a brilliant popular historical treatment of the events of 1914, see Barbara Tuchman, *The Guns of August* (New York: Knopf, 1962). One of the great virtues of this tour de force is the way the writer demonstrates the terrifying lack of control that the main actors had over the situation. Other discussions include Miles Kahler, "Rumors of War: The 1914 Analogy," *Foreign Affairs* 58 (Winter 1979–1980): 374–396; Oda Holsti, "The 1914 Case," *American Political Science Review* 49 (June 1965): 365–378; and, esp., Jack Snyder, *The Ideology of the Offensive: Military Decision Making and the Disasters of 1914* (Ithaca: Cornell University Press, 1984).

14. Again, there are numerous discussions of the problem of unintended or inadvertent nuclear war. Note that this category includes more than merely accidental war, as we see later. The first early discussion, still a masterpiece, is Thomas C. Schelling, "The Reciprocal Fear of Surprise Attack," in *The Strategy of Conflict* (Oxford: Oxford University Press, 1960), chap. 9. Some more recent useful discussions include Daniel Frei, *Risks of Unintentional Nuclear War* (Totowa, N.J.: Rowman and Allanheld, 1983). The entire book is on point, although the material that is most relevant is chaps. 4 and 5. See also Richard Ned Lebow, *Nuclear Crisis Management: A Dangerous Illusion* (Ithaca: Cornell University Press, 1987). Again, the whole book pertains, but the middle section, "Three Sequences to War," is of most pertinence.

15. See p. 55 in Scherer's Chapter 2.

16. There is yet no definitive account of this aspect of the Vietnam war. But one very good general history is Stanley Karnow, *Viet Nam: A History* (New York: Viking, 1983).

17. See Larry Berman, *Lyndon Johnson's War* (New York: Norton, 1989).

18. Obviously, this will come as no surprise to Scherer, and it adds credence to his position. We do not want to dispute the difficulty of either the conceptual job of the definition of aggression or the factual job of its application. On this point, see Gerhard von Glahn, *Law among Nations* (New York: Macmillan, 1981), p. 582, esp. n. 16.

19. See p. 59 in Scherer's Chapter 2.

20. Among adults, there may be the different problem of ambiguity when parties have each attempted to demarcate the situation in ways that legitimize their own interests.

21. This pregnant question—Does violence beget violence?—has many aspects. My discussion of it stretches over several sections, not concluding until I discuss escalation dominance.

22. This is no mere philosopher's example. These sorts of threats were exactly those made by the United States and the Soviet Union in the Cuban missile crisis of October 1962. The United States had clear superiority of conventional forces in the Caribbean theater, and several times throughout the crisis the Soviets alluded to Allied vulnerability in West Berlin as a counterpoint. See Lebow, *Nuclear Crisis Management*, pp. 131–139, for a discussion of threats and perceptions of threats during this crisis.

23. Again, mobilization and countermobilization at the onset of World War I represent the best example of this kind of escalation. See note 13. Today, escalation in alert status plays much the same role. See Lebow, *Nuclear Crisis Management*, pp. 65–68 and passim. See also Scott Sagan, "Nuclear Alerts and Crisis Management," *International Security* 9 (Spring 1985): 99–139. To demonstrate the frightening escalatory power of reciprocal increases in alert status, see Lebow, *Nuclear Crisis Management*, p. 199 n. 93; and John Steinbrunner, "Nuclear Decapitation," *Foreign Policy* 45 (Winter 1981–1982): 16–28. Both argue that on both powers reaching the highest levels of alert, war becomes virtually inevitable.

24. Richard Smoke, *War: Controlling Escalation* (Cambridge: Harvard University Press, 1977), p. 21.

25. Ibid.

26. Ibid., p. 22.

27. A good elementary treatment of the following material is Bruce Russett, *Prisoners of Insecurity* (New York: Freeman, 1983). For a more advanced but highly lucid discussion, see Steven Brams, *Superpower Games* (New Haven: Yale University Press, 1985).

28. As with so many of these problems, this is very much like the Security Dilemma. There is a large literature on reciprocal misperception, including Kenneth Boulding, "National Images and International Systems," *Journal of Conflict Resolution* 3 (June 1959): 120–131, Ralph White, *Fearful Warriors*

(New York: Macmillan, 1984). The best discussion of the topic is Robert Jervis, *Perception and Misperception in International Politics* (Princeton: Princeton University Press, 1976), pp. 62–84. Jervis carefully points out that too univocal a reading of the behavior of a state system as manifesting this sort of spiral of misperception can miss the fact that one of the states is really acting aggressively or preparing to do so.

29. Such spirals of misperception are common throughout history. They featured heavily in traditional Franco–German enmity, in the Anglo–German naval race at the turn of this century, between Japan and the United States between the world wars, and surely to some extent in the Soviet–American antagonism. The trick in all these cases, of course, is to sort misperception from accurate perception, misinterpreted aggressive motives from genuinely aggressive ones.

30. John Courtney Murray, *Morality and Modern War* (New York: Council on Religion and International Affairs, 1959), p. 13. In fairness to the present author's rediscovery of the principle, Murray did not seem to appreciate fully its importance in the face of systemic tendencies of conflict systems to escalate.

31. Brams, *Superpower Games*, pp. 66–77.

32. We rely here completely on Scherer's descriptions of the martial arts, presented in Chapter 2.

33. Notice how close Scherer comes at this point to condoning violence. Clearly, A parries B's blows in ways that A knows will enhance, or at least not diminish, the probability that B will injure himself. To the extent that A effectively enhances the probability, A increases the probability that harm to B will result. There are deep questions here about causality by commission and omission and double effects. We must ignore these in the interest of brevity and because they are not central to our concerns.

34. I use "escalation dominance" for what is more often called "deterrence." The problem with "deterrence" is that we tend to think of a means of preventing war "by deterrence." That is, of course, correct, but escalation dominance also prevents wars from starting because the first step in escalation is to begin fighting. The point is that *escalation dominance can also contain, dampen, even deescalate a conflict already under way.* We tend not to think of deterrence in that way, although conflict theorists have introduced the notion of "intrawar deterrence" to capture this notion. Nonetheless, I prefer "escalation dominance" as both more generic and more self-explanatory. There is a huge literature on deterrence and escalation dominance. A few of the classics are Bernard Brodie, *Strategy in the Missile Age* (Princeton: Princeton University Press, 1959); Hermann Kahn, *On Escalation* (New York: Praeger, 1965); Schelling, *Strategy of Conflict;*

and Thomas Schelling, *Arms and Influence* (New Haven: Yale University Press, 1966).

A comment is in order here. The notion of deterrence and escalation dominance has been discussed almost exclusively in the context of nuclear weapons and nuclear war. Even a book like John J. Mearsheimer, *Conventional Deterrence* (Ithaca: Cornell University Press, 1983), which is about exactly what its title says, is based on a background of nuclear deterrence and nuclear balance. There has been very little work done on these concepts in intrastate or interpersonal violence (as opposed to punishment as deterrence), but they clearly apply.

35. A friend and former law partner of mine served a five-year stint in the FBI as a field agent, making arrests and investigating violent crimes every day. He reports that, in five years, neither he nor any of the agents in his field office unholstered their gun in conflict. Using these techniques of overwhelming capacity for force and violence, the worst they had were a couple of minor, brief wrestling matches, and with odds of six to one, no one ever had to get very violent.

36. Lest I be accused of dwelling on Hitler and Munich, we could adduce many other examples. These include Stalin's series of postwar seizures in Eastern Europe, which finally stopped when faced with the obdurate firmness of the Allies at the Berlin blockade; a number of confrontations of the Allies with Napoleon; Poland's acquiesence in its own dismemberment by Russia, Prussia, and Austria in the eighteenth century; and others.

37. In fact, the German Siegfrid Line (opposite number to the more famous French Maginot Line) featured row upon row of huge concrete abutments called "Dragon's Teeth" to stop tanks. Patton's Third Army simply built roads over the top of them.

38. *On War*, trans. and ed. Michael Howard and Peter Paret (Princeton: Princeton University Press, 1976; original publication, 1832). See, esp., bk. 3, secs. 6, 9, and 11, and all of bk. 7.

39. It should also be noted that the price of surrender may be very high. The price will be death at the hands of a thrill killer or a racist mob. The price was the political dismemberment and literal slavery for the Czech people when the Allies surrendered to Hitler's demands at Munich.

40. See pp. 37 and 49–51 in Scherer's Chapter 2.

Chapter 6: A Viable Pacifism

1. This reading might even justify aggressive, retaliative violence against A. For instance, people might sing, "And conquer we must, if our cause it is

just," without ever considering that such conquest might be inconsistant with their sincere Just War views.

2. It is accordingly what L. Wayne Sumner calls an intuitionistic theory in his *Abortion and Moral Theory* (Princeton: Princeton University Press, 1980). Of course, logicians will be quick to see that I build the concept of a pacifist on a similarly intuitionistic concept of peace. One might note, then, that Child's objection that peace must be monistically defined relies on the same premise (the intuitionistic character of the view) as my objection. I therefore need to address why I think I can at once rebut that objection against my view and make it against Child's (see pp. 173–176).

3. Recall that in Part I, I argued that (1) the facts of the case will often so underdetermine the presumptions of the Justified Violence Theory as to be logically compatible with pacifist presumptions and that (2) data regularly underdetermine agents' intentions.

4. See pp. 144–146 in Child's Chapter 5.

5. The complementary, second phase of this argument is indicated in the final paragraph of "Escalation Dominance and the Future of Pacifism."

6. Recently, for example, in Gene Sharp, *Making Europe Unconquerable* (Cambridge, Mass.: Ballinger, 1985).

7. Even more extreme than views that allow passive resistance but argue that a passively resisting population has the force to make itself unrulable are the nonresistance views of thinkers like Tolstoy. In the same letter quoted in Part II, pp. 68–69, Tolstoy says,

> I think [this law of love] has been expressed most clearly of all by Christ who even said frankly that on this alone hang all the Law and the prophets. Furthermore, foreseeing the distortion which comes naturally to people who live by worldly interest, namely the danger of allowing themselves to defend these interests by force, i.e., as he said, returning blow for blow, taking back by force objects which have been appropriated, etc., etc. He knows, as every reasonable person is bound to know, that the use of violence is incompatible with love as the basic law of life, that once violence is tolerated in any cases whatsoever, the inadequacy of the law of love is recognized and therefore the law itself is repudiated. The whole of Christian civilization, so brilliant on the surface, grew up on this obvious, strange, sometimes conscious but for the most part unconscious misunderstanding and contradiction.

Clearly, Tolstoy's view stands in opposition to the distinction Child made between escalating and deescalating uses of violence.

8. For a good presentation of this history, see Arthur G. Gish, *The New Left and Christian Radicalism* (Grand Rapids, Mich.: Eerdmans, 1970), pp. 49–75.

9. In *The Kingdom of God Is within You* (Lincoln: University of Nebraska Press, 1984), pp. 3–8, Tolstoy quotes the "Declaration of Sentiments Adopted by the Peace Convention" in Boston, 1838, which was composed by William Lloyd Garrison.

10. Ironically, the Gulf War and its aftermath apparently exemplify both escalation dominance used under a UN mandate and the shortsightedness of fighting without a positive conception of peace to guide peacemaking.

11. The significant problem in other circumstances in which only violence will control violence is that a violent response may not control the violence. Thus, while violent responses to violence may prove deescalating, one is left with an unhappy balance to be weighed. Should one acquiesce in violence, which may be very aggressive, or should one risk the perpetuation and intensification of violence and compromise the integrity of the violent and the victims of violence? (For even the defended party must live with knowing that his or her continued life or well-being required the life or well-being of another.) In the often searing light of this dilemma, I have argued that a pacifist response is not immoral, but I have not argued that a violent response in such situations is immoral. At this level I accede to the ambivalence of the alliance builder. Later in this chapter I emphasize the value to be constructed from the differences among the dispositions and histories of different alliance builders.

12. I do not naively accept this violence-deescalation premise. Obviously, I could argue in opposition to it, sometimes persons who sincerely attempt to deescalate violence through violence-domination techniques cause increased violence because they fail to dominate violence. I could also argue that violence-domination techniques are morally dangerous especially when they are effective inasmuch as they may be used by brutal tyrants, not by police operating within a rule of law. Both arguments are important, but I bypass them because, even after I made those arguments, I would have to deal with the fact that, within the rule of law and with properly trained police forces, violence-domination techniques achieve a morally successful reduction of violence.

13. Although it does not contribute to the development of the main dialectic between us, I pause here to note my controversy with Child over the inclusion of his "delivery condition" in the definition of violence. Whether the swiftness and forcefulness of an attack effectively limits defender's options is relative to defender's background preparation. Those who have learned *aikido* and those who carry mace in their purses will have more nonviolent options than their opposites. And those who have fortified themselves with these defenses, knowing they have them, will probably face an attack with a larger measure of composure than their opposites.

I concede that a swift and forceful manner of attack minimizes response time and narrows the range of available responses. But I do not believe Child should use his definition of violence to help foreclose issues of responsibility: Those who may come under attack are prudent and clever so to have prepared themselves as not unnecessarily to have foreclosed nonviolent options. My argument is not that people falling under attack are to be blamed if they have not adequately prepared themselves to repulse the attack. I argue, not about the right, but about a good that may be had or forfeited unnecessarily.

Child also questions the practicality of *aikido* in a world of sophisticated weapons and decreasing preparation times. Abstractly, we have noted that the martial arts can create the option of responding effectively to aggression without adopting the (im)moral standards of an aggressor. We have grasped that *aikido* can create the option of ending the cycle of needing escalated force and violence in order to respond effectively to the potential violence of one's adversary. We have seen that stun guns can create options for police to subdue violent criminals nonviolently. We have observed that within a society practicing vengeance, introducing the rule of law creates the option of responding to injustices, even violent injustices, without perpetuating the cycle of violent injustices. And we may recall that increasing the street lighting (i.e., changing the physical environment) and organizing the neighbors into a neighborhood watch program (i.e., changing the social environment) also reduce the occurrence of crime. Moreover, when we move from the individual to the society, the *aikido* metaphor tells us to consider how strong deterrence might be if some individuals or technologies remain capable of retaliation, not only quickly before a blow is struck, but after an adversary's blow has landed.

Child believes the *aikido* metaphor breaks down because of its assumptions that attack makes the attacker vulnerable and that defense can exploit that vulnerability effectively. For save for the brief medieval era of the fortified city, it is not at all clear that defensive weapons (especially nonviolent ones) have been comparable, much less superior, to offensive ones.

Now I read the history of warfare no differently from Child, yet I am not inclined to see *aikido* as a curiosity of a peculiar historical moment. Why, I ask myself, have defensive weapons been so peripheral? Initially, it seems to me, the problem arose out of technologies that allowed for dramatic increases in the force with which projectiles could be propelled at targets. This force has given rise to a tradition of fortifications that obtained whatever effectiveness they had at a cost of weight and geographical fixity. In other words, offensive technologies led to defenses in which decreased mobility has created increased vulnerability for defenders. Certainly no *aikido* warrior could be effective in the armor of a knight.

But if the weight of a knight's armor limits the knight's capacities, then we can imagine a kind of electronic shield that creates the possibility of combining defense with mobility: Since fortification does not abstractly imply being weighted down, fortification need not imply decreased mobility. Do I therefore use the *aikido* metaphor to endorse the Strategic Defense Initiative (SDI)? From a certain theoretical perspective, it might appear so. For if, theoretically, we begin from the premise that the goal of SDI is to protect a nation from the missiles and bombs of its adversaries, allowing it to deflect them, as a practitioner of *aikido* also deflects blows, then it would seem that I am indeed endorsing SDI. But the assumption of that theoretical argument is that what SDI protects is the lives of people and the property with which they go about their nonaggressive living. Georgi Arbitrov has noted, however, that if the shielded territory houses offensive weapons, then the shield protects and preserves aggressive capabilities as well as defending people against aggression. Arbitrov's argument implies that SDI would be more strictly analogous to *aikido* (and defensively justifiable) if all U.S. missiles and bombs were housed outside any shield (e.g., on submarines). Indeed, the moral force of the Soviet objection to SDI would seem to evaporate if, in negotiations over intercontinental ballistics missiles (ICBMs), the United States were willing to eliminate its land-based ICBMs in return for appropriate Soviet reductions in ICBMs.

Historically, much of the superiority of offensive weaponry rests, I suspect, on the contingency that much defensive fortification, unlike *aikido*, has sacrificed mobility. Child, however, believes that at bottom there may be thermodynamic reasons for the historical prevalence of offensive weapons. The Second Law of Thermodynamics, in rough terms, Child says, tells us that "highly organized states of matter (e.g., human bodies or human cities) tend to move toward disorganization, and that when 'disorganized,' the process back toward organization is either impossible (a human being) or very difficult and expensive (a city)" (p. 160).

This reasoning seems to me altogether too speculative. I cannot pretend to show that it yields a false conclusion, but I believe I can show that reasoning no more speculative leads to contrary conclusions. For the Second Law of Thermodynamics applies to the human bodies of attackers as much as to the bodies of defenders. It applies to missiles and bombers as well as to cities. The bodies of the attacker and of the attacked are thermodynamically indifferent, except to the extent that the attack introduces a difference.

The lesson at the heart of the *aikido* metaphor is that attack magnifies the tendencies of the attacker to "disorganization" and that systems of defense can be developed to exploit these tendencies. The success of *aikido* suggests one analogy; the predominance of offensive weapons in the history of warfare suggests another. What the Second Law cannot tell us is which analogy to accept, since nothing in so abstract a law distinguishes the capacities of the offensively and defensively deployed bodies.

Perhaps a more promising line against the *aikido* metaphor would come from the potential vulnerability, not of the attacked per se, but of the ignorant. The *aikido* metaphor reflects the dedication of the *aikido* artist to make it true that the attacked can make up through previous training and preparation for any shortness of warning the attacker may provide. But in preradar days, nighttime bombing missions had a special effectiveness because of the reduced preattack knowledge of the attack. And, similarly, we may suppose a case in which the attacked dies literally never knowing what happened. Such a case undermines the assumption of *aikido* that one will always know of any imminent potentially lethal blow.

The contingency, then, which seems to me most fundamental to the viability of the *aikido* metaphor is the foreknowledge of attack. The *aikido* metaphor requires that, regardless of how late the first awareness of attack arrives, effective defense is feasible. Yet I have no argument that all attacks will inevitably provide defenders with some (ample) response time.

14. This is not the place for a full discussion of the problem of freedom of the will. But I do suppose that the human capacities for foreseeing the future and for planning are the bases not only of the extended cooperation which grounds human society but also of the ascribing and acceptance of responsibility for participating in strategic (nonparametric) plans.

15. See p. 130 in Child's Chapter 5.

16. Was it, perhaps, the enemy's for inflicting them? In some ways, it surely was. But obviously, waiting for the enemy to take that responsibility would involve waiting through the deaths of countless soldiers.

17. John T. Noonan, Jr., *Bribes* (New York: Macmillan, 1984), chap. 1., "Bending the Bonds of Reciprocity."

18. Lon Fuller, *The Morality of Law* (New Haven: Yale University Press, 1964).

19. See p. 141 in Child's Chapter 5.

20. See p. 144 in Child's Chapter 5.

21. See p. 166 in Child's Chapter 5.

22. Professor Child has asked me whether he has much changed the traditional Just War view here. He has pointed out to me that Just War theorists have traditionally insisted that war should be a last resort. But, for lack of a temporal referent, that language is ambiguous. When an attack is imminent, it is easy to argue that one's only remaining resort is war. The question of responsibility I am raising regards an earlier, preattack time, when conciliation might have been feasible if peacemaking measures other than deterrence had been employed.

In fairness, of course, it must be noted that modern means of transportation and communication make feasible standards of communication between nations for which past centuries could not be held accountable. It is, then, not surprising that traditional Just War theorists have not emphasized the foresighted discussion on which I have insisted.

23. See p. 164 in Child's Chapter 5.

24. Facts about thresholds and about synergisms suggest that even when many parties clearly contribute to some pollution, an answer to the problem of responsibility will require the invention of practices, because of being literally unresolvable at the level of desert.

25. It is, of course, a rights-based question, whereas my view that it is a bad question is teleological, contrasting the practices likely to develop out of a focus on desert versus those likely to develop out of a focus on the assignment of new responsibilities and the achievement of new goods.

It may also be a question asked by someone who prioritizes the liberty of persons not to take such responsibility over the good to be attained (and the harm to be avoided) if they do. Once we recall that social change is bound to introduce new forms of harm into human life, we see that the consequence of this prioritization is the degeneration of the quality of human life as it falls prey to new harms. This seems undesirable.

26. The sequence I have just rehearsed will surely be familiar to most as a standard cold-war sequence.

27. Professor Child suggests that I urge that attacked parties have an obligation to propose alternatives like short-term slavery in response to demands of total capitulation. Contrarily, all the new interests I propose creating compromise none of the basic human values, on which Child and I agree.

Also, if the question of desert is a rights-based question, the supposition that the burden can be taken is an altruistically motivated assumption. But I have indicated in Part II how such motivations are wont to arise on no more than evolutionary assumptions.

28. Consider the use of mace, which can have a devastating short-term effect on an attacker without any long-term effects whatsoever. A person trained in the use of such a forceful but nonviolent defense will feel much less than constrained by the circumstances of an attack.

29. Here we must remember that when Mr. Green calls the police, he calls forth not only their potentially violent capacities but also the psychological training of the SWAT team leader, who may very well talk Mr. Blue out of attacking.

30. *The Gorgias* 473ff.

31. Here the contrast between a teleological and a deontological view is most telling. Earlier I raised the rhetorical question "How else are we to en-

sure that the narrowed perspectives of those closest to the violence do not undermine promoting the positive quality of peace?" The presumption of the question is that promotion of the positive quality of peace is desirable. To this, deontologist and teleologist will agree. But only the deontologist, questioning who deserves the burden of improving social practices, will balk at the inference that some ought to pursue the improvement of social practices. On my teleological view, social structures ought to encourage diverse individuals in their inclinations to accept responsibility for improving social practices. And some persons will be moved to act by visions of an improved society.

A related shortcoming of Child's view appears when he urges that the attacked person should be held responsible only for pursuing those nonviolent options "that a *reasonable person in those circumstances* would consider and try" (my italics). For reasonable persons are reasonable relative to their own socializations, and thus relative to the prevalent practices of responsibility in their own society. In contrast, I am arguing for the reasonability of improving practices of responsibility. The conservatism built into standards of "reasonableness" thus runs contrary to the teleology I advocate.

32. By the end of Part IV it should be evident that successful interest creation is typically reciprocal, and successful reciprocal interest creation is typically mutually beneficial.

33. Although Corazon Aquino, of course, is not a pacifist, her leadership of the insurgency against the Marcos administration relied and built on the pacifistic tactics of Gandhi and King.

34. How did it happen that thousands of people gathered on the streets of Manila, February 23, 1986, in the presence of potentially violent Marcos forces, and yet virtually no violence occurred? The charismatic leadership of Corazon Aquino is well known. Much less well known is the training leaders on the streets had received through the Regional Office in Manila of the International Fellowship of Reconciliation in the nonviolent tactics of Gandhi. Similarly, Cardinal Sin, through the channel of Radio Veritas, was able to influence the masses to make their demonstrations peaceful.

35. I can only regret that the main line of my argument does not allow me to explore in detail the institutions of a free press and the power of contemporary mass communication, especially the power of television news, for the ways in which they so shape the social environment as to make pacifist programs more powerful.

36. I emphasize how empirical a segmented pacifism is by developing such a pacifist program in Part IV.

37. Quoted by Origen, *Contra Celsus*, trans. Henry Chadwick (New York: Cambridge University Press, 1953), p. 509.

38. Ibid.

39. Private letter, August 1987.
40. Briefly and roughly, these are the presumptions that any conflict is recon-cilable, that the conflicting parties have substantial interests in common, and that community-restoring, trust-developing actions can be taken.
41. Professor Child suggests that when a mugger threatens one, saying, "Your wallet or your life," the mugger has created a new interest, an interest in not being killed. I do not recognize what the mugger does as creating a new interest in my sense of the term. New interest creation, as I advocate it, is built on the compatibilist assumptions about peace and the presumptions defined in Chapter 2. That is, any acceptable new interest creation respects and does not threaten persons' basic well-being. Violence, as I define it and as Child agrees, violates the basic well-being these assumptions and pre-sumptions are designed to hold together. Therefore, the mugger's actions are not acceptable new interest creations. (Of course whether the mugger's threats can be handled nonviolently is a different question, related to my discussions of *aikido* and stun guns.)
42. What I here call historical considerations arise out of a sequence of inter-actions in which maxims of disclosure, hard-to-fake cues, and discrimi-nating perception of disclosures and cues are central. The clearest unified exposition of this important material (to my knowledge) is in Robert Frank, *Passions within Reason* (New York: Norton, 1988), chaps. 5 and 6.
43. And if a scarcity of land is unavoidably at the bottom of the questions of Northern Ireland and Israel–Palestine, then the difference between Child and me may evaporate. (For I cannot argue a priori that whatever is scarce will prove compensable to the disputants.)

    And no, I do not really think that claims to property are inalienable. But both Jewish and Palestinian spokespeople have argued that they have duties to be loyal to a heritage such that those duties of loyalty deny present per-sons the right to betray their heritage by giving up their claims to the land. At face value, these arguments make the loss of land uncompensable.
44. I am aware of the obvious dangers if providing such a lure were the pacifist's entire program.
45. I am of course mindful of the extent to which President Aquino's subse-quent problems came to be perceived as resulting from the failures of her administration to develop more appropriate distributions.
46. What, we may ask, is the status of the Secretary of State? Could not the Secretary of State seek the coordinations proposed for a Secretary of Peace-making? Ultimately, perhaps, but not easily within the world of nation-states we know. For in our world, with the few international coordinating mechanisms it has, national governments tend to presume themselves to have rights. Consequently, diplomacy tends not to get beyond the disen-tangling of (potentially) conflicting interests. The distinct role I envision

for a Secretary of Peacemaking focuses on the development of practices and institutions that lead to the development of interests that tend not to conflict but to support each other. Even very inventive Secretaries of State (Kissinger and Baker) became entangled in long-standing Middle East conflicts.

47. In this section I give only the barest outline of the work Secretaries of Peacemaking could do. I detail such work, whether under the auspices of such secretaries or not, in the opening section of Part IV.

48. An extensive discussion of what constitutes such matching is found in Chapter 8.

49. And, like other pacifists, segmented pacifists forswear any use of violence themselves.

50. Of course, the prominence of an ideal of positive peace within my view should not mislead anybody into thinking that on my view there is no peace, or no peace worth achieving, unless that peace fully achieves the positive peace that many cultures have perceived as a heavenly ideal. The ideal remains valuable if only to remind us, against the very human tendency toward complacency, of how short we fall even in our well-intended policies. The dominant groups in any society will always hear plenty about how ably they manage, about what values they so adequately realize. Without the references to ideals, they might believe what they hear!

Introduction to Part IV

1. "Legitimate security needs" means close to the same thing for each of us. Child would describe it as the protection of the basic rights of its citizens. Scherer would eschew rights language, but he would be happy with "legitimately protecting vulnerabilities of the nation's citizens." The similarity of our positions rests on the extent of our agreement (in Part I) about why violence is bad.

2. We finesse here both Scherer's Chapter 6 challenge that the Minimal Justified Violence View is, in certain circumstances, incoherent, and his fundamental Chapter 2 concerns about alienating tendencies of rights concepts, employed by the Justified Violence View. Finessing these amounts here to Scherer's assuming the reformulability of security needs solely in terms of the legitimacy of protecting vulnerable human beings.

Chapter 7: On Avoiding War

1. As I have in earlier chapters, I use "state," "nation," and "nation-state" more or less interchangeably throughout, as is typical in nontechnical discussions. There are, of course, important technical differences between the three concepts, and where important, I try carefully to distinguish. Remember, also, the existence of important nonstate actors running the gamut from terrorist organizations (e.g., the Popular Front for the Liberation of Palestine) to international institutions (e.g., the World Court).

2. In "The Soviet Union: Still an Adversary?" I discuss this assumption in the light of the history of Soviet–American relations from the time Gorbachev came to power.

3. This is true, except, perhaps in small degree, with respect to the Soviet Union, but even here the fear was of a very mild and long-term kind. He did feel that the two powers could not coexist forever in Eastern Europe and that war was eventually inevitable. Nonetheless, when Hitler invaded the Soviet Union in June 1941, his confidence in a quick and decisive victory was supreme. He believed the Soviet Union to be weak to the point of defenselessness.

4. Neither Japan's aggressive motives or subsequent aggressions in any way legitimated the European colonial regimes.

5. No public figure in Japan at that time ever expressed, or subsequently recorded, any fear of American intentions to aggress on their homeland.

6. For an excellent popular history of the expansion of the Japanese empire and of the Pacific War, see John Toland, *The Rising Sun* (New York: Bantam, 1970).

7. For a still largely accurate picture, see John M. Collins, *U.S.–Soviet Military Balance* (Washington, D.C.: Pergamon-Brassey's, 1985). Collins is senior specialist in national defense at the Library of Congress, and his report was prepared for the House and Senate Armed Services Committees. One can update these figures by consulting recent annual issues of *The Military Balance* (London: International Institute for Strategic Studies). See also Brian Moynahan, *The Claws of the Bear: The History of the Red Army from the Revolution to the Present* (Boston: Houghton Mifflin, 1989), chaps. 36–46.

8. This is by all measures except the number of men under arms, where the People's Republic of China exceeds us. See *Military Balance*.

9. For a good balanced historical picture of the Soviet Union, see Basil Dmytryshyn, *USSR: A Concise History*, 3rd ed. (New York: Scribner's, 1987); and Leonard Schapiro, *The Communist Party of the Soviet Union*, 2nd ed. (New York: Vintage, 1971).

10. See Alfred G. Meyer, *Leninism* (Cambridge: Harvard University Press,

1959); see also Dmytryshyn, *USSR*, chaps. 4 and 5. For an exhaustive treatment of Lenin in the broad context of the Russian Revolution, see Richard Pipes, *The Russian Revolution* (New York: Knopf, 1990). For a good account of the brutality of Lenin's regime, see esp. chaps. 15, 16, and 18. For a short but accurate overview, see Zbigniew Brzezinski, *The Grand Failure: The Birth and Death of Communism in the Twentieth Century* (New York: Scribner's, 1980), chap. 1.

11. See Adam Ulam, *Stalin: The Man and His Era* (New York: Viking, 1973). See Robert Conquest, *The Great Terror* (New York: Macmillan, 1968), on Stalin's purges of the party and the army and the same author's *Harvest of Sorrow* (New York: Oxford University Press, 1986), an account of Stalin's liquidation of an entire class of landed peasants in the Ukraine. He purposely starved to death several million people.

12. Mikhail Gorbachev has been awarded the Nobel Peace Prize and no doubt deserves it. The man who allowed the Berlin Wall to be torn down and who freed Eastern Europe deserves it. And he may well do more. But he may be limited in what else he *can* do.

13. The power of the notions of authority, central control, and security that pervades Soviet society is evident in several accounts by American journalists who have lived in the Soviet Union during the 1980s. See Kevin Klose, *Russian and the Russians: Inside the Closed Society* (New York: Norton, 1984); Elizabeth Pond, *From the Yaroslavsky Station: Russia Perceived*, rev. ed. (New York: Universal Books, 1984); David K. Shipler, *Russia: Broken Idols, Solemn Dreams* (New York: Times Books, 1983).

14. The obsession of the Soviet society and system with authority, order, centralized control, and security (both internal and external) seems to be a universal theme running through their (primarily *Russian*) history, culture, ideology, and political and social life. On this point, I would recommend the following analyses of the Soviet Union: Heddrick Smith, *The Russians* (New York: Ballantine, 1976), esp. chap. 10 and the wonderful diagrammatic metaphor on p. 336, using a ball and two containers to illustrate the differing characters of the United States and the Soviet Union. It is not Smith's own thought, but that of a Soviet scientist with whom he became friends. I find myself returning over and over to it as I investigate Soviet society further. Robert Kaiser, *Russia: The People and the Power* (New York: Atheneum, 1976), is also very good, especially chaps. 3 and 4.

15. See, for example, Liah Greunfeld, "The Closing of the Russian Mind," *New Republic*, February 5, 1990, pp. 30–34. Also Walter Laqueur, "From Russia with Hate," ibid., pp. 21–25, and Bill Kellar, "Russian Nationalists: Yearning for an Iron Hand," *New York Times Magazine*, January 27, 1990. More troubling is Martin Walker, "Apocalypse Moscow," *New Republic*, Decem-

ber 4, 1989, pp. 22–27. Walker, for six years the Russian-speaking Moscow Bureau chief for the *Guardian*, offers dire predictions of anarchy, fascism, or both.

Perhaps the most troubling thing written about the Soviet Union since Gorbachev's accession to power is the bitterly pessimistic, highly controversial, and much discussed "To the Stalin Mausoleum" by Z (anonymous) first published in *Daedalus*, January 1990, reprinted in William M. Brinton and Alan Rinzler, eds., *Without Force or Lies* (San Francisco: Mercury House, 1990), pp. 380–435. It is compulsory reading for all optimists in regard to the Soviet Union.

16. Anti-Semitism, always just below the surface in Russia, is rearing its head again. See Kellar, "Russian Nationalists"; and Nina Tumarkin, "Russians against Jews," *The Atlantic*, October 1990, pp. 32–45.

17. "The Two Faces of Eastern Europe" *New Republic*, November 12, 1990, pp. 23–25.

18. Gorbachev has shown only a slight tendency to slip back from his democratic (*glasnost*) reforms. But he has been much more ambivalent about the movement toward free markets (*perestroika*) or at least toward more radical economic reform. Gorbachev has rejected the radical shift to free-market economics formulated by economist Stanislav Shatalin and sponsored by Boris Yeltsin. Instead he has opted for the gradualist program of Prime Minister Nikolai Ryzhkov. Ryzhkov is generally thought to represent more conservative constituencies, such as the Communist party, the planning bureaucracy, and the military–industrial complex. Does Gorbachev's siding with him herald a shift toward reaction? It is certainly too soon to tell. Yet the possibility gives rise to concern.

19. For compelling arguments to this effect, see James L. Payne, *Why Nations Arm* (Oxford: Basil Blackwell, 1989), esp. chap. 8; and Aaron Wildavsky, "No War without Dictatorship, No Peace without Democracy," *Social Philosophy and Policy* 3 (Autumn 1985).

20. See note 7, esp. Collins, *U.S.–Soviet Military Balance*, pp. 118–124.

21. It is obvious that there is no clearly delineated class of "defensive" or "offensive" weapons. Most weapons can be turned to either use depending on intention and context. Still, some weapons are more easily used defensively or at least as deterrents (not quite the same thing). Others are almost exclusively offensive. A fixed land-based ICBM is rapidly becoming an exclusively offensive weapon. At the other extreme, a tank trap on a defensive line is almost exclusively defensive. Most weapons lie somewhere on the spectrum between these poles. I hope the discussion that follows is sensitive to this inherent ambiguity.

22. The invulnerability of a deterrent force spells safety. Vulnerability spells a

very deep and frightening kind of instability, by inviting a preemptive attack. The Soviets, for example, know that destroying our vulnerable ICBMs would mitigate potential damage to their homeland. In the case of the ICBM force, such potential mitigation to the Soviets is huge. *Now comes a particularly vicious infinite regress.* The Soviets know that we know our ICBMs are vulnerable. In their eyes, we are more prone to use them to strike first. Better to use them first than to have them destroyed. The Soviets believe that, by their knowledge of our intention, we would be tempted to strike preemptively. We know that they know that we know. . . . Thus the regress turns in ever-escalating spirals, each time inviting anew first one superpower, then the other, to strike preemptively. We may know that we never would do so. The Soviets do not know this. One vulnerable strategic offensive force tempts both adversaries to preempt. A second vulnerable strategic force only compounds the danger.

Indeed the story of destabilization is even more frightening than this. Suppose the Soviet Union is originally not tempted to strike first. But suppose the two superpowers face a serious confrontation, as they did in Cuba in 1962, before developing a counterforce capacity with its attendant destabilization. Suppose further that the Soviets fear we *might* strike them first. And suppose they already have many multiwarhead fixed ICBMs. They see that the existence of their ICBMs offers us a great first-strike premium. Or so they reason as they preempt us by attacking first. Thus they can be prompted to attack because of our destabilizing weapons; otherwise, they would not have attacked.

It gets worse. *We* will be inclined to engage in mirror-image reasoning, since they have many more missiles than we do. Now *both* powers are tempted to strike first, and each power knows of the other's temptation, further encouraging them to strike. This is the most deadly version of the Security Dilemma. Many years ago, Thomas Schelling captured its logic, which he called the "reciprocal fear of surprise attack." See his *The Strategy of Conflict* (London: Oxford University Press, 1960), chap. 9. It became terrifyingly real with the advent of superaccurate, multiwarhead counterforce missiles in the 1970s. Since then, both nuclear superpowers have been riding a very large and hungry tiger.

23. Transarmament ought not to be confused with a related but distinct concept introduced by Gene Sharp, *Making Europe Unconquerable* (Cambridge, Mass.: Ballinger, 1985), chap. 3. Sharp refers to a shift from a military system of defense to one based on civilian nonviolent resistance. Needless to say, this is *not* what I recommend. But the notion of transarmament has become broadened to mean a shift from one class of arms and its attendant strategic doctrine to a different one. Sharp's use of the term then becomes

an outer limit. What I recommend is a much more modest change, but a change that is nonetheless substantial enough to earn the name.

24. The best popular account of this phenomenon is "Nuclear Weapons: Another Age?" *The Economist*, September 1984, survey pp. 1–7. More authoritative is Theodore B. Taylor, "Third Generation Nuclear Weapons," *Scientific American* 256, no. 4 (April 1987): 30–39; and Robert Jastrow, "Reagan vs. the Scientists," *Commentary*, January 1984, pp. 31–32.

25. This point can be read as an implication, with which I agree, of Scherer's discussion of *aikido*.

26. A good account of the crisis is contained in Norman Gelb, *The Berlin Wall* (New York: Random House, 1986). See also Jack M. Schnick, *The Berlin Crisis 1958–1962* (Philadelphia: University of Pennsylvania, 1971).

27. When the Berlin Wall came down in 1989, East Germany tried the alternative solution of governmental reform. Finally, even that failed, and they gave up their existence in unification with the West. What was unthinkable in 1960 is reality today.

28. See note 22.

29. See Walter Laqueur, *Confrontation* (New York: Quadrangle, 1974); and Scott Sagan, "Lessons of the Yom Kippur Alert," *Foreign Policy* 36 (Fall 1979): 168ff.

30. Before we assess the rights and wrongs of this American maneuver, consider two things. First, American foreign policy was under the virtually unilateral direction of Henry Kissinger, probably the most intelligent and knowledgeable man since Thomas Jefferson to direct it. (Nixon was completely enmeshed in the Watergate affair and was a virtual figurehead in the situation.) Second, Leonid Brezhnev, to his eternal credit, did not put his nuclear forces on alert in response (or if he did, it was at so low level an alert as not to be detected by us).

31. See John Steinbrunner, "Nuclear Decapitation," *Foreign Policy* 45 (Winter 1981–1982): 16–28.

32. Here I follow Scherer's argument that prohibiting certain immoral means of response to an immoral action does not amount to granting an immunity to the immoral. Instead it amounts, at least in the present context, to an injunction to those who would be moral to use effective and moral means of response to the immorality of violence.

33. James W. Child, *Nuclear War: The Moral Dimension* (New Brunswick, N.J.: Transaction Books, 1986). Also see this volume for a guide to the extensive literature on nuclear weapons, nuclear deterrence, and nuclear pacifism.

34. John J. Mersheimer, "Why We Will Soon Miss the Cold War," *The Atlantic*, August 1990, pp. 35–50, discusses this explicitly. Moreover, the instabilities described in *Strategic Survey 1989–1990* (London: International Institute

for Strategic Studies, 1990), pp. 5–61, implicitly raise many of the same issues.

35. *The Fate of Nations* (Cambridge: Cambridge University Press, 1988), chap. 5.

Chapter 8: Toward an Enriched Peace

1. George Kennan, "The American–Soviet Relationship: A Retrospective," in *The Nuclear Delusion* (New York: Pantheon Books, 1982).
2. I find noteworthy the considerable extent to which Gorbachev's leadership between 1985 and 1990 employed the concepts of this chapter, culminating in his receiving the 1990 Nobel Peace Prize.
3. I wish to reemphasize my acknowledgment that this stability may in fact depend on military systems that exhibit a fair measure of the stability Child discussed.
4. As Charles Osgood wrote in his book *An Alternative to War or Surrender* (Urbana: University of Illinois Press, 1962).
5. Thus, in the realm of commerce, the considerable creativity going into the fledgling relationships between the Soviet Union and such American enterprises as PepsiCo, Occidental Petroleum, and McDonalds is immensely important to surmounting the historical differences in the economic backgrounds out of which each is accustomed to work.
6. For example, Argentina may be fearful of the trade deficit it has run with Brazil, while Brazil is in need of importing wheat and oil. Brazil could buy the wheat and oil products from many other exporting nations. But buying them from Argentina has served both to allay Argentinian fears and to symbolize the possibilities of expanded cooperation, both between Argentina and Brazil and throughout South America.
7. Consider how frequently a security adviser will be able to premise truly either that the cost to the adversary was minimal or that the benefit to "us" was small.
8. There is some evidence that the death of President Kennedy, the retirement of Chairman Khrushchev, and the escalation of the Vietnam conflict played such a role between November 1963 and January 1967. See Amitai Etzioni, "The Kennedy Experiment, *Western Political Science Quarterly* 20 (1967): 361–380.
9. Although perhaps most famous for his most extreme tactics of nonresistance, his uses of fasting and general strikes, Gandhi did not see his more extreme tactics as central to his effort.
10. I remain cognizant of the possibility that an aggressively intended adversary may not accept (or may not be guided by) this coordinative self-interest.
11. Here also is a powerful pragmatic argument for setting aside the alienating

language of rights in favor of a language of common human values.

12. Sections about (1) information; and (2) microcosmic structures follow. The reader will note how they respond to the problems I associated with defining violence in terms of intention in Chapter 2: (1) security presumptions and information restriction; and (2) national intentions and historical perspective.

13. A measure of GRIT-like progress in recent U.S.–Soviet relations is that their emphasis did not exist (e.g., in U.S. press coverage of the use of the Soviet military in Azerbaijan). Clearly, part of this difference in coverage reflects differences in Soviet response.

14. This is my translation of the assertion of Dwight D. Eisenhower in his farewell address that the people of the world want peace so much that someday their governments will have to get out of their way and let them have it.

15. For an extended discussion of salience, see Thomas Schelling, *Micromotives and Macrobehavior* (New York: Norton, 1978).

16. This argument follows the general form of David Gauthier, *Morality by Agreement* (Oxford: Clarendon Press, 1985).

17. At such moments, the evidence in favor of continued cooperation will look bleaker both because whatever history of "cooperation" has occurred will now come in for perspectival reconceptualization ("They don't really believe in peace; they only stayed with the process while it was obviously benefiting them.") and because the projected benefits of a previously presumed continuation of cooperation will be reassessed in the light of the puzzlingly "irrational" behavior of the adversary. (Indeed, the defensively minded will find this "irrational" behavior explainable only in antagonistic terms, and security advisers will be assigned to make these arguments.)

18. It is fairly standard that when incompatible means are about to be chosen, troubleshooters find new and compatible means toward legitimate ends. It is somewhat less standard that even when two ends are legitimate, troubleshooters may need to renegotiate the ends, given that the conflict over the means to the original ends is ineliminable.

19. The argument has the following form: It is desirable for those who act in good faith to create structures in which bad faith is transparent. For by the creation of such structures, they ensure that whoever should wield power within those structures, and however ambivalent or even bad may be the faith of those who come to exercise such power, the structure, by making any bad faith in which they act self-revealing, will coerce them not to act in bad faith. True, the structure will also tempt the aggressively intended to find the means of pursuing their aggressive designs covertly, evading the power of the structure. The crucial contest will thus be that of maintaining the power of the structure to keep malevolent intentions self-revealing and thus self-defeating. I believe the argument I develop here follows the same

lines Robert Frank pursues in *Passions within Reason* (New York: Norton, 1988), esp. chap. 6.

20. The demographer correlates declining birthrates most strongly with literacy and the widespread distribution of monies within an economy, just as the highest birthrates are correlated with illiteracy and pockets of poverty.

21. "Obscure" benefits may be only apparent, with the result that mutually suspicious nations will tend to frustrate a series of mutually beneficial exchanges if they offer such benefits to one another. For if the benefit is real (though obscure), it is likely to be unappreciated and unreciprocated, whereas if the benefit is merely apparent, it is likely to provoke renewed suspicion and reciprocated deceptive behavior.

22. See notes 12–14, Chapter 2.

23. For appropriate expositions of the concept of the Kingdom of Heaven, see Leo Tolstoy, *The Kingdom of God Is within You*; and Gustavo Gutierrez, *A Theology of Liberation* (Maryknoll, N.Y.: Orbis Books, 1973).

24. *The Gorgias* 473.

25. That this impulse is appropriately called altruistic is argued by Richmond Campbell in "Sociobiology and the Possibility of Ethical Naturalism," in *Morality, Reason and Truth: New Essays on the Foundations of Ethics*, ed. David Copp and David Zimmerman (Totowa, N.J.: Rowman and Allanheld, 1985), pp. 284–286.

action: aggressive, 33–34, 37–38, 136–142, 182, 197, 240–241; alienating, 48; cooperative, 242, 243; creating conflict, 31–32, 136–142; and doings, 130, 177–178, 289; escalation as an, 148–151; evaluation of, 31–34, 39–41, 52, 67–71, 100–101, 103–107, 111–113, 115–116, 119–122, 123–124, 129–135, 172–173, 277, 282, 286, 307; and integrity, 108, 286; and intention, 52–56, 61, 129–135, 136–146, 275, 289; misinterpretation of, 53–56, 57–58, 157–158; of nations, 56–58, 138–142; and pacifism, 67–71, 103–107, 153, 185–188, 196; of the pacifist, 190–195, 254–257, 259; Pareto-optimal, 252; past, as focus of problem, 38; and presumption, 48–50; reciprocal, 236–238, 261; required for rights violation, 24, 279; and Security Dilemma, 149–151; and status quo ante, 32, 38; strategic, 92–98, 149–151, 153, 176–177, 178–181, 182, 196, 198, 199, 218–221, 229, 231, 234–235, 240–241, 246–247, 250–251, 254–257, 260; and Theory of the Right, 24–26; transparent, 253–254, 259; and violence, 18, 60, 61, 67–71, 163–167, 168–169, 185–188, 277–282

adjudicative perspective, 133, 136, 143, 144, 289. *See also* party perspective; policy perspective

Agency Theory: defined, 131–135; and escalation of violence, 146–151; foundation of Justified Violence View, 136, 142; and responsibility for practice improvement, 177. *See also* Happening Theory

aggression, 33, 161–162, 291, 297; and balance of power, 240–241; and conflict, 132–133; criticism of concept of, 37–39, 56, 61–62, 136–142, 291; in contrast to defense, 56; duty not to commit, 133; and escalation, 150, 169–170, 279; excuses for, 162; and fault, 138–142, 144–146, 290; and the Happening Theory in contrast to the Agency Theory, 131–135, 187; and human nature, 78–80, 195–196, 196–197; immanent or occurrent, 34, 163–167, 185–188, 299; international, 70; and Just War standards, 44, 169–173, 182–183; obligation to resist, 118–119, 119–122, 164, 209; and pacifism, 81–82, 94, 109–110, 111–116, 153, 195–196, 241, 288, 296; response to, 44, 81–82, 94, 102–103, 164–167, 187–188, 196–197, 241, 288, 295, 296–297; and rhetoric, 55–56; right to resist, 31–34, 134–135, 165–167, 218, 277; and subjugation, 196–197; and violence, 33–34

aggressor: appeasement of the, 135; criticism of concept of the, 37–42, 48; identifiable, 134–135, 136–142; and the Justified Violence View, 138–139, 164–167, 287–288; num-

aggressor *(cont.)*
   ber of, in conflict, 134, 138–142;
   and rule of law, 136; in contrast
   to the victim, 42–43, 102–103,
   118–119, 163–167, 184–188
ahimsa, 72
aikido: and the criminal, 113–114;
   defined, 111–113; limitations of,
   119, 125, 156; moral significance of,
   115–116, 153–155, 203, 295–298;
   and response to violence, 173–176,
   295–298
alcoholism, 240, 249
alienation, 279–280; criticism of
   goods resulting from, 283; resulting from divergent presumptions,
   50; in contrast to focus on common goods, 61; resulting from liberalism, 46–47, 48; in contrast to
   love, 258; in contrast to pacifism,
   103, 173; in contrast to peace, 98,
   100, 173; and responses to cultural
   differences, 41
Alsace-Lorraine, 32, 279
Aquinas, Saint Thomas, 28
Aquino, Corazon, 190, 198, 260, 300,
   301
Aristotle, 277–278
assurance game, 82, 285
Attig, Tom, 284
Augustine, Saint, 28, 72
Austin, John, 85
Austria, 157, 263, 293
authority: limited by rules, 22, 192;
   and peacemaking, 242–243; and
   practice development, 180; of Secretary of Peacemaking, 200–201;
   in Soviet society, 304; of standards,
   277; for trouble-shooters, 248; to
   use violence, 27, 85, 192

Balkan states, 263

Beowulf, 16
Berlin, 222, 223, 286, 292, 293
Berlin Wall, 224, 304
Bible, 16
Brezhnev, Leonid, 218, 224, 225, 307
bribes, 180, 181, 184
Brinton, Crain, 284
Britain, 144, 153, 208, 211, 288
Buchanan, James, 86
Bulgaria, 229

Celsus, 190
Challenger crew, 97
Chamberlain, Neville, 135, 157
Chekhov, Anton, 46, 48, 258
Chernobyl, 97, 244
China, 95, 107, 211, 216, 262, 303
Chou Dynasty, 95, 107, 108
chun-tzu, 107
civil rights, 153, 174
Clausewitz, Karl von, 107, 116, 160
coercion: and effective mediation,
   192–193; nuclear, 226; and overwhelming force, 80; and the rule of
   law, 84–87, 192; and violence, 22,
   80
commitments, 50, 55, 61, 101, 158,
   195, 227
common goods. *See* goods in common
community, the: building, 95–99,
   119–122, 146, 199–201, 244, 260,
   261, 283, 287; and definition of
   peace, 101; ideal, 258, 259, 260;
   liberals and, 103, 283; and love,
   259; and persons as rights-bearers,
   46–47; respect for, 103, 119–122,
   283; and respect for persons, 103–
   104; and respect for practices,
   103; restoration of, 49, 51, 95, 287;
   teleological pacifism and, 51, 103,
   119–122, 199–201; value of, 38–39,

49, 95–99, 277–278
confederated republics, 267–270
conflict: and aggression, 31–34, 132–
146, 161–162, 163–167, 171–172,
181, 182–183, 195–196; alienating
analysis of, 39–40, 42–43, 287;
alternative responses to, 38–45,
47–52, 53–56, 60–62, 95, 96, 97,
98, 101, 105–107, 116, 158, 173,
181, 203–204, 237, 249–251, 280,
287; and escalation (dominance),
44–45, 85, 146–152, 155–156, 279,
291, 293; Gandhi's response to, 44–
45, 240–243, 279; that happens,
31, 132–136; hard-to-categorize
cases of, 31, 32; and the Happening and Agency theories, 132–136;
and intentions, 53–60, 133–146;
and interest creation, 126, 163–
167, 192, 195, 196; international,
34, 57–58, 59–60, 138–142, 142–
146; irreconcilable, 47–48, 51–52,
112–113, 123–124, 126, 196–199;
and pacifism, 98, 105–107, 121,
161–162, 191–196, 203–204, 288,
309; from a party perspective, 15,
133–135, 144–146, 163–167, 183,
289; and peace, 95; from a policy
perspective, 134, 163–167, 189–
190; and presumption, 47–52,
55–56; and revenge, 43–44; and
the right to resist, 31–34, 112–113;
between rights, 25; and scarcity,
123–124, 196–199; situation, defined, 31; and violence, 154–155,
158, 195–196; and war, 34, 45, 210–
218, 228–230. *See also* conflict
resolution
conflict resolution: and alienation,
46–47, 50–52; Gandhi's approach
to, 44–45, 240–243; and interest
creation, 163–167; liberal short-

comings at, 41, 101; and pacifism,
100, 101, 105, 180–183, 192–196,
257–258
Confucius, 95, 96, 97, 98, 107
Controllability, Principle of, 151–
152, 155–160, 169–173, 220, 226–
227
courts, 15, 16, 162, 278
criminals: and escalation dominance,
156; nonviolent defense against,
113–114, 296; pacifism benefits,
85, 158; and rule of law, 86; violence acceptable against, 68, 86; as
violent aggressors, 162
Cromwell, Oliver, 218
Cuba, 224, 229, 287, 301
Czechoslovakia, 135, 157, 213, 214,
215, 216, 263

Daladier, Edouard, 135
Danzig, 157
deescalation, 147, 155–156, 175, 295.
See also escalation; escalation
dominance
defense: against accidental or inadvertent war, 221–228; aggressive
or vigilant, 58, 135, 150–151; as
alienating, 199–201; alleviating
need for, 95; in contrast to aggression, 55, 56, 162; escalation
dominance as, 155–156, 157–158,
165, 169, 173–176; and interest
creation, 164–167, 184–185; and
(Minimal) Justified Violence View,
27–34, 116, 169–173, 181–183,
287; national, 26–27, 209–213,
218–230, 276; nonviolent, 111–
116, 153–155, 158–160, 165, 176,
195–196, 240–241, 287, 295–298,
299, 306; of (innocent) others,
24, 81–82, 89–90, 116, 117–122,
185–188, 207, 275; and the party

defense (*cont.*)
    perspective, 136–146, 166–167,
    185–188; passive, 158–160, 296–
    298; and peacemaking, 60–62,
    199–222, 185–188, 203, 235, 240–
    241; and moral agency, 132; police
    as providers of, 86–87, 113–114;
    in contrast to punishment, 16;
    rhetoric of, 55; rights of, 25–34,
    47, 133–134, 136, 150, 276; of self,
    24, 48, 81, 118, 150–151, 218–220,
    275–276, 287; Soviet, 214, 217–
    218; stable, 220–221; and violence,
    25–34, 135, 162, 218–220
deontological approach (ethics), 106–
    107; to pacifism, 42, 91; in contrast
    to the teleological approach, 126,
    299–300
deterrence: as escalation dominance,
    155–156, 292–293; nonviolent,
    296–298; of nuclear war, 226–228,
    307; and policy perspective,
    164–165
Dr. Strangelove, 222

Eastern Europe, 213, 216, 217, 229,
    293, 303, 304
East Germany, 223–224
East Indies, 211
Egypt, 118, 159, 225–226
Eisenhower, Dwight D., 309
El Salvador, 140
equality. *See* moral equality
escalation, 147–152, 155, 156, 157,
    158, 173, 223, 224, 225, 226, 284,
    291, 292
escalation dominance, 85, 158, 165,
    169, 170, 173, 175, 190, 192, 202,
    223, 292, 295
Europe, 211, 228, 245, 261, 262

Falkland Islands, 144
Fanon, Frantz, 17

Final Solution, 109
Finland, 263
Florida Public Services Commission,
    234
force, 109–116, 153–155, 223, 281–
    282, 285, 287, 299; and aggression,
    171–172; and *aikido*, 111–113,
    153–155, 295–298; and counter-
    force capability, 219–221; degrees
    of, 30, 68–70, 106, 294–297; and
    government, 83–84; impersonal
    or inadvertent, 32, 37; and legal
    powers, 191; military, 27, 70, 76,
    114–116, 157–160, 192, 211, 216,
    217–218, 225–226, 227, 228, 229,
    239, 300, 305–306, 307; as neces-
    sary, 77; in contrast to nonresis-
    tance, 108, 294; nuclear, 217, 222,
    226, 228; and pacifism, 68–70, 88,
    152–167, 173–176, 192, 193–201,
    288, 295–299; and paternalism,
    273–274; police, 27, 70, 76, 81, 86–
    87, 113–114, 122, 164, 166–167,
    185, 195–196, 288, 293, 299; and
    rights of defense, 26, 33–34, 83–85,
    86–87, 90, 117–118; show of, 56;
    strategic, 249; and stun guns, 114,
    115, 156, 173, 203, 279, 288, 296;
    and violence, 18, 20, 26, 84–85, 86–
    87, 88, 146–147, 155–158, 173–176,
    293
Ford Motor Company, 143
France, 32, 44, 139, 141, 159, 211, 246
Franco, Francisco, 214
Frank, Robert, 287, 301, 310
free rider, the pacifist as a, 87–88,
    116–126, 203, 207, 208
Freud, Sigmund, 75, 78, 272
Fried, Charles, 23, 26
Fuller, Lon, 131, 181

Gandhi, Mohandas. *See* pacifist:
    Mohandas Gandhi as

Garrison, William Lloyd, Sr., 295
Garver, Newton, 20, 273, 278
General Pacifist Rule, 80–82
Genovese, Kitty, 113, 124, 186
Gephardt, Richard, 217
Germany, 32, 135, 139, 141, 211, 213,
   223, 224, 229, 230, 263, 282
glasnost, 211, 213, 221, 300, 305
Glover, Jonathan, 68
Golden Age (Confucian), 95, 96, 97,
   258
goods in common, 41, 46–47, 278;
   and criticism of extant practices,
   41, 105–107, 204, 308–309; and
   definition of pacifism, 98–99, 103–
   105; in contrast to rights, 61–62;
   and teleological pacifism, 98–99,
   103–107
Gorbachev, Mikhail, 211, 213, 214,
   215, 216, 217, 218, 219, 221, 223,
   263, 264, 303, 308
GPR. *See* General Pacifist Rule
Graduated Reciprocation in Tension
   Reduction (GRIT), 235–239, 245,
   308, 309
Grotius, Hugo, 28

Hampton, Jean, 279
Happening Theory: confused invocation of, 166–167; defined, 131–135;
   and escalation of violence, 146–
   151; and responsibility, 177, 187.
   See also Agency Theory
Hegel, G. F. W., 17
Heraclitus, 17
Hersh, Seymour, M., 57, 58, 143
historical fact, and intention, 56
Hitler, Adolf, 31, 36, 44, 109, 135, 141,
   153, 157, 158, 173, 174, 182, 195,
   196, 208, 211, 215, 280, 282, 293,
   303
Hobbes, Thomas, 75

Hohfeld, Wesley Newcomb, 25, 89,
   285
Holmes, Robert L., 18, 19, 68, 77, 271
Homer, 16, 43, 118
Honda, 235, 236
human nature: criticism of the con-
   cept of, 92–93; 278–279, 284; and
   pacifism, 75–80; and the rule of
   law, 83
Hume, David, 19
Hungary, 213, 214, 215, 230, 263
Hussein, Saddam, 230
Huxley, Aldous, 287

Ibsen, Henrik, 46, 48, 258
ICBMs, 219, 297, 305, 306
Indo-China, 211
information, 244; and intentions,
   143, 144–146; and microcosmic
   structures, 241–243; and the (Minimal) Justified Violence View,
   182–183; and peacemaking, 241–
   243, 244; practices for reporting
   and disseminating, 144–146; and
   presumptions, 309; quality of, 50,
   59–60, 144–146, 150–151, 182–183,
   241–243, 254–255; and rebutting
   claims, 48; and violence, 150–151
intention: and action, 290; and
   aggression in contrast to non-
   aggression, 33–34, 61, 138–142,
   150, 157–158, 163–164, 172, 210,
   211, 220–221, 303; and conflict,
   31–34, 82, 151–162; critique of, 53–
   62, 129–131, 182–183, 281, 282,
   294; and defensive in contrast to
   offensive weapons, 305; and the
   Happening Theory in contrast
   to the Agency Theory, 131–138,
   178; in contrast to inertia, 212;
   legal conventions define, 142;
   and Minimal Justified Violence,

intention (*cont.*)
35, 138–146, 182–183, 230–231;
national, 57–60, 61, 138–146, 157–
158, 168, 182–183, 214, 220–221,
281, 282, 303, 309; and pain, 19–21,
23; in contrast to purpose, 272–
273; rhetoric of, 61; and rights,
24–26, 275; and strategic interaction, 57–59, 305–306; and social
practices, 179; transparent in contrast to opaque, 42, 61, 82, 151,
175, 220–221, 241, 249, 309–310;
and violence, 18–19, 24–26, 52,
53–60, 61, 129–131, 151, 161–162,
163–164, 175, 202, 272–273, 276
interest creation, 106, 164, 184, 192,
195, 196, 299, 300, 301, 302
interest(s): among adversaries, 54–
56, 122, 210–218, 225–227, 261;
and aggression, 32–33, 83, 163–
167, 195–196, 196–201, 247–250;
and the cause of war, 50, 210–218,
225–227; and conflict, 123–125,
163–165, 195–196, 196–199, 226,
227, 234–235, 261, 291, 301–302;
coordination of, 94–98, 110, 181–
188, 235–239, 261, 291, 301–302;
national, 34, 210–218, 225, 235–
239; presumptions about, 47–52,
123–125, 199–201; and scarcity,
123–124; security, 149–150, 208,
210–218, 220, 226, 227, 229, 231,
291, 306; in social harmony, 94–98,
122, 190–193, 235–239, 241–247,
256–257; worldly, 294
international relations: and avoiding
war, 221–230; between adversaries,
210–218, 249–251; and aggressors,
134–135, 138–142; and conflict,
32; contemporary, 262–265, 267–
270; and the control of violence,

152–153, 165–166; and intentions,
53–59; and justified violence,
34; and law, 27–28, 38, 48; and
the organization of states, 56–58,
142–146, 192–193; and pacifism,
69–70, 192–193; and peacemaking, 124–125, 199–201, 235–240,
243–247, 248–249, 301–302; and
security dilemmas, 218–221; and
violence, 132, 134–135, 138–142;
and violence-deescalating practices, 144–146, 181–183, 192–193,
204, 221–230, 301–302
Iraq, 51, 229, 230
Ireland, 45, 191, 301
Israel, 32, 45, 118, 134, 169, 191, 196,
225, 226, 227, 230, 271, 301
Israeli–Egyptian war of 1973, 192

Japan, 135, 142, 211, 235, 236, 237,
292, 303
Jen, 96–98, 107
Jesus, 68, 259
Jews, 109, 153
Joshua, 16
judges, 15, 111, 137, 180, 192
Just War Theory: applicability of, 59–
60; and the avoidance of war, 44,
170–172; coherence of, 170–172,
183; conditions of, 34, 115, 151–
152, 257, 258, 298–299; grounded
in Justified Violence View, 27–28;
and intention, 59–60; in contrast
to war as instrument of policy, 34
Justified Violence View. *See* Minimal
Justified Violence View

Kahn, Alfred, 289
Kant, Immanuel, 23, 250, 254, 274–
275
Kennan, George, 232

Kennedy, John Fitzgerald, 166, 308
KGB, 215, 217
Khrushchev, Nikita, 218, 223, 224, 308
King, Martin Luther, Jr. *See* pacifist: Martin Luther King, Jr., as
Kingdom of Heaven (Christian), 258
Kissinger, Henry, 227, 307
Kuwait, 229

law, rule of: conditions of, 56; and critical mass phenomenon, 86; and defense of rights, 26–27, 275; defined, 131; and democracy, 215; and duties to avoid violence, 164–167; evolved practice of, 43–44, 120–122; extent of, 48, 61, 136, 192–193, 278; and fault, 136–146; and immunities, 88–90; and intentions, 136–146; international, 18; and international relations, 34; and justified violence, 27–34, 36–39, 274, 295; and negligence, 152; and outlaws, 26; and the party perspective, 289; as a public good, 88, 120–122, 175–176, 296; and slavery, 22; and threats of violence or force, 77–87, 88, 117, 158, 281–283; and violence, 18, 20, 21
legal system, 281; limits of, 278; and violence, 17. *See also* law, rule of
Lehman, John, 57
Lenin, V. I., 213
liberalism, 41, 61, 101–104, 212, 274, 276
Lorenz, Konrad, 272
love, 258–260
Lyon, Bryce, 279

MacArthur, Douglas, 135
Machiavelli, 92, 107

MacIntyre, Alasdair, 277–278
Maistre, Joseph, de, 83
Mandelbaum, Michael, and theory of the Security Dilemma, 230
Manila, 153, 300
Marcos, Ferdinand, 174, 198, 300
Marshall Plan, 217, 263
Marx, Karl, 17, 215, 216
mediation, 192–193
Michnik, Adam, 215, 216
microcosmic structures, 243–247; and information, 241–243
Midgley, Mary, 76
Minimal Justified Violence View: convergence of, with Segmented Teleological Pacifism, 201–202; critique of, 43–52, 59–60, 60–61, 108, 111–116, 169–173, 181–183, 276; definition of peace, 72–75; and escalation, 146–160; exposition of, 27–34, 151–152; and Gandhi, 146–160; and the Happening Theory in contrast to the Agency Theory, 131–135; implications of, for (inter)national security, 210–213, 218–221, 221–228, 228–230; and intention, 130–146; and the party perspective, 133–138, 144; and peacemaking, 190–193, 199, 230–231, 245–246; and police authority, 80–82; strength of, in contrast to pacifism, 90; tainted by liberal concept of the self, 41, 46–47, 61, 101, 103–105, 190–193, 199, 280
missiles, 159, 212, 217, 219, 222, 225, 297, 306
Moists, 107
moral equality, 22–23; of criminal, 26; compromised by military conquest, 218; in contrast to cultural dissimilarity, 212; and historical

moral equality (*cont.*)
　wrongs, 135
moral imagination, 106, 119, 126, 159, 160
moral principles, 15, 16, 190
Murray, John Courtney, 152, 170, 292

Nagel, Thomas, 19
Napoleon, 151, 211, 293
Narveson, Jan, 25, 87, 117
NATO, 159, 224, 226, 229
Nazis, 135, 153
negligence standard, 152
new interest creation. *See* interest creation
Nicaragua, 140
Niebuhr, Reinhold, 74–75, 273
Nietzsche, Friedrich, 17
1984 (George Orwell), 75
Nixon, Richard M., 226, 307
North Korea, 229
Norway, 263

Origen, 68, 190, 191, 193, 289, 300
Osgood, Charles, 308
outlaw, 26, 70

pacifist, the: as appeaser, 135; collective choice problems of, 80–87, 107–116; commitment of, to peace, 100–107; and creating interests, 106, 123–125, 163–167; defined, 67–71, 202–204; and escalating violence, 146–160, 173–176; as a free rider, 87–88, 116–126, 203, 207, 208; and force, 109–116, 283, 288, 295–298; and human nature, 76–80, 92–93, 283; as immunizing evil, 89–90, 109–116; Martin Luther King, Jr., as, 110, 152, 189, 190, 239, 241, 256, 259, 300; Mohandas Gandhi as, 44–46, 72–74, 110, 147, 152, 173–175, 186, 189, 190, 194, 239, 240–246, 256–259, 300, 308; morality of, 87–90, 116–126, 288, 295; motivation of, 92–93, 286; and Mr. Blue and Mr. Green, 164, 166, 185, 299; and national security, 207, 208; as optimist, 209–210, 212; and pacifism as an empirical claim, 161–162, 189–201; and pacifism in personal contrast to universal, 70–71, 288; on peace, 72–75, 94–98, 294; and peacemaking, 232–265; and the policy perspective, 163–167; as practice developer, 189–201; presumptions of, 105, 294; and Segmented Teleological Pacifism, 189–195, 197, 201–204; and teleological pacifism, 5, 42, 50–52, 189–201; on violence, 25, 283, 302
pain, 18, 19, 20, 22, 23, 24, 30, 33, 39, 42, 75, 129, 130, 163, 260, 274
Palme, Olof, 97
party perspective, 136–138, 144, 163, 164, 166, 185, 188, 289; in contrast to adjudicative and policy perspective, 133–135. *See also* adjudicative perspective; policy perspective
peace: as the absence of war, 72–75, 98–100, 209, 301; and collective choice problems, 82, 107–116, 251–261; and Controllability, Principle of, 226–228; defined, 72–75, 91, 94–98; destabilized in multiparty conflicts, 228–230; and Gandhi, 240–247; and GRIT, 235–239, 245; and human nature, 75–80; monistic concept of, 72–75, 98–100, 169–173, 294; as a public good, 87–88, 119–122, 207;

and Security Dilemmas, 218–221;
seeking after, 60–63, 100–107, 123–
125, 168, 176–188, 189–201, 218,
232–265, 298, 299–300, 301, 309;
in contrast to violence, 116–117,
155–156; and worst-case thinking,
151

peacemaking: efficacy of, 193–196,
247–250; Gandhian approach to,
240–247; and GRIT, 235–239,
245; and information, 244; and
love, 258–260; and microcosmic
structures, 244–247; in contrast
to military advising, 231; pacifists
and, 193–196, 240–247, 258–260;
the practice of, 190–193, 193–201,
210–211, 233–261; and practice
development, 233–235; Secretary
of, 124–125, 199–201, 301–302; and
security, 210–211; and suspected
aggressors, 247–250; theory of,
251–260

perestroika, 213, 305

Plato, 17

Poland, 157, 211, 213, 214, 215, 230,
280, 293

policy perspective, 163–167, 183–
190, 207–218, 244–250; in contrast
to adjudicative and party perspectives, 133–135. *See also* adjudicative perspective; party perspective

practices, 277–278; alternative, 36–
41; evaluating 43–47, 48–51, 62,
116, 121–122, 165–167, 282–283,
299, 300; and the Happening and
Agency theories, 176–178; for pri-
oritizing principles, 172–173; to
promote human improvement,
102–107; for resisting violence,
107–108, 145–146, 175–176, 190–
195, 199–201; responsibility for

developing, 123–126, 178–189,
190–193, 199–201, 299, 300, 302;
to support presumptions, 99–106

Prague Spring of 1968, 216

presumptions: against aggressors,
28–34, 170–173; and alienation,
54–56, 59–63, 116, 247–249, 252,
257, 281, 282, 309; alternative, 47–
52, 54–56, 244–247; and the definition of peace, 98–101; established
by practices, 145; by pacifists,
105; and practice improvement,
188–201, 244–247; sometimes
(in)consistent, 124, 294; against
violence, 25, 29, 30, 151

Prisoners' Dilemma, 82, 151, 181,
230, 284

punishment, 16, 18, 38, 39, 43, 60, 83,
84, 102, 120, 133, 164, 271, 277, 293

rationalism, 254

Rawls, John, 88, 275

reasonable person, 29–30, 167, 300

reciprocation, 236–238, 253, 261

responsibility: assigned for wrongdoing, 38, 136–146; assumed by
pacifists, 87–88, 109–195; and
the Happening in contrast to the
Agency Theory, 131–135, 176–178;
and Just War Theory, 298; linked
to intention, 138–146; and the
party in contrast to the policy
perspective, 163–167, 185–189; promoting the taking of, 105, 115–116,
119–125, 163–167, 178–189, 199–
201, 202–204, 228–230, 240–251,
296, 298, 299, 300; and revenge,
39, 43, 44, 45, 120, 121, 122, 124,
134, 165, 175, 279, 282; wrongs
regardless of, 60

revenge: improving upon a practice of, 120–122, 279; as inferior practice, 39, 43–47, 279; justice under law as superior to, 175–176, 282–283; and relying on Agency Theory, 134; taking responsibility for improving upon, 123–125, 165–166

Rhineland, 157

Right, Theory of the, 24–25, 52. *See also* Value, Theory of

rights: and the Agency Theory, 132–135, 136; civil, 153, 174; critique of, 46–52, 53–60, 277, 287, 299, 301–302, 309; to do evil, 89–90; and estrangement, 38–39, 98, 257; in contrast to happenings, 142; immunities as, 281; to life, 274; in contrast to peace, 60–63; not bound to conflict, 198–199; not to be a victim of violence, 20–24, 118–119, 210, 275; of the police, 86; to resist violence, 25–34, 78–80, 81, 126, 136, 161–162, 163–167, 170–173, 218, 276; and responsibilities, 143–146, 158; and the rule of law, 138, 282–283; to security, 226; of self-defense, 25, 81, 86, 133, 141, 274, 275, 276

right to life, 24, 35, 52

Romania, 229, 230

Roosevelt, Franklin Delano, 213

Rousseau, Jean Jacques, 19

Russia, 211, 212, 215, 293, 305. *See also* Soviet Union

Samson, 16

Sartre, Jean Paul, 17

satyagraha, 279

scarcity, 123, 124, 162, 196, 197, 198, 199, 203, 289, 301

Schelling, Thomas, 81, 86, 284, 290, 306

Schwartz, Delmore, 286

SDI (Strategic Defense Initiative), 297

Second Law of Thermodynamics, 160, 297, 298

Security Council (United Nations), 142

Security Dilemma, theory of the, 149, 150, 209, 210, 218–221, 230, 232, 291, 306

self-defense. *See* rights: of self-defense

Sharp, Gene, 173, 306

Smoke, Richard, 149

Socrates, 260

South Africa, 229

Soviet Union, 57, 58, 139, 141, 142, 192, 211, 212, 213, 214, 215, 216, 217, 218, 219, 223, 226, 228, 229, 230, 239, 242, 263, 267–270, 291, 303, 304, 305, 309

Spain, 214

Stalin, Joseph, 82, 213, 216, 218, 293

State Pacifist Rule, 82. *See also* general pacifist rule

status quo ante, 32, 38, 48, 56, 145, 175, 281

Strategic Defense Initiative (SDI), 297

strategic interaction, 224, 298; and pacifist problems, 164; and Just War problems, 182

Sudetenland, 135, 157

Sumner, L. W., 172, 275, 294

supererogation, 33, 167

superpowers, 211–213, 220–221, 225–227, 228, 284, 306

Sweden, 263

Switzerland, 263

Syria, 225, 229

teleological approach, 39–41;

Gandhi's, 44–45; and Just War Theory, 183; to pacifism, 42, 50–52, 189–201; to peace, 94–102; to practice-improvement, 36–39, 46, 103–107, 119–122, 165–166, 178–188, 189–190, 277–278; in contrast to a rights-based approach, 46, 300
Thailand, 211
Third World, 198, 229
Tiananmen Square, 153, 174, 216
Tolstoy, Leo, 68, 258, 259, 282, 293, 294
torture, 21, 75, 83, 242, 273
transarmament, 220–221, 230, 245, 305
trouble-shooting, 246–250, 308
trust, 38, 55, 56, 82, 193, 196, 202, 221, 230, 244, 245, 248, 301

Unger, Roberto, 280
United Nations Security Council, 142
Ukraine, 153
United States, 58, 110, 111, 123, 139, 140, 141, 142, 143, 182, 183, 192, 211, 216, 219, 223, 226, 227, 228, 229, 233, 236, 237, 239, 242, 244, 258, 264, 288, 291, 292, 297

Value, Theory of, 24–25, 270; disputed implications of, 45–52, 69; monistic, 73–75, 98–100
Versailles, Treaty of, 44, 135
Vietnam, 140, 229
violence, 60–63; acquiescence to, 161–162; alternatives to invoking rights against, 36–43, 46–52, 277; and coercion, 22, 80; and collective choice problems, 80–86, 107–116; defenses against, 158–160; defensive, 83–87; defined, 17–19, 52–53, 129–131, 281–282, 301; escalation

of, 44–45, 146–158, 284, 291, 295, 305–306; in contrast to force, 109–116, 280, 293, 295–298, 299, 301; and the Happening Theory in contrast to the Agency Theory, 131–135; and human nature, 76–80, 92–93; and intention, 18, 53–60, 136–146, 272; as morally good, 16–17, 271, 272; and pacifism, 67–71, 78–82, 87–90, 98–100, 190–201, 258–262, 286, 288; and the party in contrast to the policy perspective, 163–167; and peace, 72–75, 94–98, 100–107; as opposed to punishment, 16, 292; and revenge, 43–45, 278, 282; responsibility for, 136–146; responsibility for curtailing, 87–90, 116–126, 175–188, 220–230, 240–251, 254–257, 299–300, 306, 310; rights against, 25–34, 275; and scarcity, 123–124; and social organization, 36–39, 262, 265; voluntary, 207; why bad, 19–24, 273, 294

war, 16–18, 168; accidental or inadvertent, 146, 147, 221–228, 289; aggressive, 141, 142; and *aikido*, 295; avoidance of, 115, 116, 120, 209–231, 302; defensive, 26–32, 34, 36, 50, 60, 61, 68, 69; and discerning aggression, 181; and escalation, 149, 157–158, 192, 290, 292; and escalation dominance, 292; and nonviolent force, 158–160; and intention 135, 139, 144; justification of, 183; by pacifist lights, 76, 79, 82; and the party in contrast to the policy perspective, 163–167, 179, 188; as related to peace, 72–75, 94, 95, 204; and peacemaking, 229, 230, 231, 232, 239, 241, 245,

war (*cont.*)
    250, 251, 258, 264; and revenge,
    43–45, 278; and security dilem-
    mas, 218–221; and scarcity, 198;
    submarines, 219, 297; between
    the United States and the Soviet
    Union, 209–217
Wealth of Nations (Adam Smith), 262

West Africans, 38, 39, 46, 98, 100, 103
Wilder, Thornton, 46, 48, 258
Wilson, Woodrow, 213
World Court, 143, 280, 303
World War I, 44, 50, 139, 140, 147
World War II, 135, 211, 246, 263

Zimbardo, Philip, 278